Prisons and Punishment
in America

Recent Titles in Contemporary Debates

PRISONS AND PUNISHMENT IN AMERICA

Examining the Facts

Michael O'Hear

Contemporary Debates

An Imprint of ABC-CLIO, LLC

Santa Barbara, California • Denver, Colorado

Library of Congress Cataloging-in-Publication Data

Names: O'Hear, Michael, 1968– author.
Title: Prisons and punishment in America : examining the facts /
    Michael O'Hear.
Description: Santa Barbara : ABC-CLIO, [2018] | Series: Contemporary
    debates | Includes bibliographical references and index.
Identifiers: LCCN 2018020529 (print) | LCCN 2018025353 (ebook) |
    ISBN 9781440855436 (ebook) | ISBN 9781440855429 (alk. paper)
Subjects: LCSH: Prisons—United States. | Punishment—United States.
Classification: LCC HV9471 (ebook) | LCC HV9471 .O44 2018 (print) |
    DDC 365/.973—dc23
LC record available at https://lccn.loc.gov/2018020529

ISBN: 978-1-4408-5542-9 (print)
       978-1-4408-5543-6 (ebook)

22 21 20 19 18   1 2 3 4 5

This book is also available as an eBook.

ABC-CLIO
An Imprint of ABC-CLIO, LLC

ABC-CLIO, LLC
130 Cremona Drive, P.O. Box 1911
Santa Barbara, California 93116-1911
www.abc-clio.com

This book is printed on acid-free paper ∞

Manufactured in the United States of America

Contents

How to Use This Book

Prisons and Punishment in America: Examining the Facts is the latest volume in ABC-CLIO's Contemporary Debates reference series. Each title in this series, which is intended for use by high school and undergraduate students as well as members of the general public, examines the veracity of controversial claims or beliefs surrounding a major political/cultural issue in the United States. The purpose of the series is to give readers a clear and unbiased understanding of current issues by informing them about falsehoods, half-truths, and misconceptions—and confirming the factual validity of other assertions—that have gained traction in America's political and cultural discourse. Ultimately, this series has been crafted to give readers the tools for a fuller understanding of controversial issues, policies, and laws that occupy center stage in American life and politics.

Each volume in this series identifies thirty to forty questions swirling about the larger topic under discussion. These questions are examined in individualized entries, which are in turn arranged in broad subject chapters that cover certain aspects of the issue being examined, that is, history of concern about the issue, potential economic or social impact, findings of latest scholarly research, and so on.

Each chapter features four to ten individual entries. Each entry begins by stating an important and/or well-known **Question** about the issue being studied. The entry then provides a concise and objective one- or two-paragraph **Answer** to the featured question, followed by a more comprehensive, detailed explanation of **The Facts**. This latter portion of each entry uses quantifiable, evidence-based information from respected sources to fully address each question and provide readers with the information they need to be informed citizens. Importantly, entries will also acknowledge instances in which conflicting data exists or data is incomplete. Finally, each entry concludes with a **Further Reading** section providing users with information on other important and/or influential resources.

The ultimate purpose of every book in the Contemporary Debates series is to reject "false equivalence," in which demonstrably false beliefs or statements are given the same exposure and credence as the facts; to puncture myths that diminish our understanding of important policies and positions; to provide needed context for misleading statements and claims; and to confirm the factual accuracy of other assertions. In other words, volumes in this series are being crafted to clear the air surrounding some of the most contentious and misunderstood issues of our time—not just add another layer of obfuscation and uncertainty to the debate.

1

❖

American Sentencing—Law and Practice

Beginning in the mid-1970s, prison populations in the United States rose sharply and continuously for more than three decades (O'Hear, 2017, xiv). By the end of the "imprisonment boom," the American rate of imprisonment had more than quintupled, from a long-term rate of 100 prisoners per 100,000 residents in the mid-twentieth century to a high of 527 per 100,000 in 2007.

The first half of the imprisonment boom coincided with similarly sharp increases in the rate of violent crime in the United States (O'Hear, 2017, xvi). However, crime rates have consistently fallen since the early 1990s. Still, even as crime rates dropped, imprisonment rates continued to climb for another decade and a half. This combination of a steadily declining crime rate and a steadily increasing imprisonment rate provides strong evidence that the U.S. criminal justice system became significantly tougher in the 1990s and early 2000s.

There are many actors in the system that could have contributed to this increased toughness, including (1) police officers, who decide whom to arrest; (2) prosecutors, who decide whether and how to charge the individuals who have been arrested; (3) judges, who decide how to sentence convicted defendants; (4) parole boards, which decide in many states when exactly sentenced defendants will be released from prison; and (5) community supervision agents, who decide whether convicted defendants who have been released on probation or parole should be "revoked" and sent to prison for violating the conditions of their release. In this chapter, we will focus particularly on the role of judges and prosecutors.

In addition, the work of another key player, the legislature, has to be considered. Congress and America's fifty different state legislatures establish the legal framework within which judges and prosecutors do their jobs. Since the overwhelming majority of criminal cases in the United States are prosecuted in state courts under state law, the fifty state legislatures collectively play a far more important role in criminal justice issues than Congress, which only sets the rules for the comparatively few cases that are prosecuted in federal court. In any event, for every crime in a state's criminal code, the legislature must establish a minimum and maximum sentence. These constitute the parameters within which prosecutors and judges exercise their discretionary power over punishment. For instance, for the crime of armed robbery, a given state's legislature might prescribe a penalty of five to twenty years in prison. Thus, when a defendant in that state has been convicted of armed robbery and faces sentencing, the judge has the discretion to select a prison term of five years, twenty years, or any length of time in-between.

Q1: HAVE JUDGES LOST THEIR SENTENCING DISCRETION?

Answer: In the final quarter of the twentieth century, there emerged a definite legislative trend against judicial sentencing discretion. However, the practical impact of this trend was highly uneven, varying considerably from state to state and from one type of offense to another. In most states, judges retained much of their traditional sentencing discretion in many types of cases. Since 2000, there has been a trend in favor of restoring some of the discretion that was taken away during the height of the tough-on-crime era.

The Facts: In the mid-twentieth century, criminal justice experts and policy makers favored wide judicial sentencing discretion so that punishment could be carefully individualized based on the needs and circumstances of each offender (Chanenson, 2005). The goal was to make the punishment fit for not only the crime but also the criminal. This goal, in turn, reflected the era's emphasis on rehabilitation and a prompt return to the community as the objective for most offenders. The wide discretion of the sentencing judge mirrored and served the same ends as the wide discretion of the parole boards, which were empowered to release prisoners based on their rehabilitative progress behind bars.

In the 1970s, judicial sentencing discretion came under political attack from both the right and the left. Critics on the right charged judges with excessive lenience; the feeling was that judges should be forced to give tougher sentences. Critics on the left decried the absence of clear, objective principles to guide sentencing; this raised concerns that punishment might in practice be based on arbitrary or improper grounds, such as race or economic class. In one influential critique, for instance, a federal judge famously characterized sentencing as "law without order" (Frankel, 1973). The attacks from both ideological directions were strengthened by a sudden loss of confidence in the ability of the criminal justice system to foster rehabilitation (Martinson, 1974). If the system were less focused on rehabilitation, then it seemed far less important to fit the punishment to both the crime and the criminal. Sentencing appeared a more straightforward matter that required less fine-tuned individualization and discretion.

Reforms intended to curtail discretion took two quite distinct forms: mandatory minimums and sentencing guidelines. The first high-profile minimums of the tough-on-crime era were contained in the so-called Rockefeller drug laws adopted by New York in 1973. The Rockefeller laws required judges to impose a prison term of at least fifteen years on defendants who were convicted of distributing even rather small quantities of illegal narcotics (O'Hear, 2017, 4). Mandatory minimums then proliferated rapidly across the United States for the next quarter century. They played an especially prominent role in sentencing for drug-related crimes but were also adopted by many states for violent, sexual, and other offenses.

The mandatory minimum trend reached its climax in the mid-1990s with a wave of "three strikes and you are out" laws that were adopted by at least twenty-five states and the federal government. Although the details varied from state to state, the three-strikes laws generally required the imposition of a life sentence upon an offender's conviction for a third serious felony. California's version was the broadest and most draconian, requiring a life sentence when the third conviction was for *any* felony—even if it was a low-level, wholly nonviolent theft (Zimring, Hawkins, & Kamin, 2001, 4).

For policy makers wishing to rein in judicial discretion, sentencing guidelines offered a different model of reform. In contrast to mandatory minimums, guidelines were more nuanced and preserved greater flexibility for judges. While minimums were adopted on a piecemeal basis in an effort to increase the punishment for specific offenses or particular classes of repeat offenders, guidelines represented a more systematic approach to sentencing reform, typically aiming to establish consistent, proportionate punishment in one fell swoop across many different types of offenses (Chanenson, 2005). Sometimes, guidelines are merely advisory, leaving judges with complete or nearly complete freedom to disregard the guidelines' recommendations. Alternatively, guidelines might be "presumptive," which means that judges must follow the guidelines unless there is a legally approved ground to "depart." Either way, guidelines are often drafted by an expert sentencing commission.

Guidelines were adopted in many states in conjunction with the elimination of the power of parole boards to determine when prisoners would be released to supervision in the community. Regulating the judge's sentencing discretion seemed a sensible reform once the parole board's discretion would no longer serve as a check and balance on the judge's. In other words, once the judge's sentencing decision became the final say on the severity of the punishment, it became a matter of greater importance to ensure that judges were sentencing in a reasonably consistent and principled fashion.

Minnesota's presumptive guidelines, which went into effect in 1980 and remain in force in somewhat modified form today, exemplify a durable, respected system for regulating judicial sentencing discretion (Frase, 2005). In all, eighteen states adopted presumptive guidelines (Pfaff, 2009). In contrast to the experience of Minnesota and several other states, the sentencing guidelines used in federal court beginning in 1987 proved highly controversial, drawing criticism for excessive rigidity and severity (Stith & Cabranes, 1997).

Despite the widespread adoption of mandatory minimums and guidelines in the 1970s, 1980s, and 1990s, judges still retained considerable sentencing discretion in many cases. The minimums were normally focused on very specific crimes or on offenders with especially disturbing criminal histories. In the vast number of routine cases—theft, traffic offenses, and other forms of low-level violence and disorder—sentencing judges were unlikely to encounter a minimum. Moreover, even in those cases nominally subject to a "mandatory" prison term, prosecutors often had to take affirmative steps before the minimum was triggered. If a prosecutor declined to seek a minimum—for instance, because the prosecutor traded away the minimum in plea bargaining or because the prosecutor felt it would result in an unjust sentence—then the judge's sentencing discretion would remain fully in force.

Consider the "three-strikes" mandatory minimums. Although California's version did have a big impact, resulting in more than 9,000 life sentences by

2012 (Mills & Romano, 2013), the narrower versions adopted in many other states were only applied to one or two cases per year, if even that (Dickey & Hollenhorst, 1998). Or consider the experience of the federal system. Although Congress has been quite active in adopting mandatory minimums, and although the federal criminal docket is heavily skewed toward the drug and firearm offenses that tend to draw minimums, only a small minority of federal defendants are actually subject to minimums in practice (U.S. Sentencing Commission, 2011).

As for guidelines, only the presumptive form could be regarded as a genuine constraint on judicial discretion. Judges could simply ignore advisory guidelines. And even presumptive guidelines were only truly limiting to the extent that appellate courts established and enforced rigorous standards for departures. However, state appellate courts varied considerably in their willingness to involve themselves in the sentencing process (Reitz, 1997). Federal appellate courts tended to be far more demanding of guidelines adherence than their state counterparts, but even in the federal system departures were hardly uncommon. In 1999, for instance, more than one-third of federal sentences were outside the recommended guidelines range (O'Hear, 2017, 106).

Thus, even at the height of the tough-on-crime era in the 1990s, the burgeoning network of mandatory minimums and sentencing guidelines did not come close to eliminating judicial discretion. Then, after 2000, developments on two fronts restored much of the discretion that had been taken away.

First, in 2004, the U.S. Supreme Court ruled that defendants have a constitutional right to a jury trial on the factors that increase their punishment in presumptive guidelines systems (Chanenson, 2005). Strictly speaking, this holding did not preclude presumptive sentencing guidelines, but it did make their use much more procedurally cumbersome—it is much quicker, cheaper, and easier to have a single, experienced judge make the important decisions than a jury of twelve laypeople who have little or no prior knowledge of sentencing law. In the wake of the Supreme Court's decision, several presumptive guidelines systems, including the federal system, became merely advisory (Pfaff, 2009). A few years later, in 2013, the Supreme Court ruled that defendants also have a right to a jury trial on the factors that trigger a mandatory minimum (O'Hear, 2017, 165).

Second, as the high cost of mass incarceration became a matter of concern in a growing number of states, legislatures began to soften or repeal mandatory minimums with increasing frequency after 2000. In New York, for instance, where the 1973 Rockefeller laws helped to propel the national wave of tough new sentencing provisions, almost all drug minimums were repealed through reforms adopted in 2004 and 2009 (O'Hear, 2017, 47). At least thirteen other states similarly restored judicial discretion in drug sentencing in the same time period (O'Hear, 2017, 41). Although reformers particularly targeted drug-related minimums, other sorts of minimums were also softened. Perhaps most notably, even the California three-strikes law was finally modified in 2012 so that the lowest-level felonies would no longer count as a third strike for most offenders (O'Hear, 2017, 186–87).

Despite widespread perceptions that judges are too lenient (O'Hear, 2017, 204), judicial sentencing discretion has proven remarkably durable. Judges may have benefited from the fact that their sentencing decisions actually tend not to be any less severe than those of laypeople (Tonry, 2004, 35–36). Judges have also benefitted from the fiscal pressures that have plagued state governments in recent years; policy makers see judicial discretion as a way to minimize the likelihood that expensive prison cells will be wasted on low-risk offenders. Whatever the reason, discretion has remained substantial, and current trends seem to favor its further restoration.

FURTHER READING

Chanenson, Steven. 2005. "The Next Era of Sentencing Reform." *Emory Law Journal*, 54, 377.

Dickey, Walter & Hollenhorst, Pam. 1998. *Three Strikes Laws: Five Years Later*. Washington, DC: Center for Effective Public Policy.

Frankel, Marvin. 1973. *Criminal Sentences: Law without Order*. New York: Hill and Wang.

Frase, Richard. 2005. "Sentencing Guidelines in Minnesota, 1978–2003." *Crime & Justice*, 32, 131.

Martinson, Robert. 1974. "What Works: Questions and Answers about Prison Reform." *Public Interest*, 35, 22.

Mills, David & Romano, Michael. 2013. "The Passage and Implementation of the Three Strikes Reform Act of 2012 (Proposition 36)." *Federal Sentencing Reporter*, 25, 266.

O'Hear, Michael. 2017. *The Failure of Sentencing Reform*. Santa Barbara, CA: Praeger.

Pfaff, John. 2009. "The Future of Appellate Sentencing Review: *Booker* in the States." *Marquette Law Review*, 93, 683.

Reitz, Kevin. 1997. "Sentencing Guidelines Systems and Sentence Appeals: A Comparison of Federal and State Experiences." *Northwestern University Law Review*, 91, 1441.

Stith, Kate & Cabranes, José. 1997. "Judging under the Federal Sentencing Guidelines." *Northwestern University Law Review*, 91, 1247.

Tonry, Michael. 2004. *Thinking about Crime: Sense and Sensibility in American Penal Culture*. New York: Oxford University Press.

U.S. Sentencing Commission. 2011. *Mandatory Minimum Penalties in the Federal Criminal Justice System*. Washington, DC: U.S. Sentencing Commission.

Zimring, Franklin, Hawkins, Gordon, & Kamin, Sam. 2001. *Punishment and Democracy: Three Strikes and You Are Out in California*. New York: Oxford University Press.

Q2: DO MODERN-DAY PROSECUTORS DICTATE SENTENCES FOR CRIMINAL CONVICTIONS?

Answer: Although prosecutors do not formally impose sentences, they have long had a great deal of influence over the severity of punishment imposed on people convicted of crimes. That influence increased as judicial sentencing discretion diminished in the late twentieth century. In most cases, prosecutors are not in a position simply to dictate the sentence, but their charging and plea-bargaining decisions do set key parameters within which the sentencing judge operates. It is a matter of debate whether the prosecutor's resulting power over punishment leads to excessively harsh or otherwise ill-advised sentences.

The Facts: The prosecutor has arguably become the most powerful decision maker in the American criminal justice system. Yet, it remains difficult to characterize the fundamental nature of the prosecutor's role. Prosecutors are lawyers, and lawyers typically act on behalf of clients, but who is the prosecutor's client? Sometimes, prosecutors seem to act on behalf of crime victims. Yet, many criminal cases lack a clearly identifiable victim (think, for instance, of drug or no-accident DUI cases). In many other instances, the prosecutor seems to have a rather different set of priorities than the victim (O'Hear, 2007). For instance, a prosecutor might prefer the convenience of a quick plea deal, while the victim might resist giving any break to the offender in order to induce a guilty plea.

Alternatively, it might be more helpful to think of police officers as the prosecutor's client. It is the police who initially push forward the cases that lack an identifiable, engaged victim. Indeed, in many cases, the officer who has done the investigative work may come to feel that he or she has a stake in the case's outcome and may lobby the prosecutor to handle the case in particular ways. Prosecutors often try to accommodate such preferences, if only because of their need to maintain good working relationships with the police. On the other hand, police (like victims) lack the sort of formal control over litigation objectives and strategies that a client would normally possess in an attorney–client relationship. Moreover, police-prosecutor dynamics vary tremendously from office to office, person to person, and case to case; officers may sometimes be disengaged from the litigation process or have relatively distant or subservient relationships with prosecutors (Bach, 2009, 179).

Prosecutors often say that their client is the community, or the state, or the people. These are abstractions, though, that provide little clear sense of the prosecutorial role. It would be more helpful and accurate to say that the prosecutor serves not an imaginary, monolithic "public," but rather the *voters* who elect the head prosecutor in each jurisdiction. (In the United States, the head prosecutor—typically given the title "district attorney"—is normally elected on a county level.) Prosecutors who value their careers can hardly afford to wholly disregard the values and preferences of the electorate. At the same time, the voting public tends not to have a clear idea of what prosecutors do on a day-in, day-out basis. Only a very small number of highly unusual cases reach the public's consciousness through the media. In other cases, prosecutors may or may not give much conscious attention to what the voters want.

Given the absence of any individual or group that clearly, consistently functions as a client, the prosecutor might best be thought of as a "quasi-judicial" official. In other words, the prosecutor exercises considerable discretion in the legal system, with a broad mandate, like the judge's, to do justice within the legal framework established by the legislature and the Constitution. The quasi-judicial character of the prosecutor's role is most apparent in charging and plea bargaining. American criminal codes are expansive, including many overlapping offenses. Thus, a given illegal act might be charged in many different ways, according to the prosecutor's preferences. For instance, the intoxicated patron who throws a few punches in a barroom brawl might find himself charged with aggravated assault, simple assault, disorderly conduct, or nothing at all. Assuming there is probable cause to support each of the potential charges, the prosecutor has a free hand to select which charge would be most just and appropriate in light of all of the circumstances of the case.

The prosecutor must also decide what to offer the defendant in plea bargaining. The great majority of criminal convictions in the United States come from guilty pleas, and most guilty pleas result from a deal. For instance, in return for his guilty plea, the barroom brawler may be offered a reduction in charges from the felony crime of assault to the misdemeanor charge of disorderly conduct. Again, prosecutors typically face few legal constraints on what they may offer to induce a guilty plea.

Once the guilty plea is entered, it is the judge, not the prosecutor, who formally imposes the sentence. Yet, the prosecutor's actions can potentially exert a powerful influence over the sentence in at least four different ways. First, the prosecutor's charging and plea-bargaining decisions effectively establish the maximum sentence that the judge can impose. This is important not only because the maximum may prevent the judge from imposing as harsh a sentence as he or she would like in some cases, but also because the maximum establishes an important reference point from which any punishment will be evaluated. Thus, for instance, probation may seem a perfectly reasonable sentence for a defendant who pleads guilty to a disorderly conduct charge carrying a thirty-day maximum, but far too lenient if the defendant is instead convicted of an aggravated assault carrying a thirty-*year* maximum.

Second, the prosecutor's decisions may also determine the minimum permissible sentence. In certain limited circumstances, a mandatory minimum may be triggered by a judge's findings without the prosecutor's support, but this is not normally the case. Sometimes the prosecutor-determined minimum and maximum are so close together that the judge has very little, or perhaps no, sentencing discretion. For instance, in a murder case, the prosecutor may agree not to seek the death penalty in return for the defendant's plea to a lesser murder charge that carries a mandatory minimum life sentence. In such a case, the judge's role at sentencing is merely a formality—there is nothing for the judge to do besides imposing the agreed-upon life term.

Third, in cases in which there is some judicial discretion left to exercise, the prosecutor may influence the punishment through his or her sentencing recommendation to the judge (O'Hear, 2017, 17). Whether prosecutors make such recommendations varies from jurisdiction to jurisdiction; some judges view the practice as an overstepping of the prosecutor's role. In courthouses where recommendations are made, however, they can be quite important and often become part of the plea-bargaining deal. Experienced attorneys recognize that judges don't often sentence above a prosecutor's recommendation (or for that matter below a defense lawyer's). This is consistent with the normal role of judges in litigation, which is to award one side with what it requests or to find some principled way to split the difference.

Fourth, the prosecutor may influence punishment through the information and arguments that he or she chooses to present to the judge at sentencing. The prosecutor, for instance, may or may not encourage the victim to provide a statement; inform the judge that the defendant was suspected of committing other, uncharged crimes; or draw attention to the extreme callousness with which the defendant perpetrated the charged crime. Such strategic decisions may be especially important in cases in which the prosecutor's recommendation as to the sentence is either flatly unwelcome or otherwise unlikely to carry much weight in and of itself. These decisions may also play an important role in the calculation of sentencing guidelines ranges in those jurisdictions in which guidelines are used (U.S. Sentencing Commission, 2004, 83–84). For instance, in robbery cases, the federal guidelines call for a longer sentence if a victim was physically restrained, but the defendant's guilty plea to a robbery charge does not indicate in itself whether there was such restraint. The judge must determine this at the sentencing hearing, and the prosecutor's decision about whether to present arguments and evidence in support of a physical restraint "enhancement" may effectively control how the judge finds.

These four mechanisms have long provided prosecutors with considerable power over punishment. Yet, many scholars have argued this prosecutorial power dramatically expanded in the late twentieth century (Miller, 2004).

Although there is no precise metric for prosecutorial power, it has surely grown in some important respects. Most obviously, the proliferation of mandatory minimums and presumptive guidelines effectively shifted much power from judges to prosecutors. To the extent that prosecutors make the key decisions about the application of minimums and guideline factors, they are able to exert increased direct control over sentencing outcomes, even to the point of taking away the judge's discretion entirely in some cases. (Recall the murder example discussed earlier in the chapter.) On the other hand, as explained in Q1, minimums and guidelines never completely dominated American sentencing and have undergone gradual retreat since 2000. The preservation of quite meaningful judicial sentencing discretion in most cases means that prosecutors are not able simply to dictate punishment.

Yet, there may be other, more subtle ways in which prosecutorial power has grown. With more and more new crimes on the books, and longer maximum and minimum sentences for many old crimes, the prosecutor's plea-bargaining leverage has ballooned. Consider, for instance, a defendant arrested in a public park with two grams of cocaine, a hypodermic needle, and a lawfully permitted firearm. A generation ago, the plea deal might have included the prosecutor's agreement not to argue against the defendant's request for a sentence of probation. Now, however, the defendant's sentencing exposure may look dramatically different. Depending on the state, the maximum sentence for possession with intent to distribute cocaine is apt to be far more severe, plus the prosecutor might be able to pile on several additional charges for crimes that did not exist in earlier eras: drug distribution in a public park, possession of drug paraphernalia (the needle), and possession of a firearm in connection with a drug trafficking offense. If the prosecutor pursued all of these charges, there might well be a significant mandatory minimum in play, as well as a maximum that is several *decades* longer than it would have been a generation ago. Many defendants in such circumstances would be willing to agree to almost anything to get some of these charges dropped. This might result, for instance, in a joint recommendation from the prosecutor and the defense lawyer for, say, a five-year prison term. Although judges are not required to go along with such a recommended sentence, they are typically inclined to accept joint recommendations, which, among other things, minimize the risk of appeal. In any event, when thinking about the power of prosecutors over punishment, it is important to bear in mind not only their ability to directly override judicial sentencing preferences but also their ability to pressure defendants into less favorable plea deals.

Prosecutorial control remains far from absolute, but its strengthening in the late twentieth century has prompted debate. Do prosecutors now have too much power over sentences? Critics make several different points. First, for a variety of reasons, including their close association with police and victims, prosecutors may lack the neutrality of judges and tend to favor excessively severe sentences. Second, while judges almost invariably come to the bench with significant professional and life experience behind them, prosecutors are often much younger—perhaps even fresh out of law school—and so may lack a certain wisdom or depth of understanding of human character that may helpfully inform decisions about punishment. Third, to the extent that prosecutors are shaping or even effectively determining the sentence through their charging and plea-bargaining decisions, they are doing so without the full body of information that might be available at the formal sentencing hearing. For instance, in some jurisdictions, it is common in felony cases for a probation agent to prepare an extensive presentence investigation report between the entry of a guilty plea and sentencing; this report may contain much information about the defendant's background, mental health, and family circumstances that the prosecutor did not have during plea negotiations. Fourth, and finally, there is the closed, opaque nature of prosecutorial decision making. By contrast, sentencing hearings occur in open court, for all the world to see. Defendants, and increasingly also victims, have a right to make a statement at the hearing. There is a structured process for the lawyers on both sides to present evidence and arguments. With a judge presiding and a permanent record created of who said what, the lawyers can be held accountable for dishonesty or carelessness. When the judge renders his or her sentencing decision, he or she is expected to provide a public explanation for the decision—an explanation that can be reviewed for fairness and logical coherence by an appellate court. However, charging and plea-bargaining decisions—typically made outside of public view and without any requirement of explanation—lack the procedural safeguards that we rely on to ensure that judicial sentencing decisions have both the appearance and the reality of rationality and fairness.

Prosecutors and their supporters, not surprisingly, argue that these criticisms are overblown. Prosecutors are professionals, subject to the same ethical rules that govern all lawyers. Although they sometimes work closely with victims and police officers, prosecutors retain formal independence from them. Directly or indirectly, prosecutors are answerable to the voters, which establishes another mechanism of accountability for negligence and abuse of power. Although some prosecutors may seem young and inexperienced, they typically work in offices with more seasoned lawyers, who provide training, guidance, and supervision. While plea negotiations may lack transparency and formality, that does not necessarily mean they are unfair to defendants; prosecutors normally give defense lawyers an opportunity to make a pitch on behalf of their clients, and defense lawyers are capable of gathering and presenting most of the helpful information that might appear in a presentence investigation report. There is, moreover, a hearing in court before a defendant pleads guilty; although these hearings tend to be brief and formulaic, they do create an opportunity for the judge to block gross injustices in plea bargaining. Additionally, prosecutors often find themselves up against the same defense lawyers on a regular basis; they have an incentive to treat these lawyers fairly in order to maintain cooperative working relationships in future cases. Finally, although charging and plea-bargaining decisions may shape the sentence in important ways, prosecutors only very rarely have the final say over punishment. Judges retain substantial sentencing discretion in most cases, while other actors later in the process, such as a parole board, may also ultimately serve as a meaningful check and balance on the prosecutor's power.

There is something of a middle-ground position in the debate, too. One might accept the prosecutor's current level of power in determining sentences, but still think that the plea-bargaining process should be reformed so as to include stronger safeguards against unfairness (Lynch, 2015). For instance, prosecutors might be required to create and publish specific guidelines for charging and plea bargaining (O'Hear, 2007). There might be a formalized process, then, for defendants to request supervisory review of decisions that seem to violate the guidelines. Prosecutors might also be required to justify deviations from the guidelines at guilty plea hearings. For their part, defense lawyers could be held to higher standards of competence in plea negotiations; a defendant might thus be permitted to withdraw his or her guilty plea if his or her lawyer failed to look for and present mitigating information to the prosecutor. Pretrial "discovery" rules might also be reformed so as to ensure that prosecutors share with the defense lawyer any information they have that would be favorable to the defendant at trial before a plea deal is finalized (Covey, 2016). These are just a few of the changes that might be considered to improve plea bargaining. The real challenge may lie in determining to what extent new procedural safeguards can be established without going too far toward eliminating the efficiency that makes plea bargaining so attractive in the first place.

FURTHER READING

Bach, Amy. 2009. *Ordinary Injustice: How America Holds Court.* New York: Henry Holt and Company.

Covey, Russell. 2016. "Plea Bargaining and Price Theory." *George Washington Law Review*, 84, 920.

Lynch, Gerald. 2015. "Our Administrative System of Criminal Justice." *Fordham Law Review*, 83, 1672.

Miller, Marc. 2004. "Domination & Dissatisfaction: Prosecutors as Sentencers." *Stanford Law Review*, 56, 1211.

O'Hear, Michael. 2007. "Plea Bargaining and Victims: From Consultation to Guidelines." *Marquette Law Review*, 91, 323.

O'Hear, Michael. 2017. *Wisconsin Sentencing in the Tough-on-Crime Era: How Judges Retained Power and Why Mass Incarceration Happened Anyway.* Madison: University of Wisconsin Press.

U.S. Sentencing Commission. 2004. *Fifteen Years of Guidelines Sentencing.* Washington, DC: United States Sentencing Commission.

Q3: ARE DEFENDANTS PUNISHED FOR EXERCISING THEIR CONSTITUTIONAL RIGHT TO A TRIAL?

Answer: Defendants can normally expect to receive a harsher sentence if they go to trial and are convicted than if they plead guilty. This practice has sparked considerable controversy, but many lawyers and judges view it as necessary to induce prompt guilty pleas and thereby save the courts from being overwhelmed by their caseloads.

The Facts: About 95 percent of criminal convictions in the United States come by way of a guilty plea, as opposed to a guilty verdict at the end of a trial (O'Hear, 2008). What might lead a defendant to surrender his or her right to a trial and admit guilt? In some lower-level cases, the defendant is simply motivated to "get it over with"; if the punishment is not likely to be severe, there may seem little point in investing the time and money required to contest the charges at trial. In other cases, the defendant may see a guilty plea as a way to express regret over what he or she has done. In still others, the guilty plea may result from the defendant's sense of hopelessness, or from a desire to protect a vulnerable loved one from having to testify at trial, or from some other idiosyncratic motivation. However, the primary motivation for most guilty pleas is the defendant's belief that he or she will receive a more lenient sentence from a guilty plea than a guilty verdict at trial.

This more lenient treatment is sometimes called the "plea benefit." Alternatively, and reflecting a more critical perspective, some might say that the tougher sentence after trial embodies a "trial penalty." Whether the language of "benefit" or "penalty" is more appropriate depends on the baseline of comparison—the normal post-plea sentence or the normal post-trial sentence. Since there is no clear right answer, it might be better to use more neutral terminology and simply refer to a "plea differential."

The plea differential results from the actions of one or both of two actors. First, the prosecutor may act to encourage or reward the defendant's guilty plea. As discussed in Q2, the prosecutor normally has various tools available to influence the sentence, so the prosecutor's support of a relatively lenient outcome typically matters a great deal. Second, with or without the prosecutor's acquiescence, the judge may independently choose to recognize the guilty plea. Knowing this, defendants in some cases are even willing to enter an "open plea," that is, plead guilty without the benefit of any express deal with the prosecutor. When a defendant enters an open plea in the expectation of a more lenient sentence, this is sometimes called "implicit plea bargaining."

Why would a prosecutor or judge favor a more lenient sentence for a defendant who pleads guilty? There are two competing theories. First, the guilty plea may be an indication of remorse, and the genuinely remorseful defendant seems less likely to commit more crimes in the future than the defendant who remains defiant. According to this view, the lenient sentence for the defendant who pleads guilty reflects a belief that he or she is less dangerous and hence requires less control by the state. However, there is an important objection to this theory: if we normally respond to guilty pleas with reduced sentences, then it is impossible to know whether the plea reflects true remorse or is merely an act of self-interest. The second theory thus seems more plausible—that prosecutors and judges reward guilty pleas in order to promote greater efficiency in the court system. Where a single trial might easily consume several days or even weeks of prosecutor and judge time, a guilty plea might be presented to the court and accepted in a matter of minutes. Moreover, trials normally lead to burdensome appeals and the possibility that a higher court will send the case back for yet another time-consuming trial. By contrast, many fewer appealable issues are likely to arise in a guilty-plea case. Guilty pleas, in short, permit prosecutors and judges to handle far more cases than they would be able to otherwise. Indeed, if the plea differential did not exist and most defendants insisted on a trial, the court system would likely require a massive infusion of new resources in order to avoid collapse.

Although the existence of a plea differential is widely recognized, it is difficult to ascertain the precise degree of the benefit/penalty. The magnitude does seem to vary considerably from courthouse to courthouse—and even within a single courthouse, from judge to judge, prosecutor to prosecutor, and case to case. In general, these variations are invisible to anyone who does not work regularly in the courthouse. Rarely does a judge say anything on the record as explicit as "I would have given this defendant X years in prison if he had pled guilty, but since he was convicted at trial I am going to impose a sentence of Y years."

The federal sentencing guidelines have attempted to bring greater consistency and transparency to the plea differential for defendants prosecuted in federal court. The guidelines include an "acceptance of responsibility" adjustment that was intended to provide a sentence reduction of about one-third for most defendants who plead guilty (O'Hear, 1997). However, even beyond this provision, federal prosecutors and judges have a variety of other tools available to encourage guilty pleas. For instance, in return for a guilty plea, the prosecutor might agree not to argue that a particular factor is present that would increase the guidelines sentence. Recent research suggests that the average actual plea discount in the federal system may approach 40 percent (Kim, 2015).

Evidence of state-court practices is more fragmentary, but in some jurisdictions, defendants who go to trial may routinely face prison terms that are twice or more the length they would receive if they pled guilty (Oppell, 2011). The classic Supreme Court case of *Bordenkircher v. Hayes* provides a stark illustration of this reality (O'Hear, 2006). Indicted in Kentucky for forging a check in the amount of $88.30, Paul Hayes faced a prison term of between two and ten years. During plea negotiations, the prosecutor offered to recommend a five-year sentence if Hayes pled guilty but threatened otherwise to add an habitual criminality charge carrying a mandatory minimum life sentence. Feeling that five years was excessive for his nonviolent offense, Hayes refused the deal, and the prosecutor carried through on his threat. Thus, when Hayes lost at trial, he was sentenced as an habitual criminal. In effect, for exercising his constitutional right to a trial, Hayes's punishment ballooned from five years to life in prison—an extraordinary but not unprecedented plea differential.

Critics assert that punishing a defendant differently based on his or her decision to go to trial violates the Constitution. They contend that the Sixth Amendment to the Constitution gives defendants the right to contest the charges against them at trial, and a right really isn't a right at all if the state can punish you for exercising it. Yet in a close 5–4 decision, the Supreme Court upheld the life sentence in *Bordenkircher v. Hayes*, and, by extension, nearly every other plea differential established through a prosecutor's or judge's discretion. In essence, the Court decided that plea bargaining had simply become too important to the criminal justice system to undermine through new constitutional restraints. On that ground, the Court had already approved the constitutionality of offers to *reduce* charges in return for a guilty plea, and the Court could see no logical reason to treat threats to *increase* charges any differently.

While constitutional challenges to the plea differential have gone nowhere, a lively debate over the practice continues. Because prosecutors play such an important role in establishing the differential, this controversy echoes some aspects of the debate discussed in Q2 regarding prosecutorial power over punishment.

Critics of the plea differential make three major points. First, the differential may lead to many wrongful convictions because of the pressure it exerts on innocent defendants to plead guilty. Although it may seem that a genuinely innocent defendant would always want to have an opportunity to clear his or her name at trial, no defense lawyer can ever guarantee an acquittal; trials are simply too unpredictable. Given the risks of an erroneous verdict, any rational defendant would have to think long and hard about the potential trial penalty. Indeed, if the plea differential is made large enough, there would be very few innocent defendants who are willing to take their chances with a jury. Not surprisingly, then, there are now hundreds of documented cases of defendants who pled guilty and were later conclusively exonerated (Dripps, 2016).

Second, the plea differential may result in excessive sentences for defendants who are convicted at trial. Since most people are convicted by guilty plea, the argument goes, it is the guilty-plea sentence that should be regarded as the "normal" punishment for any given crime. However, as previously discussed, the post-trial sentence may be many years longer than this norm. There is nothing about the mode of conviction (trial versus plea) that changes the seriousness of a defendant's past criminal conduct or the risk that the defendant will commit more crimes in the future, which should be the main determinants of the sentence. Thus, situations in which a defendant convicted after trial gets a much longer sentence than he or she would have received if he or she pled guilty—think again of the life term that Mr. Hayes received in Kentucky—have frequently been condemned as unjustifiably harsh and unfair.

Third, as a result of the plea differential, criminal trials have become much less frequent. As increasingly tough sentencing laws have given prosecutors more powerful tools to induce guilty pleas, trials have become increasingly rare. While about one in twelve felony cases went to trial in the 1970s, that number plummeted over the ensuing four decades to about one in forty (Oppell, 2011). From one perspective, this trend may seem a great triumph of efficiency. However, there may also be a variety of subtle costs. Trials often provide an opportunity for defendants and victims alike to tell their stories. Whatever the outcome of a trial, some observers believe that the process is apt to be perceived as fairer all around than the expedited—indeed, often rushed—plea procedures. Fairer process, in turn, promotes greater acceptance of the results (O'Hear, 2008). Additionally, interested members of the public are able to gain much more information about cases that go to trial. Moreover, jury trials, in particular, give lay people a central role to play in the determination of guilt, which may enhance the public legitimacy of the criminal justice system. By contrast, a system in which nearly every case is effectively resolved through private plea bargaining seems to be a closed system that primarily serves the convenience of the people who work in it. The fairness and legitimacy costs of a plea-dominated system are difficult to quantify, but they may be quite substantial.

Defenders of the current arrangements—who seem overwhelmingly to come from inside the system—argue that police and prosecutors normally do a good job of separating the guilty from the innocent before charges are filed, and that the efficiencies created by a sizeable plea differential allow the system to hold a far higher percentage of offenders accountable than would otherwise be the case. If trials were the norm, instead of guilty pleas, and if taxpayers were unwilling to build and staff many new court-houses, then prosecutors would likely have to decline charges in many more cases than they do now.

Perhaps the biggest challenge facing critics has been the difficulty of coming up with a workable alternative to the current system. Efforts to ban explicit prosecutorial plea bargaining have not been particularly successful in promoting higher trial rates. For instance, a ban in Alaska simply led to a large increase in open guilty pleas—that is, implicit plea bargaining (Covey, 2016). Other reformers would permit explicit plea bargaining but cap the size of the plea differential, so as to prevent sentences that are disproportionate to the severity of the offense (Bowers, 2016) or that create too great a risk that innocent defendants will plead guilty (Dripps, 2016). Such vague standards would presumably prevent a recurrence of what happened to Paul Hayes—a life sentence for a low-level property crime—but would be difficult to apply consistently in cases presenting less extreme injustices.

Given the reality of caseload pressures, it does not seem politically or practically feasible to eliminate the plea differential entirely. But once critics concede the legitimacy of *some* plea differential, it is difficult to see where exactly to draw the line. How much is too much?

FURTHER READING

Bowers, Josh. 2016. "Plea Bargaining's Baselines." *William & Mary Law Review*, 57, 1083.

Covey, Russell. 2016. "Plea Bargaining and Price Theory." *George Washington Law Review*, 84, 920.

Dripps, Donald. 2016. "Guilt, Innocence, and Due Process of Plea Bargaining." *William & Mary Law Review*, 57, 1343.

Kim, Andrew. 2015. "Underestimating the Trial Penalty: An Empirical Analysis of the Federal Trial Penalty and Critique of the Abrams Study." *Mississippi Law Journal*, 84, 1195.

O'Hear, Michael. 1997. "Remorse, Cooperation, and 'Acceptance of Responsibility': The Structure, Implementation, and Reform of Section 3E1.1 of the Federal Sentencing Guidelines." *Northwestern University Law Review*, 91, 1507.

O'Hear, Michael. 2006. "The End of *Bordenkircher*: Extending the Logic of *Apprendi* to Plea Bargaining." *Washington University Law Review*, 84, 835.

O'Hear, Michael. 2008. "Plea Bargaining and Procedural Justice." *Georgia Law Review*, 42, 407.

Oppell, Richard. 2011. "Sentencing Shift Gives New Leverage to Prosecutors." *New York Times*, September 26. Retrieved from http://www.nytimes.com/2011/09/26/us/tough-sentences-help-prosecutors-push-for-plea-bargains.html.

Q4: DO DRUG OFFENDERS GET TOUGHER SENTENCES THAN VIOLENT OFFENDERS?

Answer: On average, violent offenders are given significantly longer sentences than drug offenders in the American justice system. However, averages mask wide variation in the sentences for both groups. Some drug offenders do receive sentences comparable to those imposed for the most serious violent crimes, including life sentences.

The Facts: Beginning with New York's Rockefeller laws in 1973, American legislatures adopted a long series of tough drug sentencing laws in the late twentieth century. In general, however, drug offenders still tend to receive more lenient sentences than offenders convicted of major violent crimes. For instance, in 2009, in large urban counties, the median prison term for offenders convicted of a violent felony (forty-eight months) was exactly twice as long as the median term for those convicted of a drug felony (Reaves, 2013). Even just focusing on those convicted of the most serious category of drug offenses—trafficking—the median sentence of thirty-six months was still well short of the median for violent felonies. Another study of felony sentencing in a more representative sample of 300 counties in 2006 found a similar gap, with a median term of sixty months for violent offenses and thirty-six for drug offenses (Rosenmerkel, Durose, & Farole, 2009). Both studies also found that drug offenders were more likely than violent offenders to avoid prison with a probationary sentence.

More recent and fine-grained data are available for the federal system (U.S. Sentencing Commission, 2017). In 2016, federal defendants convicted of drug trafficking had a median sentence of forty-eight months, while those convicted of simple possession of drugs had a median sentence of only six months. By contrast, the median for murder was 210 months; kidnapping, 213; sexual abuse, 120; and robbery, 60.

Of course, averages obscure the wide range of sentences that are imposed, and a substantial number of drug offenders do receive very long prison terms. Drug type plays a major role in driving some of the longer sentences. For instance, the 2016 federal data show a median sentence of seventy-four months for methamphetamine offenses and sixty-five for crack cocaine—both longer than the median sentence for the violent crime of robbery. Nor are long drug sentences limited to federal court. The 2009 data from large urban counties indicate that 5 percent of those convicted of drug felonies received sentences of ten years or more.

Nothing more dramatically illustrates the potential severity of drug sentences than the steadily growing number of drug offenders serving life terms. Twelve states, plus the federal government, authorize sentences of life without the possibility of parole (LWOP) for drug offenders (O'Hear, 2013). As of 2016, more than 2,000 American prisoners were serving LWOP sentences for drug offenses (Nellis, 2017). If life with parole and "virtual life" (fifty years or more) sentences were included, then the number of lifers in prison for drug offenses would reach 5,308. Moreover, while the "hard" drugs tend to get the toughest punishment, at least fifty-four marijuana offenders have received LWOP sentences since 1996 in federal courts alone (Cauchon, 2015).

Long prison sentences for drug crimes have been attacked as wasteful, unjust, and even unconstitutional. However, in 1991, the U.S. Supreme Court seemed to foreclose constitutional challenges in this area in the case of *Harmelin v. Michigan* (O'Hear, 2013). Convicted of possessing more than 650 grams of cocaine, but lacking a significant prior record, Allen Harmelin received a mandatory LWOP sentence under Michigan law. He argued on appeal that such a severe sentence violated the Eighth Amendment ban on cruel and unusual punishment when imposed for a nonviolent offense. A divided Supreme Court concluded otherwise. Writing the key opinion, Justice Anthony Kennedy rejected Harmelin's contention that drug trafficking should even be considered a nonviolent offense. Kennedy identified three distinct ways that drug offenses may lead to criminal violence: (1) an intoxicated drug user may be more prone to violence, (2) an addict may have to resort to robbery or other crime in order to obtain drugs, and (3) violence may result from competition between rival drug trafficking organizations.

Kennedy's argument highlights an important difficulty in trying to compare drug and violence sentences. While it is easy enough to determine the average sentence imposed on people convicted of drug offenses, many of those individuals actually drew police attention because they were involved with violent gangs or were otherwise suspected of violence

(Stuntz, 2011, 270). However, it is often easier for prosecutors to prove a drug offense than a violent offense. For that reason, many drug prosecutions are "pretextual"; that is, they are not fundamentally motivated by a desire to punish the drug offense that was formally charged. (This is the sort of law enforcement strategy that was used most famously against the notoriously violent gangster Al Capone, who was ultimately convicted of income tax evasion.) Arguably, an effort to compare drug and violence sentences should factor out the drug cases that were really about violence. However, there is no reliable way to make this distinction in the available data.

Should drug sentencing laws be softened? Doing so would weaken some of the tools that prosecutors use to address violent crime. On the other hand, there is no requirement that tough drug laws be limited in their application to violent offenders. Prosecutors can, and sometimes do, send to prison hapless individuals who have only very minor roles in trafficking organizations or who seem merely to have possessed small quantities of drugs in the wrong place at the wrong time. There are inevitably tradeoffs—countervailing costs and benefits—when prosecutors are armed with tough sentencing laws that nominally target a large industry with millions of workers and customers spread across nearly every community in the United States. Prosecutors have a seemingly endless supply of drug offenders to go after and the legal tools to induce a quick, easy guilty plea in most cases. This is a lot of power, and such power will not always be exercised in consistent, principled ways.

Whether current laws strike the right balance is a difficult question that implicates many of the same considerations as the debate over prosecutorial power more generally, as discussed in Q2 earlier. Also implicated are such contentious matters as the dangerousness of different drugs, the effectiveness of criminal punishment as a deterrent to drug distribution and drug use, the morality of drug use, and the value of penal threats as a way to encourage addicts to enter and remain in treatment.

Since the late 1990s, the general legislative trend has been to reduce drug penalties (O'Hear, 2017, Ch. 2). The Rockefeller drug laws are gone now, as is the draconian Michigan law that gave Allen Harmelin a life sentence. A handful of states have even legalized marijuana. Still many laws remain on the books from the height of the War on Drugs, and the number of imprisoned drug offenders has been receding only very slowly. Meanwhile, America's current opioid addiction crisis seems to be fueling a renewed interest in tough responses to drug crime, especially in rural jurisdictions, where treatment resources are often scarce (Keller & Pearce, 2016).

FURTHER READING

Cauchon, Dennis. 2015. "Fifty-Four Marijuana Offenders Given Federal Life Sentences since 1996." *The Clemency Report*. Retrieved from http://clemencyreport.org/fifty-four-marijuana-offenders-given-federal-life-sentences-since-1996/.

Keller, Josh & Pearce, Adam. 2016. "This Small Indiana County Sends More People to Prison Than San Francisco and Durham, N.C., Combined. Why?" *New York Times*, September 2. Retrieved from https://www.nytimes.com/2016/09/02/upshot/new-geography-of-prisons.html.

Nellis, Ashley. 2017. *Still Life: America's Increasing Use of Life and Long-Term Sentences*. Washington, DC: The Sentencing Project.

O'Hear, Michael. 2013. "Not Just Kid Stuff? Extending *Graham* and *Miller* to Adults." *Missouri Law Review*, 78, 1087.

O'Hear, Michael. 2017. *The Failure of Sentencing Reform*. Santa Barbara, CA: Praeger.

Reaves, Brian. 2013. *Felony Defendants in Large Urban Counties, 2009—Statistical Tables*. Washington, DC: U.S. Department of Justice.

Rosenmerkel, Sean, Durose, Matthew, & Farole, Donald. 2009. *Felony Sentences in State Courts, 2006—Statistical Tables*. Washington, DC: U.S. Department of Justice.

Stuntz, William. 2011. *The Collapse of American Criminal Justice*. Cambridge, MA: Belknap Press.

U.S. Sentencing Commission. 2017. *2016 Sourcebook of Federal Sentencing Statistics*. Washington, DC: U.S. Sentencing Commission.

Q5: DO WHITE-COLLAR CRIMINALS EVER GET SERIOUS PRISON TERMS?

Answer: Sentences in white-collar cases have been on the rise since the 1980s. Incarceration has become common. Occasionally, prison terms are even in the decade-plus range. Still, as a general matter, white-collar offenders remain far more likely to get probation or just a short spell of incarceration than are "street criminals" convicted of major violent crimes or drug trafficking.

The Facts: The term "white-collar crime" is used frequently in the media and everyday conversation but lacks any precise legal meaning. Various definitions have been developed for different purposes (Strader, 2011, 1–3). Usually, the term "white-collar crime" seems to connote a crime of deceit perpetrated for financial gain, typically by a person who is either exploiting a position of trust in an organization or otherwise taking advantage of actual or pretended technical or professional knowledge. Prototypical white-collar crimes would include an employee embezzling money from his or her workplace; a "Ponzi" scheme in which a financial manager lures naïve customers with false promises of big investment returns; and a corporate accountant filing tax returns claiming nonexistent business expenses in order to minimize the corporation's tax bill. There are other crimes that might or might not be regarded as white collar, depending on the precise definition used. Consider, for example, an ordinary individual's failure to declare all of his or her income on a tax return, or the sale by a street vendor of a counterfeit Rolex watch, or a grocery store's alteration of the "sell by" date on perishable food.

Since "white-collar crime" has no specific definition and is not a legal category that the courts track, it is not possible to state with any precision what the average sentence is for these sorts of offenses. However, we may get a rough sense of where things stand by considering sentences for fraud—the basic category for offenses involving deceit. In 2015, federal fraud defendants received a median sentence of fourteen months in prison, including the 22 percent who received a sentence of probation (U.S. Sentencing Commission, 2017a). This was many years less than the median sentences for the major violent and sexual crimes, as well as drug trafficking and firearms violations. However, fraud was hardly the offense with the most lenient treatment. For instance, even lower median sentences were reported for simple possession of drugs (six months), illegal gambling (four months), and immigration violations (nine months).

State-court data also point to relatively high rates of probation, as well as average prison terms that are far shorter than those for the major violent crimes. In large urban counties in 2009, the median prison term for felony fraud was thirty-six months, *not* including the 29 percent given probation (Reaves, 2013). And, in a nationally representative sample of 300 counties in 2006, the median term of incarceration for fraud, forgery, and embezzlement was twelve months, not including the 35 percent who got probation (Rosenmerkel, Durose, & Farole, 2009).

As always, average figures can mask large variations. Among the major fraud subcategories tracked by the U.S. Sentencing Commission (2017b), the longest sentences went to those offenders who committed securities and investment fraud. Sentences in these cases averaged fifty-seven months. These tended to be large cases, with most involving fifty or more victims and total losses of more than $3 million.

Sentences have become considerably more severe in recent years, at least in federal court, where most major fraud cases are prosecuted. In the mid-1980s, about half of the federal fraud offenders received probation, but that proportion fell to less than one-third by 2001 (U.S. Sentencing Commission, 2004, 58). Then, between 2002 and 2011, median sentence lengths increased by 50 percent (Dervan, 2015). Average sentences in securities fraud cases jumped even more dramatically, more than tripling between 1997 and 2011.

These trends reflect the increasing severity of the federal sentencing guidelines for economic crimes. As originally promulgated in 1987, the maximum guidelines sentence for the fraud cases involving the largest financial losses would have been thirty months (Bowman, 2017). The comparable sentence today would be 262 months.

In order to illustrate the impact of changes to the guidelines, Professor Lucian Dervan uses the case of stockbroker Jordan Belfort, the notorious "Wolf of Wall Street" who became the subject of a popular movie (Dervan, 2015). Dervan calculated a sentencing range of seventy-eight to ninety-seven months based on the guidelines that actually applied to Belfort's 1998 prosecution. If prosecuted under the 2013 version of the guidelines, however, Belfort would have faced a sentence about three times longer at twenty years. (Dervan's calculations do not include the breaks that Belfort received for pleading guilty and cooperating with prosecutors, which brought his actual time served down to twenty-two months.)

Although the sentencing guidelines for white-collar offenses tend to be much harsher today than they were in the 1980s and 1990s, judges are highly inconsistent about following the guidelines (which shifted from presumptive to merely advisory in 2005). As a result, one can find no shortage of examples of both extreme severity and surprising lenience in white-collar cases in the 21st century. Standing out on the severe side is Bernard Madoff's 150-year prison term for an exceptionally long-running Ponzi scheme with thousands of victims. Also notable are Robert Allen Stanford's 110-year sentence for a $7 billion investment fraud, Edward Woodard's twenty-three years for concealing nonperforming bank assets, and David McMaster's 15.5 years for a $28 million bank fraud (Goodman, 2014). On the other hand, H. Ty Warner received only probation after being convicted in 2014 of using an illegal tax dodge that cost the federal government $5.6 million. Even in the area of high-level investment scams and insider trading, several sentences since 2012 have been below five years (Goodman, 2014).

In sum, white-collar offenders—especially those who are guilty of multimillion-dollar investment or securities frauds—now face a genuine risk of significant incarceration, including the possibility of the sort of decade-plus prison terms that are normally associated with major violent offenders. At the same time, white-collar offenders remain far more likely than their violent counterparts to avoid prison entirely with a probationary sentence. Based on overall averages, it seems that one is still much better off if convicted of fraud than of rape, robbery, or murder.

Hardly anyone seems happy with the current state of affairs. However, there is no consensus as to whether incarceration for white-collar crime should be made more frequent or less frequent.

Those who would like to see more incarceration emphasize that there can be very serious harm in white-collar cases. Madoff, for instance, is said to have frittered away the life savings of thousands. Moreover, white-collar offenses can be unusually difficult to detect and prosecute, which suggests that such offenses cannot readily be deterred unless all of those who are caught and convicted receive severe punishment. Additionally, some critics see race and/or class bias when white-collar offenders receive more lenient treatment than street criminals. Should the robber who steals one person's wallet really get a sentence many years longer than the corrupt financial adviser or business manager who steals a thousand or even a million times as much money—especially when the robber has not had the same advantages in life as the white-collar fraudster?

For their part, the critics of long white-collar sentences point out that these offenders tend to have little or no criminal history and are unlikely to repeat their crimes. The taint of a conviction is apt to cause the offender to be removed from positions of responsibility, which deprives her of the opportunity to reoffend even if she has not truly "learned her lesson." In this sense, incarceration may seem unnecessary. Moreover, in some cases, the offender's loss of a good name, a high social status, and a materially comfortable life will be psychologically devastating and may seem punishment enough. Additionally, major white-collar offenders are often much older than the typical street criminal. For instance, among federal securities and investment fraud offenders, the average age at sentencing is fifty-one (U.S. Sentencing Commission, 2017b). A twenty-year sentence for a sixty- or seventy-year-old is effectively a life term, and thus means something quite different from the same sentence would to a twenty- or thirty-year-old. Also, with age comes a higher likelihood of chronic illness and disability—conditions that tend to be much harder (and more expensive) to manage in prison than outside (see Q30 for additional coverage).

The debate over the proper severity of white-collar sentences touches on another contentious topic in criminal law: under what circumstances (if any) should the criminal justice system be used to enforce compliance with technical economic regulations? Over the past century, government regulation of business has grown far more complex and extensive, covering areas such as environmental pollution, labor relations, workplace safety, food and drug safety, market consolidation, and corporate finance. When some of these regulations are violated, there may be criminal liability, whether or not any particular harm is apparent. Moreover, some regulatory offenses are considered "strict liability," which means that a prosecutor does not need to prove the sort of bad intent that is traditionally required for criminal punishment, as for fraud offenses. Supporters of this system believe that a credible threat of criminal punishment for violations forms a key part of the overall business regulatory regime in the United States. Critics, however, contend that strict liability is fundamentally unfair, especially when used to enforce highly technical regulations that are difficult to understand and of questionable value. Of course, to the extent that one is skeptical of *any* criminal liability for regulatory violations, one would be even more skeptical of significant incarceration as a penalty.

As with the sentencing of drug traffickers, the sentencing of white-collar offenders implicates many difficult questions, including those related to the proper purposes of punishment, racial and class disparities in the criminal justice system, the role of government in regulating market transactions, and the limits of capitalism. However, given their shared backgrounds, legal elites seem far more likely to identify with white-collar offenders than with drug trafficking defendants. That may help to explain why, despite growing public pressure to get tough on financial crime following the recessions in 2001 and 2008, there has not been a more consistent turn to longer prison terms.

FURTHER READING

Bowman, Frank. 2017. "'Loss' Revisited: A Defense of the Centerpiece of the Federal Economic Crime Sentencing Guidelines." *Missouri Law Review*, 82, 1.

Dervan, Lucian. 2015. "Sentencing the Wolf of Wall Street: From Leniency to Uncertainty." *Wayne Law Review*, 61, 1.

Goodman, Leah. 2014. "Nonsensical Sentences for White Collar Criminals." *Newsweek*, June 26. Retrieved from http://www.newsweek.com/2014/07/04/nonsensical-sentences-white-collar-criminals-256104.html.

Reaves, Brian. 2013. *Felony Defendants in Large Urban Counties, 2009—Statistical Tables*. Washington, DC: U.S. Department of Justice.

Rosenmerkel, Sean, Durose, Matthew, & Farole, Donald. 2009. *Felony Sentences in State Courts, 2006—Statistical Tables*. Washington, DC: U.S. Department of Justice.

Strader, J. Kelly. 2011. *Understanding White Collar Crime*. New Providence, NJ: LexisNexis.

U.S. Sentencing Commission. 2004. *Fifteen Years of Guidelines Sentencing*. Washington, DC: U.S. Sentencing Commission.

U.S. Sentencing Commission. 2017a. *2016 Sourcebook of Federal Sentencing Statistics*. Washington, DC: U.S. Sentencing Commission.

U.S. Sentencing Commission. 2017b. *Quick Facts: Securities and Investment Fraud Offenses*. Washington, DC: U.S. Sentencing Commission.

Q6: IS CAPITAL PUNISHMENT "DEAD" IN THE UNITED STATES?

Answer: Capital punishment has been in slow, steady decline since the 1990s, as reflected in both the number of death sentences imposed and the number of executions carried out. In most states, the death penalty is no longer in active use. However, in a few states, mostly concentrated in the nation's southern region, capital punishment remains a notable feature of the criminal justice landscape.

The Facts: In 1972, the U.S. Supreme Court effectively declared the death penalty unconstitutional. However, this decision sparked a furious backlash, and dozens of states adopted new death penalties laws in the years that followed (Mandery, 2013, 253–58). In 1976, the Supreme Court relented and approved some of the new laws, thus inaugurating what is sometimes called the "modern era" of capital punishment in America.

The number of new death sentences and the number of executions in the United States grew, more or less steadily, between the mid-1970s and the mid- to late 1990s (Snell, 2014). Because of the lengthy appeals process in these cases—often successful for the defendant—the pace of actual executions always lagged well behind the pace of new death sentences. New death sentences peaked at 315 in 1996, while executions peaked at ninety-eight in 1999.

Since the peak years, both numbers have dropped sharply and consistently. In recent years, new death sentences have been below 100 per year, and executions below fifty. Indeed, in 2016, executions fell to just twenty—the lowest figure since 1991 (Snell, 2017).

These trends reflect a variety of interrelated legal developments (O'Hear, 2017, 149–54). A handful of states (New Jersey, New Mexico, Illinois,

Connecticut, and Maryland) repealed their capital punishment laws, while the death penalty was effectively eliminated in New York and Delaware through court decisions. Other states retained the death penalty but narrowed the range of offenders to whom it could be applied. The U.S. Supreme Court also contributed to this narrowing process by declaring it unconstitutional to execute the cognitively impaired, or to impose the death penalty for crimes that were committed by a juvenile or that did not involve homicide.

These legal developments, in turn, both reflected and amplified the impact of a broader shift in public opinion against the death penalty. After peaking at 80 percent in 1994, support fell to under 50 percent in 2016 (Chokshi, 2016). This likely resulted from a variety of considerations. For instance, as DNA analysis improved and became more readily available in the 1990s, there followed a wave of exonerations from American death rows. One study counted seventy-four death-sentenced individuals who were formally declared not guilty between 1989 and 2003 (Gross, Jacoby, Matheson, & Montgomery, 2005). The steady drumbeat of exonerations reduced public confidence in the reliability of convictions in capital cases. Additionally, the high cost to taxpayers of maintaining death rows and fighting lengthy appeals also became an increasing concern. In recent years, the average length of time from death sentence to execution has exceeded twelve years (Snell, 2014). In principle, the processes in many states could likely be expedited but probably only at a greater risk of executing the innocent.

The death penalty has also been dogged for many years by perceptions of unfair race and class disparities. More than one-third of the individuals executed in the modern era have been black—a proportion that is about three times greater than the black percentage of the overall U.S. population (Snell, 2014). Race seems to play an especially important role in cases in which a black defendant is charged with killing a nonblack victim; this is the defendant-victim combination that is most likely to result in a death sentence (Dieter, 1998). Meanwhile, there are also class disparities related to the low quality of legal representation provided in some jurisdictions to poor defendants in capital cases. Many disturbing instances of inexperienced, incompetent, and careless lawyering have emerged over the years (Bright, 1994). And even those court-appointed lawyers who have been genuinely committed to helping their clients have often been hampered by inadequate resources to investigate their cases and develop "mitigation" evidence that might lead a judge or jury to show mercy.

Views of capital punishment have also been affected by the widespread adoption of life without the possibility of parole (LWOP) as a new sentencing option. Prosecutors, judges, and juries increasingly found that they had a reasonably satisfactory alternative in most or all homicide cases to capital punishment. Policy makers also saw less need to keep the death penalty on the books when LWOP was available.

More recently, new legal, political, and practical challenges have arisen with regard to the most common method of execution in the United States, lethal injection (Berman, 2017). As several botched executions have drawn negative attention to this method, manufacturers of the lethal drugs have attempted to block use of their products for this controversial purpose. Extensive litigation has resulted. A new dimension to the messiness of this situation became apparent in early 2017, when Arkansas hurriedly scheduled eight executions in order to beat the fast-approaching expiration date for one of the key drugs in its deadly "cocktail." Elsewhere, concerns about the humaneness of lethal injection or simply the unavailability of the necessary drugs have led to a suspension of executions (St. John, 2016).

As against all of these concerns and objections to the death penalty, solid evidence of its benefits remains elusive. In particular, while a multitude of studies have considered whether the death penalty actually deters people from committing crimes, researchers have not reached any consistent conclusions. If there are deterrence benefits to the death penalty, they are not likely large (Donohue & Wolters, 2010).

Perhaps the most striking feature of the American death penalty is its intensely regional character. In 2015 and 2016 combined, executions were carried out in only seven states (Alabama, Florida, Georgia, Missouri, Oklahoma, Texas, and Virginia). All are southern or border states. This continues a long-standing trend. Those same seven states are the top seven for executions nationally in the modern era (i.e., since 1976). If the southern states of North Carolina and South Carolina are also added to the tally, the nine account for more than three-quarters of all executions in that time period (Snell, 2014).

If we consider the eleven states that formally joined the Confederacy during the Civil War, plus the two adjoining states of Missouri and Oklahoma, as a regional block, they contrast markedly with the rest of the nation. All thirteen states have carried out multiple executions in the modern era, continue to have at least a handful of individuals on death row, and maintain capital punishment as an active sentencing option in aggravated homicide cases (Snell, 2014). Outside that southern block, most states either did not adopt a modern-era capital punishment law at all or formally discontinued capital punishment through a recent legislative repeal or court order. In many of the other northern and western states that still have capital punishment on the books, actual executions have been so infrequent that the death penalty almost seems to have been informally repealed. Colorado, for instance, has carried out only one execution in the modern era, with just three inmates now on death row. Kansas has had no executions, with nine now on death row. And Washington has had just five executions, with nine now on death row. California presents perhaps the most remarkable story. The nation's largest state, with hundreds of inmates on death row, has executed only thirteen in the modern era and none in over a decade.

It would only be a little bit of an exaggeration to say that capital punishment is already dead in the United States outside the South. And even in the few states inside and outside the South that maintain an active execution practice, it is debatable how broadly important the death penalty is within the state's criminal justice system. Consider the nation's top two executing states, Texas (by total executions in the modern era) and Oklahoma (by executions per capita). In 2013, Texas arrested 648 individuals for major homicide offenses (Federal Bureau of Investigation, 2014, Table 69) but sent only nine individuals to death row. In the same year, Oklahoma arrested 156 for major homicides, but sent only one to death row. Thus, even for the worst crimes in the most active death-penalty states, the odds that any given defendant will be sentenced to death are quite low—and the odds that the sentence will eventually be carried out lower still. In both Texas and Oklahoma in 2013, three death sentences were overturned on appeal (Snell, 2014).

On the other hand, capital punishment may have important effects that are not fully reflected in the number of death sentences and executions alone. At a minimum, the threat of capital punishment often gives prosecutors much more plea-bargaining leverage than they would have otherwise, potentially leading some homicide defendants to accept much longer prison terms, in some cases even a life sentence (Thaxton, 2013). Although much harder to demonstrate, it is also possible that capital punishment generally tends to pull up sentences even for nonhomicide crimes. The death penalty serves as a prominent benchmark for sentencing severity in a state, potentially making life and other very long prison terms seem less severe than they would elsewhere.

FURTHER READING

Berman, Mark. 2017. "Arkansas Carries Out First Execution since 2005 after Supreme Court Denies Stay Requests." *Washington Post*, April 21. Retrieved from https://www.washingtonpost.com/news/post-nation/wp/2017/04/20/arkansas-plan-to-resume-executions-is-blocked-by-new-court-orders/?utm_term=.bf5f7f0768ff.

Bright, Stephen. 1994. "Counsel for the Poor: The Death Sentence Not for the Worst Crime but for the Worst Lawyer." *Yale Law Journal*, 103, 1385.

Chokshi, Niraj. 2016. "Death Penalty Loses Majority Support for First Time in 45 Years." *New York Times*, October 3. Retrieved from https://www.nytimes.com/2016/10/04/us/death-penalty-loses-majority-support-for-first-time-in-45-years.html.

Dieter, Richard. 1998. *The Death Penalty in Black and White: Who Lives, Who Dies, Who Decides*. Washington, DC: Death Penalty Information Center. Retrieved from https://deathpenaltyinfo.org/death-penalty-black-and-white-who-lives-who-dies-who-decides#.

Donohue, John & Wolfers, Justin. 2010. "Uses and Abuses of Empirical Evidence in the Death Penalty Debate." *Stanford Law Review*, 58, 791.

Federal Bureau of Investigation. 2014. *Crime in the United States—2013*. Washington, DC: Federal Bureau of Investigation.

Gross, Samuel, Jacoby, Kristen, Matheson, Daniel, & Montgomery, Nicholas. 2005. "Exonerations in the United States 1989 through 2003." *Journal of Criminal Law & Criminology*, 95, 523.

Mandery, Evan. 2013. *A Wild Justice: The Death and Resurrection of Capital Punishment in America*. New York: W.W. Norton & Co.

O'Hear, Michael. 2017. *The Failure of Sentencing Reform*. Santa Barbara, CA: Praeger.

Snell, Tracy. 2014. *Capital Punishment, 2013—Statistical Tables*. Washington, DC: United States Department of Justice.

Snell, Tracy. 2017. *Capital Punishment, 2014–2015*. Washington, DC: United States Department of Justice.

St. John, Paige. 2016. "How Riverside County Became California's Death Penalty Leader." *Los Angeles Times*, November 5. Retrieved from http://www.latimes.com/local/lanow/la-me-riverside-death-row-20161104-story.html.

Thaxton, Sherod. 2013. "Leveraging Death." *Journal of Criminal Law & Criminology*, 103, 475.

Q7: ARE THE NEEDS AND WISHES OF CRIME VICTIMS DISREGARDED IN THE SENTENCING PROCESS?

Answer: A politically powerful victims' rights movement has emerged in the United States since the 1970s, leading to a multitude of reforms in every state. These reforms have substantially increased the legal rights of crime victims. However, there remain important practical impediments to the effective exercise of these rights. Additionally, while it is often assumed that victims simply wish to maximize the severity of sentences, their actual views often include a desire for the rehabilitation of their victimizers—a desire that may be in tension with the incarceration-heavy sentencing practices that accompanied the rise of the victims' rights movement.

The Facts: Traditionally, the victim's role in criminal litigation was limited to that of a witness, deployed at the convenience of a prosecutor. The court system tended to ignore the needs and wishes of victims, aside from whatever interest the victim had in seeing an offender held legally accountable. Indeed, the system sometimes seemed so callous that victims felt as if they have been revictimized by the lawyers and judges. This "secondary victimization" was most notoriously a problem in sexual assault cases, in which defense lawyers had wide latitude to subject victims to humiliating cross-examination about their sexual histories.

A national victims' rights movement took shape in the 1970s and 1980s. The movement proved broadly popular, drawing support from across the political spectrum. To many on the left, the movement seemed a continuation of the civil rights activism that was already occurring on behalf of other traditionally marginalized groups in society. Feminists had particularly important affinities for victims' rights, given the shabby treatment so many female sexual and domestic assault victims received in the criminal justice system (Gottschalk, 2006, 121–33, 139–40). Meanwhile, to law-and-order conservatives, victims' rights seemed an appealing counterbalance to defendants' rights. In the eyes of many conservatives, defendants' rights had grown too strong as a result of the judicial activism of the 1960s.

The movement succeeded in changing American law in many res pects. Indeed, every single state has enacted victims' rights legislation, and most have put victims' rights into their constitutions (Roberts, 2009). Although efforts to add a victims' rights amendment to the federal constitution came up short, Congress did adopt an expansive Crime Victims' Rights Act (CVRA) in 2004. The CVRA and similar state laws establish new rights for victims at all stages of the criminal litigation process.

In relation to sentencing, advocates for victims have focused on procedural reforms that aim to provide victims with more meaningful opportunities to participate in court processes. Most prominently, victims have won the right to offer "impact statements" at sentencing. Although this right is now recognized in all states, courts have taken different approaches to implementation, imposing varying limitations on the amount and nature of victim views that can be presented. The most contentious question has been whether victims should be limited to a "just the facts" statement about the offense and its impact on them, or whether the victim may opine as to the egregiousness of the offense, the character of the offender, and perhaps even the sentence that should be imposed (Roberts, 2009). Other notable questions include whether victims have a right to speak in court at the sentencing hearing, as opposed to merely submitting a written statement in advance; whether all victims in a multi-victim case have a right to make a statement, as opposed to a representative subset; and whether community or neighborhood representatives have a right to submit a statement in cases lacking a discrete, identifiable victim, such as those involving open-air drug dealing.

Those who favor tighter restrictions on victim statements often emphasize efficiency considerations, as well as concerns that giving victims an expansive role may cause sentences to become too emotion-driven, unpredictable, and punitive. More broadly, critics assert that victim statements threaten to break down the traditional divide between criminal prosecutions, which are intended to further *public* interests, and civil tort claims, which are intended to further the *private* interests of an injured party. However, the supporters of victim statements respond that there is a traditionally recognized public interest in fitting punishment to the seriousness of a crime, and that impact statements can help a judge to understand more fully how serious a given crime was. Additionally, research suggests that victims may feel more satisfied with the justice system if they are given an opportunity to make a statement (Roberts, 2009).

Given ongoing uncertainties and debate regarding the scope of the victim's right to make a statement, the practicalities of enforcement of the right become important. Enforcement is reasonably straightforward to the extent that the prosecutor takes it on himself or herself to vindicate whatever victim right is at issue. Indeed, prosecutors do sometimes think of themselves more or less as the victim's attorney. However, as we saw in Q2, prosecutors often have different or more complex views of their role—views that can sometimes put a prosecutor at odds with a victim. How are the victim's rights to be enforced in such cases?

One issue has been whether victims have legal *standing* to assert claims on their own behalf. After all, the victim is not technically a party to a criminal case; the only parties are the government and the defendant. In American law, non-parties to a court case do not necessarily have standing to present and argue motions to the judge. However, victims' rights laws like the CVRA now increasingly make clear that victims do have standing to enforce their rights, although there can still be questions about who counts as a "victim" in some cases.

But, even assuming standing is not an issue, how is a given victim to know what his or her rights are, let alone make legally persuasive arguments to a judge about the meaning of those rights in the case at hand? Victims would, of course, find it quite helpful to have lawyers provide legal advice and representation in court. However, lawyers are expensive, and victims' rights laws have not yet extended to the point of guaranteeing an attorney for poor victims, in the way that the Constitution guarantees an attorney for poor defendants. A few legal service agencies and volunteer lawyers do provide assistance in parts of the country to some victims, but resources are spread thin, and lack of access to an attorney remains an important practical impediment to the enforcement of victim rights (Office for Victims of Crime, 2013, 10).

It has also been pointed out that although victim participation in the formal sentencing process has expanded, a plea bargain may as a practical matter leave the judge with little to do at sentencing. In such cases, delivering an impact statement to the sentencing judge may seem an empty formality.

Given the critical importance of plea bargaining to contemporary criminal justice, the victim's right to be heard will not be fully developed until it extends to plea deals. However, the procedural rights for victims in this area remain much less robust than they are with respect to the sentencing hearing. The inherent tension is this: the whole point of plea bargaining is to resolve criminal cases in a fast, efficient, predictable fashion, but introducing a victim into the mix increases the likelihood of delay, inefficiency, and unpredictability.

The most straightforward way to incorporate victims into plea bargaining would be at the end of the process—that is, at the court hearing in which the defendant formally enters a guilty plea. Thus, for instance, the CVRA expressly provides victims with a right to be heard at plea hearings in federal court. In theory anyway, a victim's statement might lead the judge to reject a plea deal that the victim dislikes. In practice, however, by the time of the plea hearing, it is often very difficult to derail a deal; busy judges tend to accept proposed guilty pleas with little real scrutiny, happy to clear a case from the trial schedule.

In light of these pressures, the most meaningful way for victims to participate might be earlier in the process, before the prosecutor and defendant have reached an agreement. Thus, at least twenty-two states have adopted a requirement that prosecutors try to consult with victims prior to finalizing a deal (O'Hear, 2007, 324). However, enforcement mechanisms are generally poor or nonexistent, and prosecutors have not necessarily exerted much effort to confer with victims in a timely fashion. In fairness to prosecutors, many victims are hard to reach, difficult to communicate with, or ambivalent about engaging with court processes. Few victims, it seems, have the combination of good education, stable living and work arrangements, and confidence in the fairness of court proceedings that make for relatively easy collaboration with a prosecutor. Fortunately, prosecutorial offices increasingly have specialized victim-witness coordinators, who can help to ease some of the difficulties. Even so, coordinators are often spread thin, and concerns persist that victims tend to be marginalized in plea bargaining.

Similar concerns exist with respect to release decisions from prison. Although parole boards have lost much of the power they had in the mid-twentieth century, these bodies still have wide discretion over the release dates of many prisoners in some states. In some cases, it may seem that the parole board effectively exercises as much power over punishment as the sentencing judge. Exclusion of victims from a parole hearing may thus seem about as frustrating as would exclusion from the sentencing hearing. Not surprisingly, then, most states do give victims a right to present a statement to the parole board, with more than thirty specifically authorizing *oral* statements (Young, 2016, 439). Indeed, in at least one state, Florida, the victim has a right to speak to the parole board, but the inmate himself or herself does not.

Despite the opportunity to participate, research suggests that victims attend only about 10 percent of parole hearings (Young, 2016, 456). This surely reflects simple disinterest on the part of some victims in participating, but there are also various practical impediments that can get in the way. For instance, parole hearings are typically held in centralized locations in a state, in contrast to sentencing hearings, which are normally conducted in the county in which the crime occurred—a location that will tend to be much more convenient for victims. In order to make participation in parole hearings more practically feasible, reformers have urged that states reimburse victims for their travel expenses and prohibit employers from penalizing victims for missing work on hearing dates (Young, 2016, 491). Additionally, it can be difficult to locate victims and provide them with advance notice of hearings, bearing in mind that many years—or even decades—may pass between the time of sentencing and the time that the offender is up for parole consideration.

In sum, the victims' rights movement has succeeded in creating a multitude of opportunities throughout the criminal process for victims to state their views. However, the lack of independent legal representation and various other constraints may undercut the practical value of the participation rights that now exist on paper.

Moreover, even if we assume that a victim is able to say everything that he or she would like to say in a clear, timely fashion to all of the important decision makers, there is no assurance that the decisions will be made in accordance with the victim's wishes. If the victims' rights movement is only succeeding in changing the *procedures* of the criminal justice system, and not *substantive outcomes,* can it truly be said that the criminal justice system is doing a better job of taking into account the needs and wishes of victims?

The question implicates a broader debate in legal theory: whether the quality of legal procedures matters apart from the quality of outcomes. Consider, for instance, two hypothetical criminal cases in which the victim badly wants to see the defendant incarcerated. In the first case, the victim is given an opportunity to make a lengthy oral statement at the start of the sentencing hearing, to which the judge listens attentively. In the second case, by contrast, the judge makes the victim wait until the end of the hearing, at which time the judge tells the victim, "I've already made up my mind, but the law says I have to give you a chance to speak. I'll give you two minutes." If the judge in both cases gives the defendant probation, contrary to the wishes of the victim, would we nonetheless expect the first victim to feel better about the proceeding and more accepting of the outcome than the second?

The research strongly suggests that the answer should be "yes"—to most people dealing with legal decision makers, respectful treatment and a fair opportunity to be heard matter in and of themselves (O'Hear, 2007, 326–27). Indeed, the research specifically on crime victims suggests that they give higher priority to the "expressive" value of impact statements—that is, the opportunity to make a public statement in an official forum and to confront the offender directly regarding the crime—than to the "instrumental" value—that is, the opportunity to alter sentencing outcomes (Roberts, 2009).

It is possible to conclude, then, that victim participation rights are capable of serving at least some of the needs and desires of victims without regard to whether they are substantively affecting plea deals, sentences, or parole release decisions. These "procedural justice" effects are especially important in light of research on the instrumental value of victim statements, which has tended not to find much evidence of effects on outcomes (Roberts, 2009; Young, 2016).

Still, the victims' rights movement has not limited itself to procedural reforms but has also sought to help victims through substantive changes to sentencing law. Least controversially, new laws have made it easier for victims to collect financial compensation (called "restitution") from offenders. Indeed, the federal government and about one-third of the states have made restitution "mandatory" in many cases; that is, restitution is no longer simply a matter of the judge's sentencing discretion (O'Hear, 2014, 4412). Of course, victims have long had the ability to seek compensation through civil tort suits, but civil litigation normally takes a backseat to criminal. Since restitution awards are made part of the criminal sentence, victims can get compensation more quickly. Moreover, the victim need not pay for a private lawyer to get a restitution award—a prosecutor will handle the legal work—and may enlist the help of the criminal justice system to try to make sure that the offender actually pays up.

To be sure, the restitution system is hardly perfect from a victim's perspective. For instance, a prosecutor does not have the same economic incentives that a personal injury lawyer has to maximize the size of a compensation award. Indeed, if anything, the prosecutor's economic incentive is to give priority to fines, forfeitures, and court fees, all of which are payable to the government, not the victim. Few defendants have the financial ability to pay all of the economic sanctions that may be piled on them, which puts restitution in competition to some extent with the other sanctions. Indeed, this tension points to the single greatest practical problem with restitution: whether legally mandatory or not, whether vigorously pursued by a prosecutor or not, restitution normally cannot ensure anything approaching adequate compensation to seriously injured victims—you cannot wring blood, as they say, from an onion. Still, in at least some cases, restitution remains helpful to the victim as a supplement or alternative to civil tort litigation.

More controversially, the victims' rights movement has often aligned itself with tough-on-crime sentencing laws. For instance, victim groups played a prominent role in advocating for the notoriously draconian "three strikes and you are out" sentencing law in California (Page, 2011, 112).

It is uncertain to what extent victims actually embrace such an unrestrained "lock 'em up and throw away the key" approach, either in their own cases or as a matter of general policy. While it is true that many victims feel an intense anger toward their victimizers, it is also true many have complex and sometimes conflicted attitudes about punishment. The difficulties may be better appreciated if it is understood that many crimes—including a majority of violent crimes—are perpetrated by someone who is known to the victim (Truman, 2011). The victim's feelings about punishment in these cases will inevitably be colored by the whole history of the relationship and the victim's knowledge of the offender's character, background, and needs. A victim's sense of the positive things an offender has done in the past or could do in the future if properly supported might partially or wholly offset punitive attitudes toward the crime itself.

Such perspectives seem reflected in the policy preferences of victims. For instance, according to a survey conducted in 2016, a large majority of victims would prefer for the criminal justice system to focus on rehabilitation over punishment (Alliance for Safety and Justice, 2016). The same survey also found:

- By a nearly three to one margin, victims believe that imprisonment is more likely to make offenders commit new crimes than to rehabilitate them.
- By a similar margin, victims prefer to hold offenders accountable through alternatives to prison, such as drug treatment, community service, or community supervision.
- About 60 percent of victims prefer shorter prison sentences and more spending on prevention and rehabilitation.

In short, while it might seem that the toughening of sentences that occurred nationally in the late twentieth century was a pro-victim development, victims' wishes and needs might have been better served by the adoption of more balanced responses to crime that included greater investment in drug treatment and other services that promote rehabilitation.

FURTHER READING

Alliance for Safety and Justice. 2016. *Crime Survivors Speak*. Oakland, CA: Alliance for Safety and Justice.

Gottschalk, Maria. 2006. *The Prison and the Gallows: The Politics of Mass Incarceration in America*. New York: Cambridge University Press.

Office for Victims of Crime. 2013. *Vision 21—Transforming Victim Services: Final Report*. Washington, DC: U.S. Department of Justice.

O'Hear, Michael. 2007. "Plea Bargaining and Victims: From Consultation to Guidelines." *Marquette Law Review*, 91, 323.

O'Hear, Michael. 2014. "Restitution as a Penal Aim." In *Encyclopedia of Criminology and Criminal Justice*, 4410. Edited by Gerben Bruinsma & David Weisburd. New York: Springer.

Page, Joshua. 2011. *The Toughest Beat: Politics, Punishment, and the Prison Officers Union in California.* New York: Oxford University Press.

Roberts, Julian. 2009. "Listening to the Crime Victim: Evaluating Victim Input at Sentencing and Parole." *Crime & Justice*, 38, 347.

Truman, Jennifer. 2011. *Criminal Victimization, 2010.* Washington, DC: United State Department of Justice.

Young, Kathryne. 2016. "Parole Hearings and Victims' Rights: Implementation, Ambiguity, and Reform." *Connecticut Law Review*, 49, 431.

2

◆❖◆

Alternatives to Incarceration

Even in the current era of "mass incarceration" in the United States, probation remains the most common criminal sentence. Traditional probation, though, has few enthusiastic fans. Fairly or not, probation is often seen as a mere "slap on the wrist" and not a viable sentencing option for those who have committed a major victimizing crime or multiple lower-level offenses. At the same time, many find incarceration also unsatisfactory based on its cost and its spotty record of success in rehabilitating inmates. Reformers have thus worked throughout the mass-incarceration era to try to develop good options between traditional probation and imprisonment. Some successful programs have been developed but nothing has yet emerged as a widely accepted substitute for incarceration.

Q8: IS PROBATION JUST A "SLAP ON THE WRIST"?

Answer: Many convicted offenders on probation find the supervision minimal and experience few negative consequences from the sentence per se. However, as part of the general tough-on-crime trends of the late twentieth and early twenty-first centuries, probation has tended to become more punitive in various respects. Some offenders now find probation extraordinarily onerous and frustrating. In recent years, particular concerns have been raised about the potentially devastating impact of probation on the working poor.

The Facts: In general, probation is a sentence that is imposed in lieu of incarceration and that allows the offender to remain in the community. From the perspective of the sentencing judge, there are two basic ways to structure probation. In the first approach, after a defendant is convicted, the judge imposes and "stays" a sentence of incarceration. The defendant is then given various conditions that must be satisfied over a certain period of time, typically in the range of six months to three years. If the defendant satisfies the conditions, then he or she is discharged from probation and excused from serving the stayed term of incarceration. If, however, the defendant fails to satisfy the given conditions, then his or her probation may be "revoked," in which case the defendant will be required to serve the full term of incarceration that had been stayed. In the alternative approach, sentencing is deferred while the defendant serves his or her term of probation. Again, the defendant will have certain conditions to satisfy if the defendant wishes to remain in the community. If the defendant fails and is revoked, then the defendant will return to court for sentencing, at which time the judge may impose a term of incarceration.

To simplify the present discussion, "probation" means one of these two traditional approaches to placing an offender on supervision in the community. In some jurisdictions, though, probation may also be used as part of a "split" sentence, which includes a short jail term at the start. Additionally, there are a variety of preconviction arrangements that functionally operate much like probation, even though they generally go by different names. For instance, some prosecutorial offices offer some low-level offenders "deferred prosecution agreements." In such a deal, the prosecutor will refrain from pursuing criminal charges if the offender agrees to certain conditions, such as undergoing drug treatment and avoiding any new criminal activity over a specified time period. In effect, this is probation that is under the auspices of a prosecutor instead of a judge.

In traditional probation, the offender is supervised by a probation officer (PO). In some jurisdictions, the PO works for the state department of corrections. In others, the PO is employed and managed by a unit of local government, usually the county. Either way, in the original vision for probation, the PO was supposed to work with each offender individually to try to encourage and support rehabilitation. However, the vision has been undermined by chronic underfunding. On average, states spend more than twenty-three times as much per prisoner as they do per probationer (Corbett, 2015). As a result, rehabilitative programming—treatment for addiction and mental illness, vocational training and employment assistance, relationship counseling, and so forth—is often in short supply. Indeed, given excessive caseloads, many POs struggle just to keep tabs on their offenders in even the most minimal fashion. While caseloads of 30 have been viewed as ideal, POs in recent years have often found themselves assigned to supervise more than 100 individuals at a time (Petersilia, 1998, 579). In Los Angeles, some PO caseloads have even exceeded 1,000 (Walker, 2011, 256). Given the pressures created by triple-digit caseloads, the "supervision" of many probationers might consist of little more than a single short meeting per month with the PO.

Such superficial, sporadic monitoring has contributed to the widespread perception of probation as a mere "slap on the wrist." The conditions imposed on the probationer by the sentencing judge may be demanding on paper, but without effective supervision, there is no real accountability for violations. And without accountability, the seemingly rigorous conditions may be meaningless in practice. As one veteran judge recalls the conditions he encountered when he first took the bench, "Probation officers had caseloads of up to 180, and the dynamic was that offenders would repeatedly break the rules of supervision—by using drugs, skipping probation appointments and failing treatment—because there were no real consequences" (quoted in Klingele, 2015, 1632). Even when an overworked PO is aware of a violation, the officer may take no action because of all of the paperwork burdens that go along with revocation.

In recent years, the trend has been to make probation more onerous for offenders. In effect, probation has undergone a philosophical shift echoing broader changes in American criminal justice. Where probation was once conceptualized as a rehabilitative sentence, it now seems more focused on the deterrence of violations and incapacitation of repeat violators (Corbett, 2015; Cullen, Jonson, & Mears, 2017). The overriding priority seems to be preventing probationers from committing new crimes, while they are under supervision—an objective that can be in tension with the promotion of deeper and more durable personal reform. These tendencies reflect, among other considerations, the desire of judges, POs, and other corrections officials to avoid the negative media attention that often follows when an offender who was placed on probation commits a major violent or sexual offense. Additionally, the harsh treatment of probationers may also serve a symbolic function as a way to express condemnation of the underlying criminal activity.

The new toughness in probation finds expression to differing extents and in widely varying ways from state to state, county to county, and even case to case. Major components of the new toughness include: (1) increased number and difficulty of probation conditions; (2) enhanced surveillance; (3) more aggressive responses to violations; (4) increased financial burdens placed on the probationer; and (5) heavier collateral consequences to criminal convictions. Put together, these components can make probation far more than just a slap on the wrist. Let us consider them in a bit more detail.

First, probation conditions have grown more numerous and demanding. Every jurisdiction has various mandatory and recommended conditions that apply to all or certain classes of probationers. Additionally, judges may impose special conditions at their discretion on a case-by-case basis. The standard conditions alone typically number between ten and twenty (Corbett, 2015). Many conditions are broadly framed and go well beyond the requirements that the law normally imposes on citizens (Doherty, 2016). Common conditions include:

- Be of general good behavior.
- Comply with all municipal, county, state, and federal laws, ordinances, and orders.
- Avoid persons or places of disreputable or harmful character.
- Work regularly at a lawful occupation.
- Support your dependents and meet your family responsibilities.
- Do not use or possess alcohol.

Many of these and other standard conditions are vaguely worded and effectively give POs a great deal of discretion in deciding what constitutes a violation. (It is not immediately clear, for instance, what it means to "be of general good behavior.") The number and breadth of the standard conditions in many jurisdictions, on top of any special conditions that might be imposed, can make 100 percent compliance extremely difficult—maybe even, as some critics charge, simply impossible in many cases (Klingele, 2015).

Second, surveillance has grown more intensive for many probationers, who must generally accommodate unannounced home visits by a PO and permit warrantless searches of his or her person, vehicle, and property that would violate the Fourth Amendment rights of other citizens (Doherty, 2016). As a practical matter, of course, heavy caseloads mean that POs cannot conduct frequent home visits and searches of most probationers. However, technological developments allow POs to keep closer tabs on their charges than would have been possible a generation ago. For instance, drug testing has become a routine condition, providing information about what substances a probationer has consumed over a period of hours, days, or even weeks, depending on the drug. Electronic monitoring devices can also be used to track all the movements of a probationer. Finally, alcohol use can now be detected using devices that continuously test the probationer's sweat for indications of drinking.

Third, the enforcement of probation conditions has grown stricter. In the mid-1980s, nearly three-quarters of those exiting probation had completed their terms successfully, but the figure dropped to 60 percent within a decade (Petersilia, 1998, 573). In more recent years, the figure has drifted up and down between 60 and 69 percent (Kaeble & Bonczar, 2016, 5). Revocations from probation spiked from 220,000 in 1990 to 330,000 in 2004, becoming a major driver of imprisonment growth in that time period (Corbett, 2015). Many—in some states, most—revocations resulted from so-called technical violations that did not involve the commission of a new crime. Although revocation figures have stabilized in recent years, this likely results in part from the widespread adoption of new "intermediate" sanctions for violations, including curfews, house arrest, electronic monitoring, placement in a "halfway house" (i.e., a community-based detention facility), loss of travel or other privileges, and community service (Doherty, 2016). Such sanctions can normally be imposed by the PO more quickly and with less paperwork and oversight than revocation, permitting the PO to penalize many more violations than would have been possible if revocation were the only way to formally respond to a probationer's missteps.

Fourth, the financial burdens of probation have increased considerably, with probationers now commonly required to pay fees for their supervision, including the costs of electronic monitoring and drug tests. These fees are placed on top of fines, restitution, and court costs, all of which probationers are also typically obliged to pay. One study found that forty-eight states increased fees for offenders between 2008 and 2013 (Corbett, 2015). Payment of these financial obligations is a condition of probation, meaning that an economically struggling probationer who misses a payment date faces sanctions, potentially including revocation and incarceration.

Finally, the true impact of punishment in probation cases cannot be understood without also noting the increasingly complex and burdensome web of "collateral consequences" that now follow a criminal conviction. Collateral consequences are not formally part of the sentence—that is what makes them "collateral"—but they may constitute a large part of what an offender perceives his or her punishment to be. Many collateral consequences are formally imposed by the law, with the specifics varying widely from state to state. Thus, for instance, depending on the state and the offense of conviction, a probationer might face:

- Loss of basic civil rights, including the right to vote, serve on a jury, and possess a firearm;
- Loss of eligibility for student loans, subsidized housing, and other government benefits;
- Deportation, if the probationer is not a U.S. citizen;
- Requirement to register as a sex offender;
- Suspension of driver's license; and
- Disqualification from work in a multitude of different fields.

Sometimes such consequences last only as long as the offender is serving his or her sentence, but some consequences in some states may last for years after the sentence is over—potentially, indeed, for the rest of the offender's life.

Moreover, all of these formal consequences only add to the *informal* consequences of a criminal record. The stigma of a conviction can make it far more difficult for an offender to obtain and hold onto employment, housing, and intimate personal relationships. The stigma only grows harder to escape as the Internet increasingly creates a permanent, easily accessible record of one's legal transgressions.

In sum, many offenders who receive the sentence of probation hardly perceive their punishment as a mere slap on the wrist. Indeed, while we typically think of probation as an *alternative* to incarceration, the combination of demanding conditions, enhanced surveillance, and routine revocation means that probation often functions more as a *back door* to incarceration. A failed probationer may find himself or herself serving no less time behind bars than he or she would have if he or she had simply refused community supervision at the start—with the added detriment of an anxious period of financial distress and curtailed liberty in the community under the watchful eye of a capricious PO. There should be little wonder that many offenders say they would *prefer* to "get it over with" through a short term of incarceration in lieu of a longer period of probation. For instance, one study found that nearly one-third of offenders would choose one year of prison over three years of probation (Corbett, 2015).

In recent years, there have been particular concerns that probation has become overly harsh for the working poor, who tend to have tenuous employment and housing arrangements and little or no savings. Against that backdrop, probation fees that might seem a minor irritant to a middle-class offender can prove devastating, especially when layered on top of other costs associated with criminal charges, such as paying a lawyer and making bail. Additionally, offenders with inflexible work schedules or transportation challenges may struggle to comply with various probation conditions, such as meeting with POs, giving regular urine samples for drug testing, and attending treatment programs. And, of course, the stigma of the underlying conviction may in itself endanger employment or housing.

A 2015 *New York Times* story provided a vivid illustration of this reality. After a Christmas party with family and friends in 2013, Donyelle Hall, a nurse's aide with no prior criminal history, was arrested for driving while intoxicated. Offered probation in return for her guilty plea to a misdemeanor, Hall accepted. She soon found herself in a financial nightmare. Her eighteen-month probationary sentence included $385 per month to cover the costs of supervision, drunk-driving monitoring, and alcohol education. She also faced a lawyer's fee of $1,500, a bail bondsman's fee of $2,000, and fines and court costs of $252.50. Her driver's license was also suspended, leading to the loss of her job at a rehabilitation center twenty miles from her home. Still, Hall managed to stay in compliance with her probation for several months before missing some paperwork deadlines. Her PO reported the issue to the judge, who ordered her arrest. This time, she could not post the required cash bail of $2,500 and so spent more than a month in jail, while the paperwork issues were cleared up. Another job was lost. Hall and her husband soon fell behind on their rent, car payments, and insurance (Dewan, 2015).

Hall's story illustrates the sort of sharp downward financial spiral that can result from contact with the criminal justice system, even if that contact only involves a misdemeanor conviction and probationary sentence. Of course, a defendant of greater means than Hall likely would have avoided jail and job loss. In many cases, then, the question of whether probation is just a slap on the wrist or a potentially serious financial blow depends on the defendant's income level.

FURTHER READING

Corbett, Ronald. 2015. "The Burdens of Leniency: The Changing Face of Probation." *Minnesota Law Review*, 99, 1697.

Cullen, Franics, Jonson, Cheryl, & Mears, Daniel. 2017. "Reinventing Community Corrections." *Crime & Justice*, 46, 27.

Dewan, Shaila. 2015. "Probation May Sound Light, but Punishments Can Land Hard." *New York Times*, August 2. Retrieved from https://www.nytimes.com/2015/08/03/us/probation-sounding-light-can-land-hard.html.

Doherty, Fiona. 2016. "Obey All Laws and Be Good: Probation and the Meaning of Recidivism." *Georgetown Law Journal*, 104, 291.

Kaeble, Danielle & Bonczar, Thomas. 2016. *Probation and Parole in the United States, 2015*. Washington, DC: U.S. Department of Justice.

Klingele, Cecelia. 2015. "What Are We Hoping For? Defining Purpose in Deterrence-Based Correctional Programs." *Minnesota Law Review*, 99, 1631.

Petersilia, Joan. 1998. "Probation and Parole." In *The Handbook of Crime and Punishment*, 563. Edited by Michael Tonry. New York: Oxford University Press.

Walker, Samuel. 2011. *Sense and Nonsense about Crime, Drugs, and Communities*. Belmont, CA: Wadsworth.

Q9: ARE SO-CALLED INTERMEDIATE SANCTIONS MORE EFFECTIVE IN REDUCING RECIDIVISM THAN TRADITIONAL PROBATION?

Answer: The term "intermediate sanctions" encompasses a wide variety of sentencing options, which makes broad generalizations about their effectiveness impossible. Simply making a sentence more difficult or unpleasant than traditional probation does not necessarily cut recidivism rates. However, the evidence is growing strong that some community-based correctional programs—if well-designed, well-administered, and well-funded—can achieve significant recidivism reductions.

The Facts: The term "intermediate sanctions" came into widespread use in the 1990s as a way to describe sentencing options that were more rigorous than traditional probation, but that still fell short of the extreme (and extremely expensive) physical control represented by incarceration. Reformers hoped that the development of new intermediate sanctions programs could divert some offenders away from America's then-burgeoning prison population at no cost to public safety. Protecting the public from the diverted offenders required intermediate sanctions to reduce recidivism rates relative to the prevailing norms of probation and incarceration. This became the key metric by which intermediate sanctions were (and are) evaluated.

There are, to be sure, no crisp dividing lines between probation, intermediate sanctions, and incarceration. On the one hand, probation has become more rigorous in recent years and now routinely includes "intermediate" features like electronic monitoring as a penalty for violations or even as an initial condition for release. On the other hand, programs that are framed as "alternatives" to incarceration often include substantial confinement components, either as a basic requirement or as a sanction for program violations.

Indeed, to underscore the fuzziness of the terminology, even conventional jail sentences are sometimes discussed as community-based intermediate sanctions, since the periods of confinement are shorter than would be the case with a prison sentence and the offender gets to stay in his or her home community—at least in some bare physical sense— rather than being shipped off to a distant prison. (Although laypeople sometimes use the terms "jail" and "prison" interchangeably, they are recognized by criminal justice practitioners as distinct institutions; jails are administered at the local—usually county—level and typically hold offenders who have been sentenced to one year or less of incarceration, as well as defendants with active cases who are awaiting trial or sentencing, while prisons are administered by the state, intended to hold offenders with longer sentences, and often located in rural areas far from the urban centers that tend to produce a disproportionate share of the inmates.)

Rather than attempting a more precise definition of "intermediate sanctions," it is instructive to instead take a closer look at a few of the specific programs that have generated particular interest as alternatives to prison at some point over the past three decades. Most of these programs can be fit into the criminal justice system in a variety of different ways: for instance, as a preconviction diversion, a post-conviction sentence, a condition of probation, a sanction for violating conditions of probation, or an aspect of parole release from prison.

No intermediate sanction excited more enthusiasm in the 1990s than *boot camps*. Proponents of this approach asserted that many offenders come from family backgrounds lacking in discipline and structure. Perhaps if punishment were designed to fill these needs, then recidivism would go down. And what institution better exemplifies discipline and structure than the military? This sort of thinking led to the idea that offenders could be diverted from prison into a different sort of correctional institution that aimed to replicate the military boot camp experience, with rigorous physical programs, strict rules, and tough discipline. Military drill and ceremony might also be part of program, as well as the hazing-type treatment that we often associate with the experience of new military recruits. The idea caught on quickly. By 2000, ninety-five correctional boot camps in the United States held nearly 13,000 inmates (Walker, 2011, 267). Although boot camps involved confinement, they could still be thought of as intermediate punishment because stays tended to be much shorter than conventional prison terms (usually just three or four months). Educational and substance abuse components were also typically integrated into the program, and indeed sometimes emphasized more heavily than the military aspects.

For all the enthusiasm they generated initially, boot camps proved a great disappointment. In general, boot camps did not succeed in reducing recidivism rates (Walker, 2011, 268). While the "graduates" of some boot camps were less likely to reoffend, those facilities tended to be the ones that particularly emphasized treatment services and close post-release supervision, rather than the quasi-militaristic features that were supposed to be the distinguishing mark of boot camps.

Day reporting centers, or DRCs, are another intermediate punishment. In a DRC, offenders spend the day in a correctional facility but return home in the evening. In effect, this is a sort of part-time incarceration, with a strong emphasis on mandatory participation in the rehabilitative programs offered at the DRC (Tonry, 1998, 695). DRC terms tend to be considerably shorter than prison terms, often about three to nine months. Because of the need to maintain a bricks-and-mortar facility to hold offenders during the day, DRCs are more expensive to run than conventional probation. But because they do not require 24/7 staffing and the full panoply of services necessary for full-time inmates, DRCs are less expensive than conventional incarceration. In theory anyway, these operational savings can be invested in programming for the DRC inmates, which is often in short supply in the 24/7 facilities.

Although DRCs became popular at about the same time as boot camps, with at least 114 established by the mid-1990s, there is much less consensus among researchers as to their effectiveness (Boyle, Ragusa, Lanterman, & Marcus, 2011). Some studies have found some DRCs successful in reducing recidivism, while other studies of other sites have reached different conclusions. The varying outcomes may partly reflect the wide variety among DRCs, which differ in such important respects as the nature of the programming offered, the process by which participants are assigned to the DRC, the number of weeks or months participants are required to report, the intensity of surveillance during off-hours, and the services and supervision provided after the DRC term is completed. It is not known how best to structure a DRC, but there remains hope that some types of DRCs may promote the rehabilitation of some offenders more effectively than traditional probation.

Home confinement (house arrest) and *electronic monitoring* (EM) are also common options on the menu of intermediate sanctions. Although home confinement and EM may be employed separately from one another, they are typically considered together because EM is often used as a way to enforce home confinement. Home confinement typically takes the form of a curfew; the offender may leave during the day for purposes like work or school but must be home by a prescribed time.

For many years, the dominant EM technology was the radio frequency system. In such a system, the offender wears a transmitter, typically as an ankle "bracelet," while a receiver is placed in the home. If the offender strays too far from the receiver, then connection with the transmitter is lost, and the supervising agency is automatically notified. Since 2000, the radio frequency system has been eclipsed by the rival GPS system, which permits continuous tracking of the offender's whereabouts. GPS monitoring is much more adaptable to enforcing restrictions on where an offender can go outside the home, which has contributed to a rapid increase in EM use, including use for purposes other than enforcing home confinement. For instance, for sex offenders, GPS monitoring can be used to enforce prohibitions on visiting schools and playgrounds. Reflecting the popularity of such uses, between 2005 and 2015, the number of offenders on EM grew from about 53,000 to more than 125,000 (Pew Charitable Trusts, 2016). Over the same time period, the GPS share of the EM market grew from under 6 percent to more than 70 percent.

Because home confinement and EM do not require a special detention facility, they can be much less expensive to administer than boot camps and DRCs. However, unlike boot camps and DRCs, home confinement and EM do not aim to rehabilitate, but merely to control; long-term recidivism reduction therefore seems unlikely. Nonetheless, in theory anyway, home confinement and EM may be helpful in preventing reoffense during the time that an offender is subject to one or both forms of control. In practice, however, results have been mixed, with some studies finding recidivism reduction and others not. Thus, for instance, a 2005 review of the literature concluded that "applications of EM as a tool for reducing crime are not supported by existing data" (Renzema & Mayo-Wilson, 2005). Since then, however, new studies have been more supportive of EM, which may reflect the superiority of the increasingly dominant GPS technology. For instance, a recent Florida study found that offenders on EM were 30 percent less likely to be revoked than a similar group of offenders who were supervised in the community without EM (Bales et al., 2010). The same study also found that GPS-based EM had a higher success rate than the radio frequency technology.

A lower-tech intermediate punishment that also seeks to keep closer tabs on offenders is *intensive supervision*. Rather than meeting with a PO once or twice a month, an offender on IS might have that many or more required meetings per *week*. Of course, in order for this to work, POs must be given lighter caseloads; some IS programs provide average caseloads of as few as 12.5 offenders per officer (Tonry, 1998, 690). This makes IS more expensive than traditional probation but still less than incarceration. Unfortunately, extensive research on various IS experiments has failed to find evidence that they reduce recidivism (Walker, 2011, 260–61).

Community service is another popular intermediate punishment. For instance, among those convicted of felonies and placed on probation in large urban counties in 2009, 22 percent of the sentences included a community service component (Reaves, 2013, 32). In theory, community service may reduce recidivism risk by instilling pro-social values; raising self-esteem through service accomplishments; or creating connections between offenders and other individuals who may be positive social influences. However, the research results are mixed, with some studies finding recidivism reduction and others not (Wermink et al., 2010).

Since 2000, no intermediate punishment has seemed to generate more interest than the HOPE probation model. An acronym for Hawai'i Opportunity Probation with Enforcement, HOPE was developed in 2004 by Steven Alm, a trial judge in Honolulu (Alm, 2015). Alm's vision was to establish a system of "swift, certain, fair" sanctions for probation violations. Where POs would previously have attempted to work with offenders after their first few failed drug tests, missed appointments, or other technical violations, the HOPE system called for immediate arrest and a short jail term. Although drug treatment was also part of Judge Alm's original HOPE experiment, as the model has spread to at least 160 new sites across the United States, it is the zero-tolerance approach to violations that has been most heavily emphasized (Nagin, 2016).

HOPE seemed to work remarkably well in Hawai'i. An experiment with probationers randomly assigned either to HOPE or to conventional supervision found not only a reduction in positive drug tests and other violations among the HOPE group but also fewer arrests and prison sentences for new crimes (Nagin, 2016). However, studies of HOPE-based programs in other locations have produced more mixed results. The most ambitious, involving random assignment of more than 1,500 probationers at four different sites, found no evidence that HOPE reduced recidivism. The authors concluded that HOPE is no "silver bullet," observing that "HOPE seems unlikely to offer better outcomes and lower costs for broad classes of moderate-to-high-risk probationers" (Lattimore, MacKenzie, Dawes, & Tueller, 2016, 1131–32).

Two additional innovations merit note here: *problem-solving courts* and *restorative justice*. Both will be discussed in more detail later in this chapter. For now, suffice it to say that research finds some recidivism-reducing potential for both types of programs.

In sum, there is extensive experience now in the United States with a variety of intermediate sanctions. Rigorous studies have found that several different programs have succeeded in reducing recidivism rates in some settings. On the other hand, no program has proven foolproof. The research makes clear that any given program might be successfully implemented in one setting but fail in another.

Although many different factors determine the success or failure of intermediate sanctions, a few key ideas have found wide support among researchers. First, programs that most heavily emphasize surveillance, control, and deterrence tend to be ineffective (MacKenzie & Farrington, 2015). Second, those including a robust treatment component stand a better chance of success (Cullen, Smith, Lowenkamp, & Latessa, 2009). Third, programs should focus attention and treatment resources on high- and medium-risk offenders; rigorous supervision and programming requirements are likely to be ineffective or even counterproductive with low-risk offenders (Latessa & Reitler, 2015). Fourth, treatment should focus on the identified crime-causing needs of each offender, making use of one of the several scientifically validated risk-needs assessment tools that have been developed since the early 1980s. Fifth, not all treatments are equally effective; programs should match offenders with treatments that have proven crime-reducing benefits. Finally, even programs that are conceptually sound may fail if they are not administered with integrity, including, for instance, adequate training and supervision for staff and continuous assessment of whether the program is meeting recidivism-reduction and other goals.

Given the need for high-quality treatment services and highly capable professional administration, intermediate sanctions programs are not apt to succeed if done "on the cheap." However, with an adequate investment of resources, such programs could likely handle a sizeable share of the offenders we are currently sending to prison without large, adverse effects on public safety. Continuing research on "what works" in reducing recidivism will doubtlessly further improve the capabilities of intermediate sanctions over time.

FURTHER READING

Alm, Steven. 2015. "HOPE Probation and the New Drug Court: A Powerful Combination." *Minnesota Law Review*, 99, 1665.

Bales, William et al. 2010. A Quantitative and Qualitative Assessment of Electronic Monitoring. National Criminal Justice Reference Service

Document 230530. Retrieved from https://www.ncjrs.gov/pdffiles1/nij/grants/230530.pdf.

Boyle, Douglas, Ragusa, Laura, Lanterman, Jennifer, & Marcus, Andrea. 2011. Outcomes of a Randomized Trial of an Intensive Community Corrections Program—Day Reporting Centers—For Parolees. National Criminal Justice Reference Service Document 236080. Retrieved from https://www.ncjrs.gov/pdffiles1/nij/grants/236080.pdf.

Cullen, Francis, Smith, Paula, Lowenkamp, Christopher, & Latessa, Edward. 2009. "Nothing Works Revisited: Deconstructing Farabee's *Rethinking Rehabilitation.*" *Victims and Offenders*, 4, 101.

Latessa, Edward & Reitler, Angela. 2015. "What Works in Reducing Recidivism and How Does It Relate to Drug Courts?" *Ohio Northern University Law Review*, 41, 757.

Lattimore, Pamela, MacKenzie, Doris, Dawes, Debbie, & Tueller, Stephen. 2016. "Outcome Findings from the HOPE Demonstration Field Experiment: Is Swift, Certain, and Fair an Effective Supervision Strategy?" *Criminology & Public Policy*, 15, 1103.

MacKenzie, Doris & Farrington, David. 2015. "Preventing Future Offending of Delinquents and Offenders: What Have We Learned from Experiments and Meta-Analyses?" *Journal of Experimental Criminology*, 13, 565.

Nagin, Daniel. 2016. "Project HOPE: Does It Work?" *Criminology & Public Policy*, 15, 1005.

Pew Charitable Trusts. 2016. *Use of Electronic Offender-Tracking Devices Expands Sharply.* Philadelphia, PA: Pew Charitable Trusts. Retrieved from http://www.pewtrusts.org/en/research-and-analysis/issue-briefs/2016/09/use-of-electronic-offender-tracking-devices-expands-sharply.

Reaves, Brian. 2013. *Felony Defendants in Large Urban Counties, 2009—Statistical Tables.* Washington, DC: U.S. Department of Justice.

Renzema, Marc & Mayo-Wilson, Evan. 2005. "Can Electronic Monitoring Reduce Crime for Moderate to High-Risk Offenders?" *Journal of Experimental Criminology*, 1, 215.

Tonry, Michael. 1998. "Intermediate Sanctions." In *The Handbook of Crime and Punishment*, 683. Edited by Michael Tonry. New York: Oxford University Press.

Walker, Samuel. 2011. *Sense and Nonsense about Crime, Drugs, and Communities.* Belmont, CA: Wadsworth.

Wermink, Hilde et al. 2010. "Comparing the Effects of Community Service and Short-Term Imprisonment on Recidivism: A Matched Samples Approach." *Journal of Experimental Criminology*, 6, 325.

Q10: DO DRUG TREATMENT COURTS AND OTHER PROBLEM-SOLVING COURTS REALLY WORK?

Answer: Drug treatment courts, which require drug-involved offenders to undergo treatment under close judicial supervision, have been extensively studied. While not all drug courts have been successful, some do seem to have contributed to significant reductions in drug use and recidivism relative to what would have been expected from conventional criminal case-processing. Based on this positive track record, a multitude of other specialized "problem-solving" courts have appeared in recent years. However, much less research has been done on these courts, leaving their potential effectiveness uncertain.

The Facts: Miami created the nation's first drug treatment court (DTC) in 1989, at a time of explosive growth in drug prosecutions (O'Hear, 2017, 27). Local criminal justice leaders had grown frustrated with the failure of enforcement and incarceration to achieve any apparent improvement with the city's drug problems. They settled on a new approach that was centered on the delivery of drug treatment under judicial supervision.

In some respects, the DTC closely resembled a familiar sentence: probation with drug treatment as a condition of release to the community. As with this sort of conditional probation, the DTC held a threat of incarceration over the head of the offender undergoing treatment; in either setting, failed drug tests or missed appointments with treatment providers could result in arrest and jailing. However, the DTC differed from probation insofar as the judge remained closely involved in supervising the offender during the period of treatment. In probation, the PO was the offender's primary ongoing point of contact with the criminal justice system; the judge would only get involved if the offender was failing to comply with release conditions and the PO decided that revocation or some other judicial sanction had become necessary. By contrast, in the DTC, offenders would come back to court on a regular basis—perhaps weekly at first—and speak with the judge about their successes and failures. The judge was supposed to recognize and provide positive reinforcement for signs of progress—for instance, going a certain amount of time without a failed drug test—but also deliver sanctions for failures.

The regular court appearances permitted a system of swift, certain, graduated responses to violations, ranging from a scolding in court to an order for more frequent court appearances or drug tests to short stints behind bars (referred to as "motivational jail"). A pattern of failures over time could lead to an offender's expulsion from the DTC and a return to "regular" court for conventional prosecution and punishment.

Early results in Miami were encouraging and the DTC model spread quickly. Indeed, by 2015, about 3,400 DTCs were in operation in all fifty states, with about half focused on adult offenders and the other half on juveniles (O'Hear, 2017, 29). However, while DTCs tend to have certain basic features in common, there can also be a great deal of variation from court to court. For instance, some function as a preconviction diversion, while others are structured as a post-conviction sentence—basically, as a sort of enhanced probation. Some take only defendants charged with simple drug possession, while others take a wider range of drug-involved offenders, such as those who have been committing petty thefts in order to support a drug habit. Some have strict, clear eligibility rules, while others leave admission in an open-ended way to the discretion of judges and prosecutors. Some make heavy use of "motivational jail," while others treat it as more of a last resort.

With so many DTCs now in operation, some for two decades or more, it should not be surprising that there is a large body of published research on the effectiveness of these courts. However, many of the DTC studies, especially in the early years, have not been of high quality. Consumers of DTC research should be wary of certain common pitfalls. Ideally, an assessment of the quality of any criminal justice intervention should involve random assignment of individuals to the intervention and to a control group; participants in each group should thus be about equally likely to succeed at the outset, making for a valid comparison of outcomes. Without random assignment, a study that finds better outcomes for DTC participants than for ordinary probationers might simply mean that the DTC "cherry-picked" the offenders who were most likely to succeed— individuals, in other words, who might also have done perfectly well on conventional probation. If random assignment is not possible, then a good study should at least control for variables like criminal history, drug of choice, employment, and education that are known to correlate with success in drug treatment.

An accumulating body of well-designed studies now confirms that DTCs are capable of producing reduced drug use and recidivism when compared to conventional criminal case-processing. For instance, one particularly ambitious study sponsored by the National Institute of Justice compared the outcomes after eighteen months of more than 1,100 DTC participants at twenty-three sites in eight states with those of more than

600 drug-involved offenders at six sites without a DTC, controlling for pertinent variables (Rossman et al., 2011). Results included the following:

- a lower proportion of DTC participants at the eighteen-month mark reported using drugs in the past year (56 percent versus 76 percent for the comparison group);
- a lower portion also reported using "serious" drugs in the past year (41 percent versus 58 percent);
- drug tests seemed to confirm the differences in self-reported drug use, with a higher proportion of the comparison group testing positive for recent drug use (46 percent versus 29 percent);
- a lower proportion of DTC participants reported committing a crime in the past year (40 percent versus 53 percent); and
- of those who self-reported criminal activity, the DTC participants reported about half as many criminal acts on average.

At least three caveats are in order. First, DTCs are relatively expensive to administer compared to conventional probation, reflecting the need for frequent court appearances and drug tests, active case management, treatment services, and motivational jail. Second, because of the use of motivational jail and the harsh sentences that can result when a person fails out of drug court, some studies find that DTC participants may, on average, spend about as much or even more time behind bars than similarly situated offenders outside of drug court (Csete & Tomasini-Joshi, 2015, 9). Finally, although some studies find recidivism reductions in some DTCs, other studies of other DTCs do not (O'Hear, 2017, 34). As discussed in Q9, just because a concept has been implemented successfully in one jurisdiction does not mean the concept will necessarily achieve similar results in another jurisdiction, especially if the program is designed or administered somewhat differently, as often seems to happen when general concepts are adapted to fit the specific circumstances of a particular local justice system. Researchers are now beginning to identify what features are most important for a DTC to succeed (Rossman et al., 2011, 7–8).

Inspired by the success of some DTCs, reformers have developed a multitude of other "problem-solving" courts that deal with other specific types or causes of crime. Thus, one can now find DUI courts, mental illness courts, truancy courts, homelessness courts, domestic violence courts, child support courts, parole violation courts, and gambling courts (Huddleston & Marlowe, 2011, 37). There is likely even more variation in the way these courts are designed and administered than there is with the

DTCs, but they tend to share certain features, including the provision of treatment under ongoing judicial supervision, with positive recognition of progress and graduated sanctions for failures. Appearing more recently and in smaller numbers, these other problem-solving courts have been studied much less extensively than the DTCs. However, a few studies are beginning to show positive results for DUI and mental illness courts (Huddleston & Marlowe, 2011, 12–13; Sarteschi, Vaughn, & Kim, 2011).

As more favorable studies appear, support will likely increase for a further proliferation of specialized problem-solving courts. However, some critics urge caution. Rather than continuing to develop new specialized courts, it would arguably be better to make all of our existing general criminal courts more treatment-oriented and problem-solving, making systematic use of the scientifically validated risk-needs assessment tools that are now available, as discussed in Q9. The more fragmented approach may be lavishing scarce treatment resources on groups of offenders who are not among those who would most benefit from treatment.

FURTHER READING

Csete, Joanne & Tomasini-Joshi, Denise. 2015. *Drug Courts: Equivocal Evidence on a Popular Intervention*. New York: Open Society Foundations. Retrieved from http://www.hr-dp.org/contents/1100.

Huddleston, West & Marlowe, Douglas. 2011. *Painting the Current Picture: A National Report on Drug Courts and Other Problem Solving Court Programs in the United States*. Alexandria, VA: National Drug Court Institute.

O'Hear, Michael. 2017. *The Failure of Sentencing Reform*. Santa Barbara, CA: Praeger.

Rossman, Shelli et al. 2011. *The Multi-Site Adult Drug Court Evaluation: Executive Summary*. Washington, DC: Urban Institute. Retrieved from https://www.ncjrs.gov/pdffiles1/nij/grants/237108.pdf.

Sarteschi, Christine, Vaughn, Michael, & Kim, Kevin. 2011. "Assessing the Effectiveness of Mental Health Courts: A Quantitative Review." *Journal of Criminal Justice*, 39, 12.

Q11: DOES RESTORATIVE JUSTICE REALLY WORK?

Answer: Restorative justice processes, which center on mediated dialogue between an offender and a victim, tend to produce higher levels of satisfaction among victims and offenders than does conventional criminal case-processing. There is also research suggesting that restorative processes may help to lower recidivism rates. These processes have been employed most widely and successfully with juvenile offenders and low-level property crimes. It is not clear whether restorative justice can be brought to bear as successfully as an alternative to conventional case-processing in other sorts of cases.

The Facts: Restorative justice (RJ), which finds inspiration in the age-old dispute-resolution practices of many tribal cultures around the globe, first emerged as a distinctive alternative to conventional case-processing in the United States in the 1970s (Umbreit, Vos, Coates, & Lightfoot, 2005). A leading RJ theorist has described the basic approach this way: "Restorative justice is a process to involve, to the extent possible, those who have a stake in the specific offense and collectively identify and address harms, needs, and obligations, in order to heal and put things as right as possible" (Zehr, 2002, 37). As a result of its emphasis on meeting the needs of victims and other particular stakeholders in the offense, RJ tends to favor different responses to crime than does the conventional system, which is more oriented to broad public interests as they are understood by prosecutors and judges. The RJ movement has thus drawn strength from the long-standing dissatisfaction many victims feel with the conventional system, as discussed in Q7.

The theory of RJ can be implemented in a variety of different ways, including two types of RJ process that have been widely adopted and studied. First, victim-offender dialogues involve a face-to-face, mediated conversation between the victim and the offender, in which both sides have an opportunity to discuss the offense and its aftermath. The offender may come to a deeper understanding of the consequences of his or her actions and may wish to offer an apology. However, the offender is not required to apologize and nor is the victim obligated to accept any apology that is offered. The two sides might also try to come to an agreement about how the offender may make amends. For instance, if the offender has vandalized the victim's property, the offender may agree to repair the damage.

Group conferencing, the second major type of RJ process, adds community representatives to the mix. They are able to describe the broader "ripple effects" of a crime that carry beyond the immediate victim. For instance, in a residential burglary case, the conference might include not only the burglar and the victimized homeowner but also neighbors who now feel more fearful about threats to their homes. In any event, all participants in the conference are able to share their perspectives. As with victim-offender dialogues, successful group conferences may culminate with an offer and acceptance of apology and an agreement about how the offender may make amends.

RJ processes may be structured in a variety of different ways in relationship to court processes. For instance, police or prosecutors might refer a complaint to an RJ program in the hope that the victim and offender can work things out without the need for any court involvement. Alternatively, RJ might be integrated more fully into court processes. For instance, probation might be conditioned on the offender's participation in a group conference. Finally, RJ processes might occur after the conclusion of court processes and without any implications for the offender's sentence.

A large body of research finds that RJ processes can produce positive results (Luna & Poulson, 2007). On average, victims and offenders alike rate RJ processes as fairer than conventional court processes, and outcomes as more satisfactory. In RJ processes, offenders are more likely to apologize and victims to forgive. Additionally, victims who participate in RJ are less upset about crime and less afraid of revictimization. For their part, offenders who participate in RJ tend to pay more in reparations. There are also some studies that find lower recidivism rates among RJ participants, although that advantage may diminish over time (Saulnier & Sivasubramaniam, 2015).

For all of the potential benefits of RJ, it is not clear whether RJ can or should function as a general alternative to conventional sentencing and punishment. Existing programs in the United States have mostly been limited to low-level offenses, especially those perpetrated by juveniles. In more serious cases, RJ tends to be used more sparingly and to take the form of victim-offender dialogues unconnected to court processes. RJ may still have considerable value in this setting for its ability to promote psychological healing and reconciliation. Still, this form of RJ does not function as a true alternative to normal case-processing; it is just a sort of add-on that occurs after the court system finishes its work.

Some RJ supporters believe that RJ should be used much more frequently as an alternative—even in most cases of serious crime. The court's role might be limited to enforcing victim-offender agreements or imposing a regular sentence in cases in which the victim and offender do not reach an agreement. However, there are concerns that such use of RJ might sacrifice important public interests in favor of victim and offender interests. For instance, in a case in which there is a strong public interest in incarceration, a victim and offender might nonetheless agree that the offender should be allowed to remain free so that he or she can earn money to pay reparations. More generally, there are deep tensions between the RJ ideal of leaving it up to the RJ participants to work out agreements on a case-by-case basis and the public interest in ensuring that punishments for serious crimes are proportionate and reasonably predictable (O'Hear, 2007). For victim-offender dialogues or group conferences to play a central role in a wider range of cases, it may be necessary to develop new hybrid forms of RJ in order to ensure adequate protection of public interests.

FURTHER READING

Luna, Erik & Poulson, Barton. 2006. "Restorative Justice in Federal Sentencing: An Unexpected Benefit of *Booker?*" *McGeorge Law Review*, 37, 787.

Saulnier, Alana & Sivasubramaniam, Diane. 2015. "Restorative Justice: Underlying Mechanisms and Future Directions." *New Criminal Law Review*, 18, 510.

Umbreit, Mark, Vos, Betty, Coates, Robert, & Lightfoot, Elizabeth. 2005. "Restorative Justice in the Twenty-First Century: A Social Movement Full of Opportunities and Pitfalls." *Marquette Law Review*, 89, 251.

Zehr, Howard. 2002. *The Little Book of Restorative Justice.* Intercourse, PA: Good Books.

Q12: ARE COLONIAL-STYLE "SHAMING" SENTENCES AN APPROPRIATE ALTERNATIVE TO INCARCERATION?

Answer: Shaming sanctions, which are intended to publicize and encourage condemnation of an offender's misconduct, can be administered much less expensively than incarceration and may in some circumstances have a more powerful impact on the offender and on the public than either conventional probation or other alternatives to incarceration. However, critics warn that this impact may not be entirely positive. Indeed, there are good reasons to fear that shaming forms of punishment may in some cases increase recidivism risk.

The Facts: Colonial Americans famously employed a rich array of shaming punishments, such as the stocks and pillory (which held the offender immobile for a period of time in a public place), the scarlet letter, branding, and the ducking stool (Friedman, 1993, 37–38). Such punishments served as a public condemnation of the offense, marking the offender in a painfully visible way as a person whose status in the community had been diminished. However, colonial-style shaming penalties fell into disfavor in the decades following American independence and were replaced by incarceration and probation.

Shaming made a surprising comeback in the late twentieth century. In a sense, of course, shame never disappeared from punishment. Criminal convictions in themselves are public records that tend to stigmatize the offender. Moreover, whether probation, incarceration, or something in between, sentences diminish the offender's liberty and symbolically mark the offender as a person who cannot be trusted with the full range of freedom enjoyed by other citizens. Still, these shaming aspects of conventional sentences have seemed more incidental than intentional. What seemed new in the shaming revival of the late twentieth century was the deliberate use of sentences that held up the offender for public condemnation in unusually direct ways.

The new shaming sanctions have typically been cooked up by individual judges and made a condition of probation. A prominent illustration comes from the prosecution of twenty-four-year-old Shawn Gementera for the theft of letters from a mailbox in San Francisco in 2001 (Goldman, 2015). As a condition of his supervised release from jail, the sentencing judge required Gementera to spend eight hours standing outside a post office wearing a signboard stating, "I stole mail. This is my punishment." Other examples include:

- drunk drivers have been required to affix "DUI" bumper stickers to their cars;
- offenders convicted of soliciting prostitutes have been required to sweep the streets;
- offenders' names have been published in the newspaper; and
- offenders have been required to wear T-shirts announcing their crimes (Goldman, 2015; Harris, 2014, 4811).

Two major arguments are advanced in favor of shaming punishments. First, shaming is a low-cost method of adding to the pains of punishment, especially when compared to the expense of incarceration—a sort of deterrence on the cheap. Indeed, because of the inherent tendency of shaming punishments to publicize themselves, such penalties may convey deterrent messages to a much wider audience than other punishments can reach. For instance, it is likely that many more people learned of Shawn Gementera's punishment by seeing him standing in public with his sandwich board than would have heard of the case if a more conventional sentence had been used.

Second, because shaming enlists the public in condemnation of the offense, the punishment conveys the message that the offense violates the community's sense of right and wrong. Shaming can thus help to build "internalized controls or conscience" (Harris, 2014, 4810). This crime-reducing mechanism is subtly different from deterrence. A deterrent message is successful to the extent that it simply scares away the offender from repeating (or others from committing) the offense being punished. But shaming, advocates argue, also activates a different and more powerful mechanism of self-control by proclaiming the offense morally wrong and appealing to the innate desire most people have to do the right thing.

However, critics have raised a number of practical and ethical objections (Harris, 2014, 4811–4812; Kahan, 2006). For instance, shaming sanctions could endanger the safety of offenders. They are also sometimes seen as demeaning and cruel.

Most important, though, has probably been the argument that shaming is not effective at reducing crime and may actually prove counterproductive in many cases. The basic concern is this: shaming stirs up a complex stew of strong psychological responses, which judges and other criminal justice officials are not well suited to manage constructively. For instance, psychological researchers distinguish between the emotions of "guilt" and "shame" (Harris, 2014, 4813). Feelings of guilt focus on a specific act or type of behavior, while shame is a negative feeling about one's whole self. Some individuals are more prone to guilt and others to shame. A shaming penalty is thus apt to produce varying degrees of guilt and shame in different offenders. The shame responses, though, should be of concern because they are associated with feelings of anger and hostility—feelings that seem inconsistent with the rehabilitative aims of shaming sentences. Indeed, some research finds a link between an individual's difficulty in managing feelings of shame and undesirable behaviors like bullying and repeat-offending (Harris, 2014, 4815).

Shame threatens an offender's feelings of self-worth and sense of identity as a good person. An offender who no longer thinks of himself or herself as a fundamentally good person will not likely be very motivated to do the right thing for its own sake. The difficulties are compounded if the stigma of punishment interferes with the offender's ability to establish and maintain relationships with people who would be a positive influence (Harris, 2014, 4810).

Underscoring the concern that shaming penalties may be ineffective or counterproductive, Shawn Gementera himself stole mail a second time just one month after his stint wearing the sandwich board (Goldman, 2015).

In light of the risk that sanctions might make some offenders are *more* likely to reoffend, one of the leading proponents of shaming, John Braithwaite, has distinguished between "reintegrative" and "disintegrative" shaming (Braithwaite, 1989, 55). Disintegrative shaming stigmatizes and isolates the offender, diminishing the likelihood of reform and improvement. By contrast, "reintegrative shaming means that expressions of community disapproval, which may range from mild rebuke to degradation ceremonies, are followed by gestures of reacceptance into the community of law-abiding citizens." Reintegration, another commenter observes, "can be seen to have occurred when shaming is respectful, distinguishes between the person and their actions, [and] concludes with forgiveness or decertification of deviance" (Harris, 2014, 4810). Put differently, reintegrative shaming tries to elicit feelings of guilt, rather than feelings of shame. In theory, this allows the offender to take responsibility for his or her actions without developing deeply negative self-perceptions that might increase recidivism risk. Indeed, some research does support the prediction that reintegrative shaming may help to reduce recidivism rates (Saulnier & Sivasubramaniam, 2015).

It does not appear that the sentencing judges who have embraced shaming in recent years have been especially mindful of reintegration. If shaming penalties are to be employed more widely as an alternative to incarceration, reintegrative measures should be developed and implemented in a systematic way. The principles and practices of restorative justice, with their emphasis on reconciliation, may provide helpful guidance.

FURTHER READING

Braithwaite, John. 1989. *Crime, Shame and Reintegration*. New York: Cambridge University Press.

Friedman, Lawrence. 1993. *Crime and Punishment in American History*. New York: Basic Books.

Goldman, Lauren. 2015. "Trending Now: The Use of Social Media Websites in Public Shaming Punishments." *American Criminal Law Review*, 52, 415.

Harris, Nigel. 2014. "Shame in Criminological Theory." In *Encyclopedia of Criminology and Criminal Justice*, 4809. Edited by G. Bruinsma & D. Weisburd. New York: Springer.

Kahan, Dan. 2006. "What's Really Wrong with Shaming Sanctions." *Texas Law Review*, 84, 2075.

Saulnier, Alana & Sivasubramaniam, Diane. 2015. "Restorative Justice: Underlying Mechanisms and Future Directions." *New Criminal Law Review*, 18, 510.

Q13: HAVE FINES AND OTHER FINANCIAL PENALTIES IN CRIMINAL CASES DRAMATICALLY INCREASED SINCE THE LATE 1990s?

Answer: Yes, the financial consequences of a criminal conviction have grown far more severe over the past generation. Whether these consequences have grown excessive is a matter of opinion, but there are mounting concerns about the potentially devastating economic impact of a criminal case on poor families, even if the charged offense is relatively minor. Critics assert that severe financial penalties violate the ideal of proportionality in punishment, and they point to some research suggesting that such penalties increase recidivism risk.

The Facts: Fines have always been an important aspect of criminal sentences in the United States. In the very lowest-level cases, a fine might be the entirety of the sentence. In other cases, fines are coupled with incarceration, probation, or other sanctions. As with other aspects of the sentence, the judge has traditionally had wide discretion in setting the severity of the fine.

A variety of other financial consequences have been layered on top of the fine in recent years. Much of this takes the form of *fees* for court or correctional services, such as the fees for probation supervision and treatment noted in Q8. Additionally, as discussed in Q7, *restitution* for victims is now increasingly a mandatory component of criminal sentences. It has also become easier under *forfeiture* laws for the government to seize property that was used in the commission of a crime or that constitutes the proceeds of a crime. For instance, a defendant might lose his or her car if it was used to transport drugs.

These various financial consequences have become a weightier burden for defendants in recent years. For instance, one study found that 66 percent of prison inmates in 2004 had been assessed with monetary sanctions by the court, as opposed to only 25 percent in 1991 (Harris, Evans, & Beckett, 2010). Another study found that forty-eight states increased fees for offenders between 2008 and 2013 (Corbett, 2015). Reflecting these trends, the U.S. Department of Justice estimates that the total amount of outstanding criminal debt rose from about $20 billion in 2001 to $100 billion in 2014 (Greenberg, Meredith, & Morse, 2016).

It is important to remember that, in addition to any financial exactions mandated by the judge, a criminal prosecution is likely to carry a variety of other economic consequences for the defendant. Perhaps, most important, there is the challenge of securing pretrial release. After arrest, defendants are typically required to post bond in order to be able to leave jail, while their cases are being processed in the court system. A judge normally determines the financial commitment that the defendant must make as a guarantee that he or she will return to court to stand trial. Although the defendant is not usually required to pay the full amount upfront, he or she will typically have to pay something—often about 10 percent—either in the form of a fee to a bail bondsman or a deposit with the court. If he or she cannot do so, then he or she is apt to remain incarcerated for the days, weeks, or months that his or her case remains pending. This pretrial detention is likely to cost the defendant his or her job if he or she has one, which may make satisfaction of any other financial obligations impossible.

Furthermore, the cost of legal representation might easily run into thousands of dollars. To be sure, the Constitution guarantees that the government will provide a lawyer to the defendant who is too poor to hire one, but states have considerable freedom to decide what counts as too poor, and some set the cutoff at a very low level. Just because a defendant has too many resources to qualify for a public defender does not mean that he or she can comfortably bear the financial burden of competent, experienced representation. Moreover, even for those defendants who are poor enough to get a state-provided lawyer, states increasingly charge application fees in order to get a public defender or try to extract at least partial reimbursement for the costs of representation.

Additional expenses might include:

- booking fees following arrest,
- bail administration fees,
- interpreter fees for defendants who do not speak English,
- room and board for time spent behind bars,
- post-release supervision fees, and
- interest, penalties, and collection fees for defendants who fall behind in paying off all of the foregoing debts (Appleman, 2016).

Combined with all of these fees and expenses, the fine and other financial consequences of a conviction may have a devastating economic impact on the defendant and his or her family. A struggling family may find itself threatened with the loss of housing, transportation, utilities, and other necessities. Yet, if the defendant skips a court-ordered payment in order, say, to keep his or her landlord at bay for one more month, then the defendant is likely to be in violation of the terms of his or her probation, which can lead to arrest and incarceration—and hence possibly a loss of job, income, and the capacity to make any future court-ordered payments.

In theory, the Equal Protection Clause of the Constitution prohibits incarceration based on a person's poverty. In practice, however, this right is not very effectively safeguarded. Indeed, few defendants are even aware of the right, and judges tend not to inform them of it (Appleman, 2016). Yet, if an impoverished defendant does not request a hearing on his or her ability to pay, the judge may not know that the defendant is incapable of covering a substantial fine and assessment of fees. Moreover, even if the defendant does get a hearing on his or her financial situation, the constitutional standards are murky and lax. For instance, some courts have decided that a defendant cannot get out of a fine that he or she agreed to pay as part of a plea deal, no matter how unrealistic the amount.

Given the weakness of the constitutional protections, some critics charge that a two-tier, class-based system of justice has developed for lower-level offenses: middle-class defendants quickly and easily pay off their fines, fees, and other expenses, while working-class and poorer defendants struggle with payment plans, escalating financial distress, and eventually incarceration.

The current web of financial consequences developed on an *ad hoc* basis, with fees often created or increased to meet immediate needs of courts and corrections agencies. There was no grand plan or unifying vision. Yet, broadly speaking, one might defend the system to the extent that it attempts to make offenders bear the full costs of their misconduct. Restitution, of course, shifts the victim's losses to the offender, while court fees and other financial consequences might be thought of as a way to make offenders take responsibility for the costs to the criminal justice system of responding to their crimes. Why, we might wonder, should innocent taxpayers be made to shoulder these burdens? Additionally, stiff financial consequences might help to deter some crimes, especially those motivated by the hope for economic gain, such as drug trafficking and white-collar crime.

On the other hand, the current system may be in tension with the goal of proportionality in punishment—the ideal that the severity of the punishment should match the seriousness of the crime. If the financial consequences of a conviction do not take into account the offender's ability to pay, then the poor person who commits a crime will have to pay the same amount as the rich person who commits the same crime. Yet, the practical significance of each dollar is very different to the family living on, say, $20,000 per year than it is for the family living on $200,000 per year. It hardly seems proportionate when, say, a $1,000 fine delivers a crushing blow to one offender but is laughed off by another who was convicted of the same crime—the penalty in the first case must be too heavy, or the penalty in the second must be too light, or perhaps both are missing the mark. The proportionality problem seems even more starkly apparent when the poorer offender is jailed for failure to pay an unrealistically high fine; an offense that was initially adjudged not suitable for incarceration is now effectively punished with time behind bars.

Some recent research suggests that heavy financial consequences may also contribute to recidivism. For instance, offenders have been known to engage in criminal activity in order to try to pay off their debts to the legal system (Harris, Evans, & Beckett, 2010). Another study of juvenile offenders found that the imposition of economic sanctions was associated with higher recidivism rates, even controlling for offense type and offender demographics (Piquero & Jennings, 2016). Such results are not surprising: financial penalties can imperil housing and employment, and a loss of either is thought to make recidivism more likely (Lutze, Rosky, & Hamilton, 2013; Graffam, Shinkfield, Lavelle, & McPherson, 2004).

There are also concerns that the priorities of the criminal justice system can become warped once the system comes to see offenders as an important source of financial support; revenue-generation may be elevated over public safety. This was, for instance, a central problem with the police department and courts in Ferguson, Missouri, as identified by the U.S. Department of Justice in its report after extensive civil unrest in the city (U.S. Department of Justice Civil Rights Division, 2015).

Some of the problems with current arrangements might be alleviated with the "day fine" system that is routinely utilized in some European countries (Lappi-Seppälä, 2013). In this system, the fine is set as a number of days of the offender's income; lower-income offenders are thus required to pay less in absolute terms than higher-income offenders who are guilty of the same crime. However, while there have been a few localized experiments with day fines (also called "structured fines") in the United States, the idea has yet to gain a real foothold on this side of the Atlantic.

FURTHER READING

Appleman, Laura. 2016. "Nickel and Dimed into Incarceration: Cash-Register Justice in the Criminal System." *Boston College Law Review*, 57, 1483.

Corbett, Ronald. 2015. "The Burdens of Leniency: The Changing Face of Probation." *Minnesota Law Review*, 99, 1697.

Graffam, Joe, Shinkfield, Alison, Lavelle, Barbara, & McPherson, Wenda. 2004. "Variables Affecting Successful Reintegration as Perceived by Offenders and Professionals." *Journal of Offender Rehabilitation*, 40, 147.

Greenberg, Claire, Meredith, Marc, & Morse, Michael. 2016. "The Growing and Broad Nature of Legal Financial Obligations: Evidence from Alabama Court Records." *Connecticut Law Review*, 48, 1079.

Harris, Alexes, Evans, Heather, & Beckett, Katherine. 2010. "Drawing Blood from Stones: Legal Debt and Social Inequality in the Contemporary United States." *American Journal of Sociology*, 115, 1753.

Lappi-Seppälä, Tapio. 2013. "Fines in Europe." In *Encyclopedia of Criminology and Criminal Justice*, 1637. Edited by G. Bruinsma & D. Weisburd. New York: Springer.

Lutze, Faith, Rosky, Jefferey, & Hamilton, Zachary. 2013. "Homelessness and Reentry: A Multisite Outcome Evaluation of Washington State's Reentry Housing Program for High Risk Offenders." *Criminal Justice & Behavior*, 41, 471.

Piquero, Alex & Jennings, Wesley. 2016. "Research Note: Justice System-Imposed Financial Penalties Increase the Likelihood of Recidivism in a Sample of Juvenile Offenders." *Youth Violence and Justice* 15, 325. Retrieved from http://journals.sagepub.com/doi/pdf/10.1177/1541204016669213.

U.S. Department of Justice Civil Rights Division. 2015. *Investigation of the Ferguson Police Department.* Washington, DC: U.S. Department of Justice.

3

The Experience and Consequences of Incarceration

American judges have been sentencing criminal defendants to prison for two centuries, but the practical significance of such a sentence has varied dramatically from one time and place to another. While the overall trajectory of the past century has been away from the dungeon-like austerity and brutal treatment of inmates that we associate with nineteenth-century institutions, reform has hardly followed a consistent, uniform path. The experience of imprisonment in the United States remains highly varied. Some inmates find themselves in institutions that are reasonably safe and orderly—perhaps more so, in fact, than some of their home neighborhoods—and that offer a number of constructive ways of passing the time, including employment, education, vocational training, and treatment for substance abuse and other mental health disorders. Other inmates are not so fortunate, experiencing endless empty days punctuated by periodic spasms of violence. Persistent, and not unjustified, concerns remain that too many inmates leave prison severely damaged by their time behind bars—especially those who are mentally ill, youthful, or otherwise an easy target for predatory sexual behavior—and that their negative and sometimes harrowing experiences while incarcerated ultimately make them *more* likely to commit new crimes.

Q14: HAS IMPRISONMENT IN THE UNITED STATES GOTTEN TOO SOFT?

Answer: In some important respects, American prisons did tend to become more humane in the mid- to late twentieth century. However, the national imprisonment boom that began in the 1970s created chronically overcrowded conditions in many institutions, which undermined or off-set many of the gains that prisoners had achieved through litigation and other means. Overall, it is difficult to assess the "softness" of contemporary imprisonment. Conditions today vary tremendously from institution to institution, and, even within a single institution, some inmates can have dramatically different experiences than others.

The Facts: There is no precise, generally accepted metric for evaluating the relative harshness of imprisonment in different times and places. In part, this results from the wide variety of different ways that imprisonment can be hard on inmates.

Roughly speaking, the difficulties of imprisonment can be divided into four types. First, there is the basic loss of liberty that is inherent to imprisonment. Second, there are the many additional deprivations and indignities that are imposed on inmates, not as inherent aspects of imprisonment, but because they are seen as administratively expedient or otherwise conducive to the aims of imprisonment. For instance, many institutions require newly admitted inmates to undergo a strip search. Such an invasive, degrading practice is not, strictly speaking, an inherent aspect of imprisonment, but it is a convenient way for prison administrators to restrict the flow of troublesome contraband into the institution, as well as a symbolically powerful way to convey to inmates the loss of social status that has resulted from their offenses. Third, there are the sanctions formally imposed on inmates in response to violations of institutional rules. Fourth, and finally, there are the many informal acts of violence, intimidation, and coercion that are directed against inmates either by fellow inmates or by correctional officers.

By the reckoning of some scholars, the first prison in the United States opened in Philadelphia in 1790 (Friedman, 1993, 78). The institution was seen as a more humane alternative to the corporal punishments that were common in colonial America. The prison concept spread across the United States in the ensuing decades and became widely accepted as a standard form of punishment for serious crime. However, while the nineteenth-century prisons may have originated in a spirit of liberal reform, they tended in practice to be dismal, cruel places. Prison rules prohibited any interaction among inmates and mandated course clothing, simple food, and generally austere living conditions (79–80). Moreover, prison discipline involved frequent whippings and a variety of other, more exotic forms of physical torture. Severe overcrowding also exacerbated the misery of prison life. Cells were typically designed to hold only one inmate apiece, but often ended up with two or more. In New Jersey in 1867, for instance, as many as four prisoners were packed into cells of seven by twelve feet (158).

In the early decades of the twentieth century, periodic exposes of the horrors of prison life produced short-lived bursts of reform activity, but more fundamental changes did not occur until after World War II (Friedman, 1993, 310).

In the middle decades of the twentieth century, prisons evolved under the influence of the rehabilitative ideal, which played a leading role in correctional thinking at the time. In order to better prepare inmates for a successful return to free society, institutions offered increasingly rich educational programming and vocational training (Blomberg & Lucken, 2010, 112). States also developed new minimum- and medium-security facilities as less restrictive alternatives for some inmates to the high-security institutions built on the nineteenth-century model. California's new Soledad Prison exemplified progressive thinking about prison design in the postwar period, with its day rooms, cheerful paint colors, and well-equipped libraries, gyms, and educational facilities. New institutions like Soledad also helped to ease the overcrowding that had bedeviled American prisons almost from the start.

The rehabilitation-oriented reform movement of the 1940s through the 1960s was embraced by different states to varying degrees, and in many places little meaningful change occurred (Walker, 1998, 176–77). By the 1960s, however, courts had become receptive to lawsuits brought by inmates to improve prison conditions—a sharp break from the "hands-off" doctrine that had long restrained court interference in the administration of prisons. During the "golden age" of prisoner rights litigation from the 1960s to the 1980s, courts recognized constitutional rights for inmates in such areas as:

- exercise of religion,
- mail censorship,
- access to legal assistance and legal resources,
- due process for inmates accused of violating institutional rules,

- health care,
- use of force by guards, and
- sanitation and access to basic hygiene materials (Blomberg & Lucken, 2010, 151–56).

Court involvement undoubtedly improved conditions in many prison systems, but it is easy to overstate the practical significance of prisoner rights. Most fundamentally, the basic deprivation of liberty that is inherent to imprisonment has remained untouched. Additionally, while the courts overturned some prison policies and practices, they generally upheld any rules that were "reasonably related to legitimate penological interests" (Branham, 2013, 267).

This turned out to be a low bar for prison officials to meet. Inmates thus routinely continue to face many important restrictions in such areas as contact with family and friends; receipt of food, hygiene supplies, and other goods from the outside; clothing and personal adornment; alcohol and tobacco use; and privacy of possessions and of the body. On the other hand, whipping and similar forms of corporal punishment for rules violations have largely become a thing of the past. Yet, prison administrators have a range of other quite substantial sanctions at their disposal, including, as we will see in Q19, solitary confinement. The courts have also tried to crack down on informal staff violence against prisoners, permitting inmates to proceed with lawsuits when they have been harmed "maliciously and sadistically" by guards. Moreover, prisons are now generally prohibited from simply ignoring substantial risks of serious inmate-on-inmate violence (Branham, 2013, 408, 412).

By and large, it is probably true that the average inmate today experiences better conditions than his forebears did a century or even a half-century ago. However, it is also true that the trend toward improved conditions has waned—perhaps even entirely ended—since the 1980s. In part, this reflects a disengagement of the courts from prison affairs, as will be discussed in greater detailed in Q15. In part, this also reflects the influence of tough-on-crime politics and a general shift in correctional thinking away from rehabilitation and toward deterrence and incapacitation. If one is more concerned with scaring people away from committing crimes and less with preparing prisoners for life in the free world, then one might well favor a return to the grim, austere institutions of earlier generations. Thus, American politicians of the late twentieth century increasingly demanded what they sometimes called "no frills prisons" (Committee on Causes and Consequences of High Rates of Incarceration, 2014, 163). In one southern state, for instance, that meant the removal of air-conditioning, a ban on televisions in cells, the end of intramural sports, and new rules against long hair and beards. But perhaps nothing better expressed the harsh ethos of the 1990s than the "supermax" prisons that sprouted up across the United States. These institutions are designed to hold inmates alone in their cells for twenty-three hours a day, with few or no programming opportunities or other privileges.

Overall, though, the single most important force working against further improvement in prison conditions has probably been the chronic overcrowding that resulted from the late twentieth-century explosion in prison populations. While prison construction also boomed, new prisons could not be brought on line fast enough to keep up with demand. Indeed, despite the stabilization in national incarceration rates since 2000, many institutions remain jam-packed. As of the end of 2015, the prison systems of at least nineteen states had more inmates than they were designed to hold, including at least five states (Alabama, Delaware, Hawai'i, Illinois, and Nebraska) that were *more than 50 percent* above design capacity (Carson & Anderson, 2016, 27). At least six additional state systems were overcrowded based on other capacity measures.

Overcrowding adversely affects the quality of prison life in a multitude of different ways, beginning at the most basic level of reduced personal living space. In the mid-1970s, the typical maximum-security inmate resided in a single cell covering about sixty square feet (Committee on Causes and Consequences of High Rates of Incarceration, 2014, 179). Within a few years, though, double-celling had become the norm. Triple-celling also became more common, as did the use of makeshift dormitories in converted gyms and dayrooms. As new prisons were built in this era, they tended to have somewhat larger cells, reflecting the new expectation of double-celling, but they still fell far short of the earlier norm of sixty square feet per inmate (Committee on Causes and Consequences of High Rates of Incarceration, 2014, 180). Indeed, new standards promulgated by the American Correctional Association permitted as few as eighty square feet per double-bunked cell—in other words, just forty square feet of living space per inmate.

Overcrowding affects more than just the amount of living space. A greater number of inmates generally mean longer waiting lists to get into rehabilitative and other programs, thereby contributing to inmate idleness. Indeed, the urgent need for beds may require the conversion of activity areas into dorms, leading to a reduction in programming and other out-of-cell opportunities even as demand burgeons. Overcrowding can also stretch an institution's medical care and mental health treatment resources to the breaking point. At the height of California's overcrowding crisis, for instance, it was estimated that one inmate needlessly died every six to seven days as a result of failures of the state prison system to deliver timely, effective treatment (O'Hear, 2017, 175). More subtly, but perhaps no less importantly, overcrowding can increase the stress of day-to-day life as inmates must navigate a more complex social environment involving many more interactions with other inmates of unknown character and allegiances (Committee on Causes and Consequences of High Rates of Incarceration, 2014, 181). Race-based prison gangs flourish in this sort of environment, providing inmates with a greater sense of personal security as long as they stick with members of their own group (Dolovich, 2012, 1012). However, gang-dominated institutions have their own drawbacks, including periodic outbreaks of group violence.

Research finds associations between overcrowding and a variety of physical and mental health problems. Some studies, for instance, have found that overcrowding is correlated with elevated blood pressure, an increase in illness complaints, and heightened stress and arousal. There also seem to be associations between overcrowding and in-prison drug use and suicide (Committee on Causes and Consequences of High Rates of Incarceration, 2014, 180, 181).

Any attempt to assess the "softness" of contemporary imprisonment must reckon with the harsh realities of overcrowded institutions. Any such attempt must also take into account the extreme variation found from prison to prison in the United States, and also in the capacity of different inmates to adapt to life in the institutions in which they find themselves. The white-collar offender who has financial resources, a supportive family, and placement in a well-run minimum-security facility may adjust to incarceration with relative ease. But many others will find life behind bars almost unbearably difficult—the youthful or effeminate male who is serially raped, the sick inmate who cannot get treatment, the mentally ill inmate who struggles to conform with prison rules, the inmate caught in the middle of a violent gang rivalry, and the inmate sent to "supermax," to note just a few examples.

While the complexity and diversity of American prison experiences defy easy generalization, a comparison with life in some Western European institutions may nonetheless be instructive. In countries like Germany and the Netherlands, rehabilitation and a successful return to free society are recognized as the overriding aims of incarceration (Subramanian & Shames, 2013, 7). In order to better prepare inmates for release, efforts are made to make prison life as similar as possible to life in the community. For instance, inmates have the opportunity to wear their own clothes and prepare their own meals (12). From the standpoint of physical design, institutions tend to be more comfortable and welcoming than American prisons, with lots of windows and wide hallways. Additionally, inmates are encouraged to maintain and develop relationships with others both inside and outside the institution. For instance, many inmates are permitted short periods of home leave during their prison terms (13). Also, solitary confinement is only very rarely used.

Norway's maximum-security Halden prison provides an especially stark contrast with American norms. As one visitor recently noted, "There were no coils of razor wire in sight, no lethal electric fences, no towers manned by snipers—nothing violent, threatening or dangerous" (Benko, 2015). She further observed that "guards socialize with the inmates every day, in casual conversation, often over tea or coffee or meals. Inmates can be monitored via surveillance cameras on the prison grounds, but they often move unaccompanied by guards. . . . Nor are there surveillance cameras in the classrooms or most of the workshops, or in the common rooms, the cell hallways or the cells themselves." She concluded, "To anyone familiar with the American correctional system, Halden seems alien. Its modern, cheerful and well-appointed facilities, the relative freedom of movement it offers, its quiet and peaceful atmosphere—these qualities are so out of sync with the forms of imprisonment found in the United States that you could be forgiven for doubting whether Halden is a prison at all."

Despite decades of reform efforts in the United States, the contrast with Halden and other Western European institutions serves to underscore that American prisons, for better or worse, remain considerably harsher than they need to be in order to achieve the basic objective of physically separating their residents from free society.

FURTHER READING

Benko, Jessica. 2015. "The Radical Humaneness of Norway's Halden Prison." *New York Times*, March 26. Retrieved from https://www.nytimes .com/2015/03/29/magazine/the-radical-humaneness-of-norways-halden-prison.html.

Blomberg, Thomas & Lucken, Karol. 2010. *American Penology: A History of Control*. New Brunswick, NJ: Transaction.

Branham, Sheila. 2013. *The Law and Policy of Sentencing and Corrections*. St. Paul, MN: West Academic Publishing.

Carson, E. Ann & Anderson, Elizabeth. 2016. *Prisoners in 2015*. Washington, DC: U.S. Department of Justice.

Committee on Causes and Consequences of High Rates of Incarceration, National Research Council of the National Academies. 2014.

The Growth of Incarceration in the United States. Washington, DC: The
National Academies Press.
Dolovich, Sharon. 2012. "Two Models of the Prison: Accidental Human-
ity and Hypermasculinity in the L.A. County Jail." *Journal of Criminal
Law and Criminology*, 102, 965.
Friedman, Lawrence. 1993. *Crime and Punishment in American History.*
New York: Basic Books.
O'Hear, Michael. 2017. *The Failure of Sentencing Reform.* Santa Barbara,
CA: Praeger.
Subramanian, Ram & Shames, Alison. 2013. *Sentencing and Prison Prac-
tices in Germany and the Netherlands: Implications for the United States.*
New York: Vera Institute of Justice.
Walker, Samuel. 1998. *Popular Justice: A History of American Criminal Jus-
tice.* New York: Oxford University Press.

Q15: DO JUDGES PLAY A SIGNIFICANT ROLE IN THE ADMINISTRATION OF PRISONS?

Answer: Yes. To the extent that American prisons became more humane
between the early 1960s and early 1990s, prisoner rights litigation likely
played an important role. Prisoner rights cases drew judges into the business of prison administration. Institutions in nearly every state became
subject to court orders covering many aspects of institutional life. Indeed,
in more than half the states, the entire prison system became subject
to some level of judicial control at some point in time. However, court
orders have declined considerably since the early 1990s in both number
and scope. A recent, controversial order requiring California to dramatically reduce its overcrowding serves as a reminder that courts still can,
and sometimes do, play an active role in overseeing prison administration.
However, such sweeping orders are highly uncommon.

The Facts: As discussed in Q14, courts abandoned the "hands-off"
doctrine in the 1960s and began to recognize and enforce constitutional
rights on behalf of prisoners. The litigation took two distinct forms. First,
there were the lawsuits in which plaintiff-inmates sought a court order, or
"injunction," requiring an institution to change some policy or practice.
Typically, if an injunction is granted, the court will stay involved for a
period of time to ensure satisfactory compliance with its order. Second,
there were the lawsuits in which inmates sought monetary compensation,
or "damages," for violations of their rights. Although the latter type of lawsuit may not directly change the way that institutions are administered,

they can have indirect effects to the extent that institutions have incentives to modify policies or practices that expose them to legal liability. Thus, as they became more common through the 1970s and 1980s, both types of lawsuits contributed to prison reform.

By 1984, there were active federal court orders governing aspects of the administration of at least one prison in forty-four states, including nine states in which the *entire prison system* was subject to an injunction (Schlanger, 2006, 577). On average, states held more than one-third of their prisoners in institutions that were under court order (578).

The most ambitious court intervention in this "golden age" of prisoner rights litigation was doubtlessly that of Judge William Wayne Justice in Texas. After an epic 159-day trial concluding in 1979, Judge Justice found broad, system-wide violations of the constitutional rule against cruel and unusual punishments, particularly in regard to overcrowding, security and supervision, health care delivery, discipline, and access to the courts. His remedial order touched on nearly all aspects of prison administration. Justice then appointed a "special master" with a small, full-time professional staff to monitor implementation of the order over a nine-year period (Deitch, 2012, 237). These emissaries of the court were a constant presence in the prisons, documenting violations of Justice's orders and ensuring that recalcitrant officials would be held accountable. This remedial phase of the litigation represented an extraordinary assertion of judicial authority over the nation's largest state prison system, but one that was at least arguably justified by a long history of brutal violence, official callousness, and needless suffering in Texas penal institutions.

As the 1980s gave way to the 1990s, the volume of court-order litigation continued unabated. In 1995, forty-one states had at least one prison under an injunction (Schlanger, 2006, 577). However, the raw number of court orders masks a subtle shift in the nature of the injunctions, which tended to grow more narrowly focused over time (604). The massive orders like Judge Justice's covering many different aspects of prison administration grew rarer. In part, this likely reflected general improvements in prison conditions in the United States in that time period. However, the change also likely reflected the growing conservatism of the federal judiciary as the appointees of Presidents Nixon and Reagan played increasingly prominent roles on the Supreme Court and in the lower federal courts. Both presidents often railed against "activist" judges, and there was probably nothing a judge could do that seemed more activist than taking over the management of a state prison system. A series of Supreme Court decisions thus laid the groundwork for a new, more limited approach to prisoner rights litigation. These decisions affected both the scope of the rights themselves and the procedural rules for enforcing rights. For instance, as discussed in Q14, the Supreme Court held that restrictions on the basic liberties of prisoners were generally constitutional as long as the restrictions were minimally reasonable.

Individual suits by prisoners for money damages followed an historical trajectory that was similar to that of the court-order cases. The number of federal prisoner rights lawsuits jumped from just 2,245 in 1970 to its all-time high of 39,053 in 1995 (Schlanger, 2015, 157). To be sure, this was to some extent simply a reflection of the national imprisonment boom in the same time period. However, if the number of lawsuits is divided by the number of prisoners, we can still see clear evidence of increased prisoner litigiousness. Lawsuit filings per 1,000 inmates rose from 6.2 in 1970 to an all-time high of 29.3 in 1981, and then remained above 20 per 1,000 every year through 1996 (157). The plateauing after 1981 likely resulted in large part from the combination of improved prison conditions and less receptive judiciary. These factors may also have been reflected in the low success rate of prisoner rights cases. While inmate-plaintiffs have probably always had much lower winning percentages than most other plaintiffs, their success rate dropped steadily from 16.8 percent in 1988 to just 12.7 percent in 1996 (164).

Thus, by the mid-1990s, there were already indications that the golden age of prisoner rights litigation was winding down. In 1996, however, Congress adopted legislation that even more swiftly and sharply curtailed prisoner rights lawsuits. Responding to claims that a wave of frivolous prisoner lawsuits was overburdening both the federal courts and state prison officials, the Prison Litigation Reform Act (PLRA) established a variety of unique procedural hurdles for prisoner cases that did not apply to any other type of federal civil rights litigation (Herman, 2012, 265). A few of the more important aspects of the PLRA include:

- more rigorous requirement for inmates to take their complaints through internal prison grievance procedures before initiating litigation in court;
- increased filing fees for launching a lawsuit;
- reduced ability for inmate-plaintiffs to recover compensation for their attorney fees if successful in court;
- reduced ability for inmate-plaintiffs to recover damages for nonphysical injuries;
- new limitations on the scope and duration of injunctions; and
- new restrictions on the ability of courts to impose prison population caps in order to deal with severe overcrowding (Schlanger, 2015, 153–54).

The PLRA had an immediate impact on prisoner rights litigation. The proportion of state prisons under court order fell from 32 percent in 1995 to 18 percent in 2005 (Schlanger, 2015, 169). The number of lawsuit filings fell from 24.6 per 1000 inmates in 1995 to 9.6 in 2007—the lowest level since 1971 (157). Success rates dropped below 10 percent in 2002 and have remained well under pre-PLRA levels (164). By any measure, rights litigation has become a much less significant part of the prison administration landscape than it was in the 1980s.

This does not mean, however, that courts are entirely irrelevant. Recent litigation in California provides a vivid illustration of the potential impact of the courts, even in a legal environment that is much less favorable to inmates than back in the day when Judge Justice effectively seized control of the Texas prison system. The California litigation dates back to the 1990s, when a group of mentally ill inmates sued the state, claiming that lengthy delays and poor quality in their treatment constituted cruel and unusual punishment (O'Hear, 2017, 175). Physically ill inmates then sued in 2001, raising similar concerns about the treatment available to them. Although the inmate-plaintiffs in both cases succeeded in establishing constitutional violations, and although the courts entered orders requiring improvements in treatment quality, California struggled to comply, overwhelmed by a burgeoning prison population and crushing institutional overcrowding—inmates numbered more than twice what the system was designed to hold. As the years passed with little improvement in conditions, the judges overseeing the litigation grew frustrated and eventually saw no alternative to addressing the overcrowding problem directly. In 2007, the judges referred the cases to a special three-judge panel for consideration of a population-reduction order, as required by the PLRA. The panel ordered California to bring its population down to 137.5 percent of design capacity within two years, constituting a net reduction of about 46,000 inmates if the state did not create any new prison space in the interim (179). After California appealed, the U.S. Supreme Court affirmed the panel's order in a closely divided, ideologically polarized 5–4 decision in 2011.

The overcrowding order led California to adopt an array of fundamental structural reforms to its criminal justice system (O'Hear, 2017, 180–90). Although these particular changes were not, strictly speaking, required by the courts, the aggressive timeline set for a massive population reduction effectively required California to do something radical. Early indications are that the reforms have succeeded in bringing overcrowding down without any corresponding increase in crime.

With its prisons at twice their design capacity and numerous well-documented, often lethal failures in the treatment of inmates suffering from severe mental illness and other major medical problems, California represented an extreme outlier in American corrections in the early 2000s. Thus, despite its profound practical impact in the nation's most populous state, the judicial intervention in California does not likely presage a broader revival of the golden age of prisoner rights. Still, as the sharply worded dissenting opinions in the California case might remind us, prisoner rights remain a highly divisive concept. Some critics regard even the existing, relatively restrained patterns of judicial intervention as overly intrusive.

FURTHER READING

Deitch, Michelle. 2012. "The Need for Independent Prison Oversight in a Post-PRLA World." *Federal Sentencing Reporter*, 24, 236.

Herman, Susan. 2012. "Prison Reform Litigation Acts." *Federal Sentencing Reporter*, 24, 263.

O'Hear, Michael. 2017. *The Failure of Sentencing Reform*. Santa Barbara, CA: Praeger.

Schlanger, Margo. 2006. "Civil Rights Injunctions over Time: A Case Study of Jail and Prison Court Orders." *New York University Law Review*, 81, 550.

Schlanger, Margo. 2015. "Trends in Prisoner Litigation, as the PLRA Enters Adulthood." *UC Irvine Law Review*, 5, 153.

Q16: DOES TIME IN PRISON LEAVE INMATES MORE LIKELY TO REOFFEND?

Answer: Imprisonment can make some inmates more likely to reoffend, but the impact of imprisonment varies from institution to institution and from inmate to inmate. Concerns about increased risk may be greatest with respect to maximum security and other particularly harsh institutional environments, especially with respect to offenders with limited criminal history. However, certain types of rehabilitative programming may counter the tendency for time behind bars to increase the risk of recidivism.

The Facts: The effect of imprisonment on crime rates has long been a matter of debate. There are a variety of different mechanisms by which a sentence of imprisonment might tend either to increase or decrease crime. For instance, a prison term given to one offender might deter other people from committing the same crime. Also, for however long the offender is imprisoned, he or she will be incapacitated from committing fresh crimes on the outside. (Of course, the social benefits of such incapacitation may be offset if there is a corresponding increase in crime behind bars—a real concern since the surveillance and control of inmates is never perfect, as discussed in Q18.)

In order to fully understand the long-term impact of imprisonment, though, it is also important to consider how the experience of imprisonment might change the offender. After all, the vast majority of prisoners are released within a few years. If incarceration tends to increase their recidivism risk, then prison sentences might produce little overall net reduction in crime.

Theorists have identified several reasons why imprisonment might make some offenders worse. For instance, there is the long-standing criticism that prisons function as "schools of crime"; that is, by putting less-experienced offenders in proximity to more experienced, hardened criminals, the less experienced are able to learn from their elders and refine their craft. Additionally, imprisonment tends to weaken the inmate's relationships with noncriminal friends and acquaintances on the outside and to foster the development of new relationships with other offenders— relationships that may then form the inmate's core social network after release. The stigma of imprisonment, moreover, may serve to further isolate the former inmate from positive social influences and opportunities, including opportunities to secure lawful employment (Hutcherson, 2012).

More subtle psychological effects might also play an important role. Adaptation to prison life may require some inmates to develop certain habits of thought or conduct that are detrimental to the successful resumption of life as a law-abiding citizen in free society. For instance, in some male prison environments, inmates may expose themselves to predatory behavior if they do not project a façade of "hypermasculinity" (Dolovich, 2012, 1003–10). This may involve the suppression of "soft" emotions, heightened and more frequent expressions of contempt for women, anxiety about status relative to other males, and the use of violence in response to any perceived slight. Such tendencies are probably not shed as quickly and easily as the orange jumpsuit and may play a role in the criminal assaults perpetrated by some inmates after they are released.

Additionally, poor treatment in prison—as through unnecessarily restrictive rules, assaults by guards, or unfair disciplinary processes—can reinforce feelings of distrust and anger toward legal authorities. Such attitudes may leave the offender with little sense of motivation to obey the law beyond the bare fear of getting caught (Tyler, 2003).

Research increasingly bears out the validity of these theoretical concerns (Committee on Causes and Consequences of High Rates of Incarceration, 2014, 193–95). For instance, one recent study found a statistically significant, positive relationship between past incarceration and a person's amount of recent illegal earnings from drug dealing, theft, and other remunerative crime, holding constant such variables as age, gang membership, and employment status (Hutcherson, 2012). Another study sought to determine the effect of prison releases on crime rates in forty-six states over a period of twenty-eight years. The researchers found a statistically significant, positive relationship between a state's number of returning prisoners and its crime rate, holding constant the state's imprisonment rate, as well as other variables relating to age, race, poverty, education, and so forth (Vieraitis, Kovandzic, & Marvell, 2007, 606). Because increases in prisoner releases were associated with increases in crime through a time period when prison admissions were generally increasing even more quickly than releases, the researchers concluded that the experience of imprisonment was likely adding to the recidivism risk posed by inmates. Thus, although there are a limited number of high-quality studies with appropriate controls, the overall weight of the evidence supports the view that imprisonment tends to increase recidivism risk (Cullen, Jonson, & Nagin, 2011, 60S).

The research also suggests certain factors that may exacerbate the criminogenic (crime-producing) tendencies of imprisonment. For instance, life in higher-security institutions and harsher prison conditions is associated with greater post-release recidivism (Committee on Causes and Consequences of High Rates of Incarceration, 2014, 195). The adverse effects seem especially strong with respect to those inmates who have relatively few prior convictions. Age may also play a role; one recent study of former supermax inmates found that the younger subjects were more likely to recidivate, holding race, criminal history, disciplinary infractions, and other variables constant (Pizarro, Zgoba & Haugebrook, 2014, 192).

Length of time served also seems to play a role. One recent study of Florida inmates found that those with the shortest time behind bars (under six months) tended to have the lowest recidivism rates, taking into account offense type, criminal history, and other variables (Mears, Cochran, Bales, & Bhati, 2016, 111). Recidivism risk peaked with a one-year term, and then very slowly dropped with longer terms, but remained higher than for the offenders with the shortest terms at least to the six-year mark. This pattern suggests that the criminogenic aspects of the prison experience are not necessarily fully activated upon entry to the institution, but instead gather steam over the first several months behind bars. This would be consistent, for instance, with the hypothesis that recidivism risk increases with the inmate's progressive adaptation to the deleterious pressures of prison life.

The modest reductions in risk that occur after the first year in prison may partly reflect the positive influence of rehabilitative programs, which inmates must normally participate in for a period of time before benefits become apparent. Other studies point even more clearly to the potential of well-designed, well-administered institutional programs to reduce risk. More specifically, the research finds significant potential benefits from cognitive-behavioral therapy, drug treatment, educational programs, and vocational training (Committee on Causes and Consequences of High Rates of Incarceration, 2014, 197). Of course, there is no program that can entirely eliminate recidivism risk for all inmates, but, with adequate funding and institutional support, some programs may help to offset the risk-enhancing aspects of the prison experience.

FURTHER READING

Committee on Causes and Consequences of High Rates of Incarceration, National Research Council of the National Academies. 2014. *The Growth of Incarceration in the United States*. Washington, DC: The National Academies Press.

Cullen, Francis, Jonson, Cheryl, & Nagin, Daniel. 2011. "Prisons Do Not Reduce Recidivism: The High Cost of Ignoring Science." *The Prison Journal*, 91, 48S.

Dolovich, Sharon. 2012. "Two Models of the Prison: Accidental Humanity and Hypermasculinity in the L.A. County Jail." *Journal of Criminal Law and Criminology*, 102, 965.

Hutcherson, Donald. 2012. "Crime Pays: The Connection between Time in Prison and Future Criminal Earnings." *The Prison Journal*, 92, 315.

Mears, Daniel, Cochran, Joshua, Bales, William, & Bhati, Avinash. 2016. "Recidivism and Time Served in Prison." *Journal of Criminal Law & Criminology*, 106, 81.

Pizarro, Jesenia M., Zgoba, Kristen M., & Haugebrook, Sabrina. 2014. "Supermax and Recidivism: An Examination of the Recidivism Covariates among a Sample of Supermax Ex-Inmates." *Prison Journal*, 94, 180.

Tyler, Tom. 2003. "Procedural Justice, Legitimacy, and the Effective Rule of Law." *Crime and Justice*, 30, 283.

Vieraitis, Lynne, Kovandzic, Tomislav, & Marvell, Thomas. 2007. "The Criminogenic Effects of Imprisonment: Evidence from State Panel Data, 1974–2002." *Criminology & Public Policy*, 6, 589.

Q17: DO PRISONERS HAVE OPPORTUNITIES TO WORK, LEARN, OR OTHERWISE SPEND THEIR TIME PRODUCTIVELY DURING INCARCERATION?

Answer: Most prisoners participate regularly in some sort of structured work or educational activity. However, overcrowding and tight corrections budgets have strained resources in these areas, and there are substantial concerns about both the quantity and the quality of offerings.

The Facts: As an expert panel observed in 2006, "Few conditions compromise the safety and security of a correctional institution more than idle prisoners" (Commission on Safety and Abuse in America's Prisons, 2006, 27). Moreover, beyond the institutional dangers posed by bored inmates with too much free time on their hands, idleness also presents a problem insofar as it constitutes a wasting of time that might have been spent on constructive activities that can help to prepare inmates for a successful return to free society.

Prison administrators have long recognized these concerns and, to varying degrees, have embraced programs that provide inmates with structured opportunities to work and learn behind bars. Although comprehensive, high-quality data about prison programming are not available, it is probably the case that most prisoners do participate regularly in some type of work or education (Committee on Causes and Consequences of High Rates of Incarceration, 2014, 191).

A survey of state and federal correctional facilities in 2005 found that 88 percent had work programs, 85 percent had educational programs, and 92 percent had counseling programs (Stephan, 2008, 5). The most common work programs were in the area of facility services (e.g., food preparation and janitorial work in the prison). Secondary-level (high school) instruction was the most common type of educational program, with college-level courses available in barely one-third of institutions. For counseling, most institutions offered programs in the areas of life skills and community readjustment, drug/alcohol dependency, and employment.

Although institutions continued to offer programs as a matter of course throughout the period of the imprisonment boom, overcrowded institutions and thin budgets have left many programs unable to meet inmate demand. The challenges can be seen, for instance, in the ratio of inmates to educational staff, which jumped from 53 to 112 inmates per teacher between 1974 and 2005 (Phelps, 2011). As might be expected with an overstretched educational staff, inmate participation rates in academic programs dropped from 43 percent in 1991 to 27 percent in 2004. Participation in vocational training also dropped modestly over the same time period. However, participation in counseling programs remained more consistent or even increased. For instance, the number of inmates who reported having participated in professional drug or alcohol treatment fell only very slightly from 11 percent in 1997 to 10 percent in 2004.

Work participation has been consistently higher. About two-thirds of state prisoners were working in 2005 (Committee on Causes and Consequences of High Rates of Incarceration, 2014, 192). However, the median number of hours worked per week has fallen from forty to twenty over the past four decades.

In addition to concerns about the *capacity* of work and educational programs behind bars, there may also be important deficiencies in their *quality*, especially from the standpoint of preparing inmates for success after release. For instance, with most work assignments in low-skill areas like food preparation and laundry, few inmates are gaining experience that will readily translate into good jobs on the outside (Committee on Causes and Consequences of High Rates of Incarceration, 2014, 192). Pay is also typically extremely low—often just cents per hour. The disappearance of college courses behind bars, resulting in part from Congress's decision in 1994 to exclude inmates from Pell grants, also diminishes the long-term value of the educational programs in prisons. (One recent study of Minnesota inmates found that while obtaining a secondary [high-school-level] degree in prison did *not* reduce recidivism risk, earning a post-secondary degree was indeed associated with less reoffending [Duwe & Clark, 2014].) Resource constraints can also undermine the effectiveness of programming in a multitude of other ways. Vocational training in technical fields, for instance, may lose much of its value if the inmate-students are trained on out of-date equipment, or if prisons do not pay enough to attract and retain knowledgeable, competent instructors (Committee on Causes and Consequences of High Rates of Incarceration, 2014, 193).

FURTHER READING

Commission on Safety and Abuse in America's Prisons. 2006. *Confronting Confinement*. New York: Vera Institute of Justice.

Committee on Causes and Consequences of High Rates of Incarceration, National Research Council of the National Academies. 2014. *The Growth of Incarceration in the United States*. Washington, DC: The National Academies Press.

Duwe, Grant & Clark, Valerie. 2014. "The Effects of Prison-Based Educational Programming on Recidivism and Employment." *The Prison Journal*, 94, 454.

Phelps, Michelle. 2011. "Rehabilitation in the Punitive Era: The Gap between Rhetoric and Reality in U.S. Prison Programs." *Law & Society Review*, 45, 33.

Stephan, James. 2008. *Census of State and Federal Correctional Facilities, 2005.* Washington, DC: U.S. Department of Justice.

Q18: ARE INCIDENTS OF VIOLENCE AGAINST INMATES AND COERCED SEX COMMON OCCURRENCES IN PRISONS?

Answer: Prison violence has likely declined over the past generation but remains common in some institutions. Most assaults of inmates go unreported, which makes it hard to determine violence levels with precision. Some studies suggest that about one in five male prisoners will be assaulted in any given six-month period. Sexual assaults, a special concern among policy makers in recent years, are somewhat less common overall but are a particular risk for certain segments of the prison population, including the mentally ill and the nonheterosexual. Nor are attacks from fellow inmates the only serious threat to prisoner safety. Abuse by correctional staff, whether in the form of excessive force or unlawful sexual contact, may be just as big a problem in some institutions.

The Facts: It is difficult to measure the frequency of violence in prisons because so much of it goes unreported. Facing strong taboos against "snitching," inmates normally keep experiences of victimization to themselves. Researchers estimate that only about 10–20 percent of prison assaults are reported (Pritikin, 2008).

The most extreme form of violence, homicide, is the easiest to study; dead bodies are much harder to conceal from the authorities than bruises. The rate of in-prison killings dropped sharply in the late twentieth century, from 54 homicides per 100,000 state prisoners in 1980 to just 4 in 2002 (Commission on Safety and Abuse in America's Prisons, 2006, 24). By 2014, the figure has rebounded to 7 per 100,000 but remained far below the level of a generation ago (Noonan, 2016, 5).

Nonlethal assaults are far more common. In 2000, for instance, there were 2,632 reported inmate-on-inmate assaults per 100,000 prisoners, and 1,375 reported inmate-on-staff assaults (Stephan & Karberg, 2003, v). However, because of the high rate of non-reporting, the former figure almost certainly understates the actual level of inmate-on-inmate violence by a wide margin.

Inmates seem more willing to disclose incidents of violence to researchers than to prison officials. Thus, through various types of survey efforts, researchers have produced a variety of estimates of assault frequency that are probably more accurate than the officially reported figures. These estimates suggest a six-month assault rate of somewhere in the neighborhood of 20 per 100 inmates (Wolff & Shi, 2009). Since not all assaults are serious, it is also helpful to get a sense of the frequency of injury-causing violence. For instance, one survey of a representative sample of nearly 15,000 state prisoners found that about 15 percent had sustained at least one violence-related injury behind bars (Sung, 2010).

Such studies also provide a sense of what inmate and institutional characteristics are most associated with violent victimization. For instance, inmates who are younger or suffering from mental illness are more likely to be victimized (Wolff & Shi, 2009), as are those with physical disabilities and those who were convicted of violent offenses (Sung, 2010). Female inmates are less likely to be physically assaulted than male. At the institutional level, some prisons are more prone to violence than others, based, for instance, on the demographics of their inmate populations and the effectiveness of the violence-control measures adopted by their administrators (Steiner, 2009).

In male institutions, where most of the prison violence occurs, one study found that weapons were involved about 46 percent of the time in inmate-on-inmate attacks (Wolff & Shi, 2009). Most victims say that they do not know their attacker's motive. In those cases in which the victim does seem to have a sense of the motive, race, religion, or ethnicity are cited close to half the time. More than 40 percent of the male victims of inmate-on-inmate attacks say they suffered a physical injury. About one-third of victims received medical attention for injuries.

More impressionistically, a prisoner rights lawyer has summarized the driving forces behind prison violence this way:

> If you put poor, underprivileged young men together in a large institution without anything meaningful to do all day, there will be violence. If that institution is overcrowded, there will be more violence. If that institution is badly managed . . . [including by offering] poor mental health care, there will be more violence. (Commission on Safety and Abuse in America's Prisons, 2006, 22)

While less common than other forms of violence, sexual assaults in prison have received more attention in recent years from both researchers and policy makers. In 2003, Congress adopted the Prison Rape Elimination Act, which mandated data collection on sexual assaults, as well as the development of national standards for corrections administrators in the hope of eventually ending these sorts of attacks (National Prison Rape Elimination Commission, 2009). About 10 percent of former state prisoners report that they were sexually victimized during their most recent incarceration (Committee on Causes and Consequences of High Rates of Incarceration, 2014, 225). In a survey of current state and federal inmates, 4 percent said that they had been sexually victimized in the past twelve months while institutionalized (Beck, Berzofsky, Caspar, & Krebs, 2013, 6). A somewhat higher proportion of inmates reported incidents involving staff (2.4 percent) than incidents involving fellow inmates (2.0 percent).

When it comes to inmate-on-inmate victimization, the survey indicated that female inmates were at greater risk than male, whites than blacks, and inmates with a college degree than those who did not finish high school (Beck, Berzofsky, Caspar, & Krebs, 2013, 6). Mental illness was another risk factor, as was having a sexual orientation other than heterosexual (7).

As to sexual incidents with staff, male and female inmates were about equally likely to be victimized (Beck, Berzofsky,Caspar & Krebs, 2013, 17). Risk factors included being black, over the age of thirty-four, mentally ill, and nonheterosexual (17, 24, 30). Close to half of the incidents were reported as "willing" (9). However, even though the inmate may have consented to the sexual activity or touching, all such incidents with staff are unlawful. Whether willing or unwilling, the great majority of sexual incidents with staff went beyond mere touching.

If sexual contact between staff and inmates is always considered improper, nonsexual contact presents a more complicated legal problem. Staff are permitted to use force against inmates in a variety of circumstances, such as when force is necessary to prevent one inmate from hurting another. However, the legal lines are not always clear. Additionally, even when some force is initially permissible, the force used may eventually exceed what is proper either in intensity or duration, for instance, if a lethal chokehold is used against an inmate who could have been restrained in a less dangerous manner.

While not necessarily always unlawful, it is clear that assaultive behavior by staff happens with some frequency. For instance, one survey found that more state prisoners had been attacked by staff than by other inmates (Wolff & Shi, 2009). In all, about 21 percent of the prisoners reported that they had been assaulted by staff in the previous six months. A weapon was used in almost one-third of the attacks—more than half the time including a gun or Taser. Physical injuries were somewhat more common in attacks by staff than in attacks by fellow inmates. Moreover, as to most of the incidents, the inmate-victim claimed not to know the reason for the assault. Putting these results together with the data on inmate-staff sexual contacts, it seems that some inmates may have more to fear from staff than they do from other prisoners.

FURTHER READING

Beck, Allen, Berzofsky, Marcus, Caspar, Rachel, & Krebs, Christine. 2013. *Sexual Victimization in Prisons and Jails Reported by Inmates, 2011–12.* Washington, DC: U.S. Department of Justice.

Commission on Safety and Abuse in America's Prisons. 2006. *Confronting Confinement.* New York: Vera Institute of Justice.

Committee on Causes and Consequences of High Rates of Incarceration, National Research Council of the National Academies. 2014. *The Growth of Incarceration in the United States.* Washington, DC: The National Academies Press.

National Prison Rape Elimination Commission. 2009. *Report.* Washington, DC: National Prison Rape Elimination Commission.

Noonan, Margaret. 2016. *Mortality in State Prisons, 2001–2014—Statistical Tables.* Washington, DC: U.S. Department of Justice.

Pritikin, Martin. 2008. "Is Prison Increasing Crime?" *Wisconsin Law Review,* 2008, 1049.

Steiner, Benjamin. 2009. "Assessing Static and Dynamic Influences on Inmate Violence Levels." *Crime & Delinquency,* 55, 134.

Stephan, James & Karberg, Jennifer. 2003. *Census of State and Federal Correctional Facilities, 2000.* Washington, DC: U.S. Department of Justice.

Sung, Hung-En. 2010. "Prevalence and Risk Factors of Violence-Related and Accident-Related Injuries among State Prisoners." *Journal of Correctional Health,* 16, 178.

Wolff, Nancy & Shi, Jing. 2009. "Contextualization of Physical and Sexual Assault in Male Prisons: Incidents and Their Aftermath." *Journal of Correctional Health Care,* 15, 58.

Q19: DO PRISONS USE SOLITARY CONFINEMENT TOO MUCH?

Answer: There are likely tens of thousands of prisoners in the United States held in conditions of extreme isolation (locked in a cell for at least twenty-two hours per day). In the late twentieth century, prison officials increasingly used special, highly restrictive housing units as a punishment for misbehavior by inmates and as a way to limit violent conflict. More recently, corrections experts and administrators have come to recognize that depriving inmates of human contact and sensory stimulation on a long-term basis can exacerbate mental illness, increase disciplinary and other management difficulties, and enhance recidivism risk after release. A few states have explicitly adopted policies intended to reduce the use of solitary confinement, although about half of the states continue to hold more than 5 percent of their inmates in restricted housing.

The Facts: Although commonly used by laypeople, the term "solitary confinement" has no precise, uniform definition among corrections professionals. For official purposes, those working in the field are more likely to refer to "segregation," "special housing unit" (SHU), or "restricted housing." Depending on the jurisdiction and the institution, such terms can refer to a wide range of different living arrangements, not all of which necessarily include the extreme isolation that is normally connoted by "solitary confinement."

Because of these definitional problems, there is no precise figure available for the number of inmates currently held in solitary. The best approximation may come from a 2016 study sponsored by the Association of State Correctional Administrators and the Arthur Liman Public Interest Program at Yale Law School. The researchers surveyed prison system directors from around the country about their use of restricted housing, which they defined as a system holding inmates separate from the general prison population and in their cells for at least twenty-two hours per day for at least fifteen continuous days (Association of State Correctional Administrators & the Arthur Liman Public Interest Program, Yale Law School, 2016, 6). Inmates could be single- or double-celled. Using this definition, as of October 1, 2015, the forty-eight jurisdictions that provided information held more than 67,000 inmates in restricted housing (7). The median state held 5.1 percent of its prison population in this status. About a quarter of the inmates in restricted housing had been there for a year or more.

Most inmates in restricted housing are there for one of two reasons: either as punishment for rule breaking (disciplinary segregation) or as a form of preventive detention for inmates who are thought to present a safety threat to others (administrative segregation). Disciplinary segregation accounts for most of the inmates who are in restricted housing for shorter stays (less than a month); however, most of the longer-term residents are there for administrative segregation (Association of State

Correctional Administrators & the Arthur Liman Public Interest Program, Yale Law School, 2016, 30).

There have been particular concerns regarding solitary confinement of mentally ill inmates, both because such inmates may find it especially difficult to understand and obey prison rules, and because solitary may exacerbate their mental conditions. The ASCA/Yale study attempted to determine how many inmates with serious mental illness are held in restricted housing but ran into difficulties because states define serious mental illness in a variety of different ways (Association of State Correctional Administrators & the Arthur Liman Public Interest Program, Yale Law School, 2016, 48). Thirty-four jurisdictions reported data on their number of male inmates with serious mental illness, using somewhat varying definitions of the term. In these jurisdictions, there were more than 5,000 such inmates in restricted housing, amounting to nearly 10 percent of the total number of male inmates with serious mental illness (49).

The current restricted housing numbers reflect the legacy of a more aggressive use of segregation in the late twentieth century. For instance, between 1995 and 2000, as the overall prison population grew by 28 percent, the number of inmates in segregation increased by 40 percent (Commission on Safety and Abuse in America's Prisons, 2006, 56). Consistent with the toughening trends of the time period, inmates could find themselves in disciplinary segregation for relatively minor violations like talking back to an officer or possessing cigarettes (53). Meanwhile, indefinite administrative segregation could be imposed on an inmate for certain risk factors, like a gang affiliation, even when the inmate had never done anything wrong in prison (54).

The trends toward greater use of segregation and harsher conditions in segregation reached their zenith with the widespread creation of new "supermax" institutions, which were designed to hold inmates in their cells for twenty-three hours per day on a long-term basis, typically in conditions of exceptional austerity (Mears & Reisig, 2006, 33). For instance, an inmate recently released from the federal supermax prison in Florence, Colorado, described the experience this way:

> It wasn't like any of the prisons I'd been to, and I've been to a lot of prisons. I've been locked up in some isolated, rural places, but at least at those places I could always see a highway, see the sky.
>
> But at [Florence], you can't see nothing, not a highway out in the distance, not the sky. You know the minute you get there you won't see any of that, not for years and years. You're just shut off the world. You feel it. It sinks in, this dread feeling.

. . .

It's just the harshest place you've ever seen. Nothing living, not so much as a blade of grass anywhere. My cell was all concrete. Every single thing, made out of concrete. The walls, floor, the desk, the sink, even the bed—a slab of concrete. Then you get a little fortified [recreation cage] that's outside that you get to go walk around in for an hour a day. (Hager, 2016)

Critics have described such environments as solitary confinement on steroids. By 2000, more than thirty states were operating such supermax facilities (Mears & Reisig, 2006, 33).

Since 2000, correctional experts and administrators have increasingly come to question the utility and appropriateness of supermax institutions and other forms of long-term inmate isolation. For instance, in 2006, the Commission on Safety and Abuse in America's Prison, a panel of distinguished criminal-justice leaders, drew attention to the issue with a report that condemned the excessive use of solitary confinement. The commission identified several areas of concern. First, there was little evidence that the advent of supermax facilities reduced violence in state prison systems (Commission on Safety and Abuse in America's Prisons, 2006, 54). Second, some research suggested that segregation could make problem inmates *more* prone to violence. Third, many inmates were being held in solitary confinement right up to the end of their prison terms; with no opportunity to transition in a controlled manner to regular interaction with other people; these straight-to-the-street confinees seemed at higher risk of recidivism and failure in free society (55). Fourth, a considerable body of research had found that several adverse psychological effects were common among those held in solitary confinement, including "overwhelming anxiety, confusion and hallucination, and sudden violent and self-destructive outbursts" (58). One study, for instance, found highly elevated rates of self-mutilation in Virginia's segregation units, while another found highly elevated rates of suicide in California's segregation units (58, 59). Finally, research also indicated that isolation could exacerbate preexisting mental illnesses and make the problems more difficult to treat after release (60). The commission's chief recommendations were: (1) make segregation a last resort and more productive form of confinement, and stop releasing people directly from segregation to the streets; (2) end conditions of isolation; and (3) protect mentally ill prisoners.

By 2015, the Association of State Correctional Administrators could observe that "insistence on change [to solitary confinement] comes not only from legislators across the political spectrum, judges, and a host of private sector voices, but also from the directors of correctional systems at both state and federal levels" (Association of State Correctional Administrators & the Arthur Liman Public Interest Program, Yale Law School, 2016, 5).

The same year, President Barack Obama ordered a review of the use of solitary confinement in the federal prison system. The resulting report by the U.S. Department of Justice concluded,

> [T]here are occasions when correctional officials have no choice but to segregate inmates from the general population, typically when it is the only way to ensure the safety of inmates, staff, and the public and the orderly operation of the facility. But as a matter of policy, **we believe strongly this practice should be used rarely, applied fairly, and subjected to reasonable constraints**. The Department believes that best practices include housing inmates in the least restrictive settings necessary to ensure their own safety, as well as the safety of staff, other inmates, and the public; and ensuring that restrictions on an inmate's housing serve a specific penological purpose and are imposed for no longer than necessary to achieve that purpose. When officials determine that an inmate must be segregated from the general population, that inmate should be housed in safe, humane conditions that, ideally, prepare the individual for reintegration into both the general prison population and society at large. (U.S. Department of Justice, 2016, 1 [emphasis in the original])

At about the same time as the DOJ report, the American Correctional Association (ACA), the leading national accrediting body for jails and prisons, adopted new standards discouraging the use of extended restricted housing for juveniles, pregnant women, and inmates with serious mental illness (Association of State Correctional Administrators & the Arthur Liman Public Interest Program, Yale Law School, 2016, 9). The ACA also called for more rigorous review procedures to minimize excessive use of restricted housing, more frequent mental and physical health examinations and treatment of inmates in restricted housing, living conditions that "approximate those of the general inmate population," and stepdown programs to ease the transition from restricted housing (9–10).

In recent years, several states have responded to calls for reform by adopting new restrictions on solitary confinement, particularly for juvenile inmates (Association of State Correctional Administrators & the Arthur Liman Public Interest Program, Yale Law School, 2016, 11–12). In some states, including California, Indiana, and New York, change has resulted from class action litigation. International law has also increasingly turned against solitary confinement (13–14). In 2015, for instance, the United Nations General Assembly declared that solitary confinement should only be a "last resort" and condemned its use against physically or mentally disabled prisoners whose conditions would be worsened by such measures.

FURTHER READING

Association of State Correctional Administrators & the Arthur Liman Public Interest Program, Yale Law School. 2016. *Aiming to Reduce Time-in-Cell: Reports from Correctional Systems on the Numbers of Prisoners in Restricted Housing and on the Potential of Policy Changes to Bring About Reforms.* Retrieved from https://law.yale.edu/system/files/area/center/liman/document/aimingtoreducetic.pdf.

Commission on Safety and Abuse in America's Prisons. 2006. *Confronting Confinement.* New York: Vera Institute of Justice.

Hager, Eli. 2016. "My Life in the Supermax: Finger Handshakes, the Toilet Phone, and the 'Shoe Bomber.'" The Marshall Project. Retrieved from https://www.themarshallproject.org/2016/01/08/my-life-in-the-supermax#.grHb5eBIF.

Mears, Daniel & Reisig, Michael. 2006. "The Theory and Practice of Supermax Prisons." *Punishment and Society*, 8, 33.

U.S. Department of Justice. 2016. *Report and Recommendations Concerning the Use of Restrictive Housing.* Washington, DC: U.S. Department of Justice.

Q20: DO PRIVATE PRISONS DELIVER BETTER RESULTS AT LOWER COST THAN PUBLIC PRISONS?

Answer: Since the 1980s, private prisons run by for-profit corporations have rapidly proliferated in the United States. More than 8 percent of American prisoners are now held in private prisons. While some government agencies have been able to save money by sending prisoners to private institutions, there have been persistent concerns that such institutions have an inherent tendency to maltreat inmates and skimp on rehabilitative services. There is no doubt that some private prisons are poorly run, but the same could be said of some public prisons. Rigorous comparisons taking into account all of the relevant variables have not yet been performed, but the available research suggests that private prisons offer few, if any, clear advantages over public institutions. Some studies indicate that not even cost savings can be taken for granted as a benefit of privatization.

The Facts: Over the past generation, various political, legal, and economic trends in the United States have pushed government agencies to downsize their payrolls and contract with private corporations for the provision of public services. Corrections agencies have hardly been immune to these pressures. While all aspects of corrections, including community supervision, have been touched by privatization, it is the for-profit corporate prison that has attracted the most public attention and criticism.

For almost as long as there have been prisons in the United States, private businesses have found ways to reap profits from them, most notoriously in the nineteenth century by purchasing convict labor from state agencies and subjecting the inmates to brutal working conditions (Dolovich, 2005, 450–52). After the abuses and scandals of the nineteenth century, states became more leery of those seeking to exploit the penal system for private financial gain. However, reflecting the broader "neoliberal" turn of the United States in the late twentieth century, as well as the particular fiscal pressures created by booming prison populations, state governments proved increasingly amenable to contracting with private prisons in the 1980s and 1990s.

Founded in 1983, the Corrections Corporation of America (recently renamed Core Civic) is often identified as the first private prison provider of the modern era (Dolovich, 2005, 459). Other businesses soon entered the field as the potential for profits became clear. By 2000, thirty states and the federal government were holding prisoners in private facilities (Sentencing Project, 2016). Since then, the number of inmates in these facilities has continued to swell, reaching 126,272 in 2015, or more than 8 percent of the nation's total prison population. Indeed, in two states, New Mexico and Montana, more than 40 percent of the inmates were in private institutions in 2015.

The basic theory of privatization for any government service is simple. Driven by a profit motive that government lacks, private firms will find ways to deliver services more efficiently than existing agencies. With lower costs, a firm can undercut government providers, offering to do the same work at less expense to taxpayers. While some government bureaucrats might lose their jobs, everyone else benefits: the greater efficiencies of the private sector produce a surplus that can be enjoyed by corporate shareholders and taxpayers alike. Indeed, along with these advances, supporters of privatization contend that greater efficiencies will also translate into more or higher-quality public services.

The basic critique of privatization is no less straightforward. Driven by the profit motive, firms have an incentive to cut costs as deeply as possible. This almost inevitably means a diminished quality or quantity of services, at least if there is not a responsible government agency keeping close tabs on the firm and holding it accountable for its performance. Yet, a legislature that is looking to save money by shifting resources from an agency to a private contractor seems unlikely to support robust oversight, which would cut into the anticipated cost savings. And, of course, firms can help to ensure that oversight is minimal through lobbying and other appropriately targeted political efforts.

These are some generic arguments for and against privatization. However, some critics of for-profit prisons suggest that the objections to privatization may be uniquely compelling in this context. For instance, prisons are closed institutions, which greatly complicate the oversight task (Dolovich, 2005). If, say, a private firm providing garbage collection for a municipality does a poor job, the deficiencies will be quite evident to members of the public, who will make their ire known to the officials responsible for oversight. By contrast, poor prison administration may be largely invisible to members of the public. Inmates may complain, of course, but their views are less likely to be taken seriously by the authorities than are those of taxpaying voters. Moreover, even if serious deficiencies are known, a state may not realistically be able to threaten to cancel the contract of a failing institution because of a lack of viable alternatives for housing the inmates.

On a more philosophical level, some critics also argue that, by its very nature, punishment is not something that government may delegate to private parties (Harel, 2008). Indeed, the Supreme Court of Israel accepted such an argument in ruling that private prisons were unconstitutional, although other commentators remain unconvinced on this point (Feeley, 2013).

There are also concerns about creating economic incentives for wealthy, influential corporations to favor greater use of incarceration. For instance, leading prison firms played a prominent role in the 1990s in an organization called the American Legislative Exchange Council, which pushed for tough-on-crime sentencing policies in state legislatures (Mason, 2012, 12–13). A far more blatant example of the potentially corrupting influence of the profit motive in criminal justice comes from Luzerne County, Pennsylvania, where two juvenile court judges were given large kickbacks for steering youthful defendants to private detention facilities (16).

Putting aside the troubling potential for privatization to warp sentencing policies and practices, how have private prisons actually performed?

Critics have no shortage of anecdotal evidence of neglect and abuse. To note just one example, in its rush to fill beds after its opening in 1997, a private medium-security prison in Youngstown, Ohio, accepted a number of high-risk inmates that it was not equipped to handle; over the next year and a half, the facility experienced more than forty-four assaults, including two fatal stabbings (Dolovich, 2005). Yet, it must be noted, some *public* institutions are also violent and irresponsibly managed.

More systematic, comparative research is harder to find (Volokh, 2013). Existing studies are of varying quality and provide mixed results, with no decisive advantage apparent for either public or private prisons. Part of the difficulty lies in the multitude of different variables by which prison performance might be assessed, some of which defy easy measurement.

Cost, of course, is one variable of interest; after all, the case for privatization rests largely on expectations of greater operational efficiency and hence reduced cost. However, rigorous cost comparisons between public and private prisons have been bedeviled by various technical accounting challenges, as well as differences in the age, size, and inmate risk levels of the competing facilities (Volokh, 2014). It would be much more expensive, for instance, for anyone to run a decades-old maximum-security prison than a brand-new minimum-security facility. Studies that attempt to take into account such considerations tend to find some cost advantage on the private side but not uniformly so and often by only small margins (Volokh, 2014; Mason, 2012, 7–8; Spivak & Sharp, 2008).

To the extent there have been reduced costs, these seem mostly attributable to the lower salaries and benefits that are offered to the (generally nonunionized) private prison employees (Dolovich, 2005). There are concerns, though, that cheaper private employees may be less qualified, less experienced, and less committed to their work than their better-compensated public counterparts. This possibility makes it especially important to determine whether private prisons are providing service quality that matches that of public institutions.

The available research provides some support for the critics, but definitive conclusions about the quality of private prisons remain elusive. For instance, the Office of the Inspector General of the U.S. Department of Justice gathered data from 2011 to 2014 from fourteen private prisons that house federal prisoners and fourteen comparable institutions run by the federal government itself. The OIG found that the private prisons had higher rates of both inmate-on-inmate and inmate-on-staff assaults, as well as more frequent lockdowns and disciplinary actions against inmates (U.S. Department of Justice Office of the Inspector General, 2016, ii). However, the OIG also found fewer positive drug tests and incidents of

sexual misconduct in the private facilities. Additionally, the OIG con-
ceded that it was "unable to evaluate all of the factors that contributed
to the underlying data, including the effect of inmate demographics and
facility locations" (ii). Other studies also find elevated levels of violence
in private prisons (Mason, 2012, 10–11), although such results are hardly
uniform (Volokh, 2013). Meanwhile, any number of other variables of
potential interest, such as the quality of care for physical and mental
health, seem even less well-understood.

Some researchers have also attempted to assess the long-term impact
of a stay in private prison by measuring post-release recidivism rates. Different studies have reached different conclusions, although the best studies, conducted in Florida and Oklahoma, found either little difference
between private and public institutions, or a possible advantage for the
public institutions (Spivak & Sharp, 2008).

Interestingly, some research outside the United States finds more
clearly positive results for private prisons. Australia, in particular, seems
to have found success with the privatization of punishment—which may
explain why it leads the world with about 20 percent of its prisoners in
private institutions (Feeley, 2013). However, there are a variety of reasons
to question whether the Australian experience could be replicated in the
United States, including differences in the dangerousness of the inmate
populations and the caliber of the public agencies providing oversight of
private contractors. One researcher has observed, "Private prison administration succeeds in Australia because Australian public administration
is a success. It may be that the quality of privately provided public services
in a jurisdiction is a function of the quality of public services and public
administration more generally" (1425).

On the other hand, if privatization has been something of a disappointment so far in the United States, that may result from a failure to structure
the incentives of the private facilities more effectively. The contracts that
states enter into for imprisonment services normally center on the *per
diem*—a flat rate that the state pays to the contractor per inmate per day.
When the contractor's payment is determined mostly by the *per diem*,
the contractor's profit-maximizing incentives are (1) to take as many
prisoners as possible, and (2) to spend as little as possible on caring for
them—in other words, to operate like a warehouse. However, if compensation were based more on appropriate performance measures, such as a
facility's post-release recidivism rate, then the potential for private-sector
innovation might be more powerfully stimulated. The United Kingdom,
which utilizes private prisons more heavily than the United States, is currently experimenting with just this sort of performance-based contracting
(Volokh, 2013). As more such experiments take place, it is possible that

the research will start to provide clearer support for the capacity of private prisons to deliver reliably better outcomes at lower cost.

FURTHER READING

Dolovich, Sharon. 2005. "State Punishment and Private Prisons." *Duke Law Journal*, 55, 437.

Feeley, Malcolm. 2013. "The Unconvincing Case against Private Prisons." *Indiana Law Journal*, 89, 1401.

Harel, Alon. 2008. "Why Only the State May Inflict Criminal Sanctions: The Case against Privately Inflicted Sanctions." *Legal Theory*, 14, 113.

Mason, Cody. 2012. *Too Good to Be True Private Prisons in America*. Washington, DC: Sentencing Project.

Sentencing Project. 2016. Fact Sheet: Private Prisons in the United States, http://www.sentencingproject.org/publications/private-prisons-united-states/.

Spivak, Andrew & Sharp, Susan. 2008. "Inmate Recidivism as a Measure of Private Prison Performance." *Crime & Delinquency*, 54, 482.

U.S. Department of Justice Office of the Inspector General. 2016. *Review of the Federal Bureau of Prisons' Monitoring of Contract Prisons*. Washington, DC: U.S. Department of Justice.

Volokh, Alexander. 2013. "Prison Accountability and Performance Measures." *Emory Law Journal*, 63, 339.

Q21: ARE CHILDREN HARMED BY THE INCARCERATION OF A PARENT?

Answer: Most prisoners in the United States are parents, and most of these parent-inmates were involved in the lives of their children before being incarcerated. Prison sentences thus often have a direct effect on the lives of children. The nature, intensity, and duration of the impact will vary considerably from case to case, but a growing body of research is now demonstrating that troubling negative effects on children are common. These negative effects include, among others, family financial distress, strained or broken parental relationships, greater risk of homelessness, diminished academic achievement, and increased behavioral problems, including juvenile delinquency.

The Facts: Surveys of prisoners show that a sizeable number have minor children. Research conducted in 2007 found that about 52 percent of state inmates and 63 percent of federal inmates have minor children

(Glaze & Maruschak, 2010, 1). Between them, these inmates had an estimated 1.7 million children under the age of eighteen—accounting for close to one in every forty children in the United States. Most of these children of incarcerated parents were under the age of ten (3).

Most imprisoned parents reported at least some pre-incarceration involvement in the lives of their children. More than half indicated that they were the primary source of financial support (Glaze & Maruschak, 2010, 5). Additionally, nearly half reported living with their children prior to their arrest or incarceration (4). Imprisoned mothers, in particular, played a vital role as caregivers. Among those who lived with their children pre-incarceration, more than three-quarters reported that they provided most of the daily care (5). However, many of the fathers also indicated that they played a significant caregiving role. For instance, among those who lived with their children, nearly 90 percent reported at least some level of participation in their daily care.

Given such data, we might expect that sentences of imprisonment would routinely affect the lives of children. However, it has been difficult for researchers to identify and quantify the effects in a precise way. Because imprisonment is disproportionately associated with a number of problematic personal characteristics, including poverty, mental illness, substance abuse, and low educational achievement, many children of imprisoned parents would be at higher risk of various forms of adversity even without the imprisonment. Any attempt to isolate the impact of parental incarceration on children must try to control for all of these related, but distinct, variables.

Despite the methodological challenges, a growing body of research provides substantial support for the hypothesis that parental incarceration contributes to a variety of negative outcomes and life experiences for children. Most extensively studied has been the impact of *paternal* incarceration. For instance, numerous studies find that a father's incarceration often leads to a weakening of his relationship with the mother and a decreased likelihood of the parents staying together (Committee on Causes and Consequences of High Rates of Incarceration, National Research Council of the National Academies, 2014, 264–65; Western, Lopoo, & McLanahan, 2004, 25–26). A breakdown in the relationship between the parents, in turn, can contribute to reduced father–child contact. As one researcher observes, based on her studies of young male parolees, "Men see mothers and children as a 'package deal.' When the bond between men and their children's mother weakens, or if it is weak to begin with, the father separates himself from both the mother and the child" (Nurse, 20004, 81).

Incarceration has a direct and immediate effect on relationships by creating physical barriers to contact and communication. However, the adverse impact can continue even after the prisoner returns home, given the likelihood of personal change and the development of new relationships during the period of separation (Nurse, 20004, 83, 86). Many former inmates find it difficult or impossible to restore important relationships to their pre-incarceration status. At least one study finds that the impact of incarceration on parental relationships is similar to that of a military deployment (Committee on Causes and Consequences of High Rates of Incarceration, 2014, 266). However, other research suggests that the post-release impact of incarceration on family relationships can be lessened through corrections policies that make it easier and less costly for family members to visit their loved ones behind bars (Mowen & Visher, 2016).

The research also indicates that the incarceration of a parent may contribute to family financial distress, often putting families that were already struggling over the edge into economic crisis. One study of families with an incarcerated member found a multitude of financial burdens associated with the conviction and sentence, including:

- attorney costs,
- court fees and fines,
- telephone charges,
- visitation expenses,
- loss of income from the incarcerated member, and
- mental health treatment needs.

The researchers observed that the direct costs alone "often amount to one year's total household income for a family" (deVuono-powell, Schweidler, Walters, & Zohrabi, 2015, 7). Most of the families in the study struggled with meeting basic food and housing needs.

Consistent with these observations, several controlled studies have found that parental incarceration is associated with a heightened risk of child homelessness (Committee on Causes and Consequences of High Rates of Incarceration, 2014, 267–68). Other studies find an association between a father's incarceration and the mother's receipt of food stamps and other forms of welfare.

A number of controlled studies also find an increased incidence of behavioral problems, particularly aggression, among children with an incarcerated father (Committee on Causes and Consequences of High Rates of Incarceration, 2014, 271). The effects are especially clear for boys; the research has produced less consistent results as to girls. Similarly, several studies find an association between paternal incarceration and rates of delinquency and arrest among their male children (272). Research on academic achievement is more mixed, but parental incarceration (maternal or paternal) does seem associated with the completion of less schooling for the children (273–74).

To be sure, parental incarceration is not always harmful to the child. Indeed, some research suggests that children with violent or addicted fathers may *benefit* from paternal incarceration (Committee on Causes and Consequences of High Rates of Incarceration, 2014, 270, 272). Still, the incarceration of a parent seems more commonly to have a negative impact on the child. Most troubling may be the potential for incarceration to feed on itself across generations, with the father's imprisonment increasing the likelihood of the son falling into criminal behavior.

FURTHER READING

Committee on Causes and Consequences of High Rates of Incarceration, National Research Council of the National Academies. 2014. *The Growth of Incarceration in the United States.* Washington, DC: The National Academies Press.

deVuono-powell, Saneta, Schweidler, Chris, Walters, Alicia, & Zohrabi, Azadeh. 2015. *Who Pays? The True Cost of Incarceration on Families.* Oakland, CA: Ella Baker Center, Forward Together, Research Action Design.

Glaze, Lauren & Maruschak, Laura. 2010. *Parents in Prison and Their Minor Children (Revised 3/30/10).* Washington, DC: U.S. Department of Justice.

Mowen, Thomas & Visher, Christy. 2016. "Changing the Ties That Bind: How Incarceration Impacts Family Relationships." *Criminology & Public Policy,* 15, 503.

Nurse, Anne. 2004. "Returning to Strangers: Newly Paroled Young Fathers and Their Children." In *Imprisoning America: The Social Effects of Mass Incarceration,* 76. Edited by Bruce Western, David Weiman, & Mary Pattillo. New York: Russell Sage Foundation.

Western, Bruce, Lopoo, Leonard, & McLanahan, Sara. 2004. "Incarceration and the Bonds between Parents in Fragile Families." In *Imprisoning America: The Social Effects of Mass Incarceration,* 21. Edited by Bruce Western, David Weiman, & Mary Pattillo. New York: Russell Sage Foundation.

4

◆❖◆

Release and Life after Prison

Life in prison is marked by deprivation and hardship. Few inmates would choose to stay behind bars any longer than necessary. However, the opportunities for early release are more limited now than they were a generation ago. Still, in most states, many inmates can earn at least modest reductions in their prison terms through good behavior and rehabilitative progress. Yet, whatever the circumstances of their release, former prisoners (returning citizens) typically find themselves confronted by a wide array of profound challenges to their efforts to successfully reintegrate into free society. Unemployment, homelessness, mental illness, and substance abuse are common among recently released prisoners. Given these harsh realities, many become involved in new criminal behavior, with about half returned to prison within three years of release. High recidivism rates support a cautious approach regarding both early release policies and the supervision of ex-prisoners after their release. However, uniformly strict policies that minimize early releases and maximize returns to prison are probably counterproductive over the long run. Research supports drawing distinctions among offenders for purposes of release and supervision based on their objectively measured levels of risk.

Q22: CAN PRISONERS STILL ACCELERATE THEIR RELEASE THROUGH GOOD BEHAVIOR AND REHABILITATIVE PROGRESS?

Answer: During the late twentieth century, nearly all states adopted laws that diminished the flexibility of prison terms, leaving many inmates with little or no opportunity to earn an early release through good behavior and rehabilitative progress behind bars. However, opportunities for early release were never eliminated entirely, and they have increased in many states since 2000. Today, whether a given inmate has a realistic chance to reduce his or her prison term depends a great deal on the state and the offense for which they have been convicted. In many states, early release is still common, especially for inmates who are serving time for nonviolent offenses, but the amount of reduction in the length of prison terms is generally modest.

The Facts: In the middle decades of the twentieth century, prison terms in the United States were typically "indeterminate," meaning that one could not say for certain at the time of sentencing how long the defendant would actually spend behind bars (O'Hear, 2017, 6). In some states, the judge would express the sentence as a range. For instance, a robbery defendant might be sent to prison for a term of three to six years, with the actual release date determined later by a parole board, based in part on the robber's rehabilitative progress and behavior in prison. In other states, the judge would impose a prison term of a specified length, but the parole board would be permitted to release the inmate before the term had been fully served. Indeed, release might be *required* by a particular point in the term. In Wisconsin, in the 1990s, for instance, inmates could be considered for release after serving one-quarter of the judge-imposed sentence and had to be released after serving two-thirds. Thus, a robber with a six-year prison sentence could be paroled after serving one and a half years, and would have to be returned to the community after serving four years. The balance of the prison term (somewhere between two and four and a half years) would be spent on parole supervision, with a potential return to prison for violations of the conditions of release.

Although parole release was structured a bit differently from state to state, the same basic idea animated each state's system: flexibility with release dates gave correctional authorities a powerful mechanism for encouraging and recognizing rehabilitative progress and good behavior. To the same end, additional flexibility came from "good time"—a system of credits toward early release that inmates could earn by staying out of trouble behind bars. In some states, inmates might be able to cut their sentences in half simply by following prison rules (O'Hear, 2012).

Indeterminate sentencing fell out of favor beginning in the 1970s. Critics generally sounded one or more of three themes. First, many charged that the parole system was premised on false assumptions about the ability of corrections officials to promote rehabilitation and track inmates' progress. Prison-based programming at the time was increasingly viewed as ineffective, while parole boards had no demonstrably reliable means of distinguishing those inmates who could be safely returned to the community from those who could not. Second, some critics—especially those on the political left—also accused parole boards of racial bias against minority inmates. Finally, other critics—especially those on the political right—accused parole boards of excessive lenience and disregard for public safety.

By the 1990s, "truth in sentencing" (TIS) had emerged as a popular ideal. Proponents argued that sentencing judges should impose specific terms of imprisonment, rather than a range, and that, once imposed, there should be little or no variability in the length of the term, regardless of how well the inmate seemed to be doing behind bars. It was thought that TIS would provide greater reassurance to victims, deter prospective offenders more effectively, and keep dangerous individuals in prison for longer periods of time than the old system of indeterminate sentencing. By 2000, fifteen states had abolished parole altogether, while twenty additional states had otherwise scaled back the availability of parole (O'Hear, 2017, 6). TIS laws also tended to eliminate or reduce the generosity of "good time" credits for prisoners.

While most states made sentences significantly more determinate in the late twentieth century, few states entirely eliminated all flexibility from prison terms. Even at the height of the TIS movement, most prisoners retained some ability to accelerate their release dates through good behavior and rehabilitative progress.

More recently, the pendulum has swung back in favor of indeterminate sentencing. Although the extreme indeterminacy of the mid-twentieth century has not returned, many states have created new mechanisms, or expanded existing mechanisms, that permit prisoners to earn an earlier release. For instance, since 2000, at least seven states have liberalized their parole rules, and at least nineteen states have expanded their good-time programs (O'Hear, 2017, 64, 68). Several other states have adopted or expanded "earned-time" opportunities, which allow inmates to accelerate release through participation in education, employment, or other programming (65–66). Similarly, other states have created a new "risk-reduction" sentencing option for judges; if a judge imposes such a sentence, then the defendant may earn an earlier release by completing certain rehabilitative programs behind bars (79).

Thus, on paper at least, most prisoners do have opportunities to reduce their time behind bars. However, not all are so fortunate. These include the prisoners serving sentences of life without the possibility of parole (LWOP). The number of LWOP inmates in the United States has been steadily increasing and now exceeds 50,000 (Sentencing Project, 2016, 9). Absent a change in the law or a grant of executive clemency, these inmates can expect to spend the rest of their lives behind bars regardless of how much good behavior and rehabilitative progress they can demonstrate. Additionally, depending on the state, there may also be a number of additional non-LWOP inmates who are serving time under TIS laws with no flexibility. In Wisconsin, for instance, defendants who have been convicted of certain serious violent offenses like armed sexual assault have no opportunity to earn an early release—whatever the prison term ordered by the sentencing judge, the law dictates that it must be served in full.

Moreover, even for those inmates who are theoretically able to accelerate their release date, it is important to realize that many have little realistic hope of getting out early. Parole boards tend to be politically sensitive and averse to controversy. Inmates convicted of homicide or other major violent or notorious offenses are apt to find the parole board unreceptive to their pleas for early release. Even for lower-profile inmates, parole boards may err on the side of caution; there is rarely any political downside to keeping a low-risk, parole-eligible offender behind bars a little while longer, but a disquieting possibility of public condemnation if the offender unexpectedly perpetrates a serious violent crime after being paroled. As a former member of the New York parole board has put it, "It's always safer to deny than to parole; it takes no courage and is the safest route to job security. One doesn't want to find oneself in the headlines" (Schwartzapfel, 2015, 80–81).

Such thinking does not always carry the day, but it has sometimes seemed a dominant force in the parole decision making in some states. For instance, during the governorship of Gray Davis in California (1999–2003), out of thousands of parole-eligible inmates who had been convicted of murder, only six were actually released (Ball, 2011). Similarly, over a five-year period in the early 2000s, Michigan released parole-eligible lifers at a rate of only 0.2 percent per year (Alexander, 2008). More recently, Wisconsin has been holding about 400 parole-eligible inmates in minimum-security institutions; they are deemed safe enough by prison officials so as to require little supervision—some are even allowed to leave the institution without guard during the day for jobs in the community—but they are still unable to obtain parole release (Barton, 2014).

A recent national survey of parole officials underscores the challenges that face inmates convicted of major violent offenses in trying to earn early release through good behavior and rehabilitative progress (Ruhland, Rhine, Robey, & Mitchell, 2016). The survey participants were asked to rank several factors by their importance to release decisions. The top two factors, by far, were the nature and the severity of the offense for which the inmate was serving time. Moreover, the third item on the list, prior criminal record, is another fixed consideration—once in prison, there is nothing the inmate can do to change his or her criminal history. The inmate's disciplinary record behind bars appeared only fourth in the ranking, while participation in prison programs was sixth.

Despite all of the formal and informal restrictions on eligibility, discretionary parole releases are hardly rare in the United States. In 2015, for instance, nearly 200,000 inmates were released through discretionary parole, amounting to about half of the total releases from prison to community supervision (Kaeble & Bonczar, 2017, 22).

In most of the states that have formally eliminated parole, good time remains available as an alternative mechanism by which at least some inmates can accelerate their release dates. Overall, about half of the states have good time, although the generosity of these programs varies greatly from state to state (O'Hear, 2012). A few offer "day for day" credit to some categories of inmates, which can effectively cut a prison term in half. However, at the other extreme, some states offer no more than three or four days of credit per month. In such states, sentence reductions for even the best-behaved inmates will normally be a matter of months, rather than years. Moreover, even in some of the most generous states, a significantly lower rate is established for inmates convicted of violent or other serious offenses. Indeed, nearly half of the good-time states have categorical exclusions that bar any credit at all for inmates convicted of certain specified offenses.

For those inmates who are unable to benefit from parole, good time, or other statutory mechanisms for earning early release, executive clemency may serve as a last resort. State governors—and, in the federal system, the president—have traditionally had broad powers to grant pardons and commute (reduce) sentences. Many states have adopted a variety of procedural requirements to restrain the exercise of executive clemency, but the power remains on the books and could, at least in principle, be used to recognize prisoners' good conduct and rehabilitation. President Obama highlighted the potential for clemency through an extraordinary commutation push in his final two years in office. In all, Obama reduced the sentences of 1,715 federal prisoners (Osler, 2017, 436). However, President Trump did not continue the initiative, and few governors have shown any greater willingness than Trump to utilize clemency in a systematic way to reduce unnecessary incarceration. Of course, the same political sensitivities and calculations that tend to make parole boards cautious also influence the exercise of clemency. Thus, one researcher has found "frequent and regular" clemency grants in only fourteen states (421). In short, the prisoner who is forced to rely on clemency for early release is not likely to find this last resort to be of much assistance.

FURTHER READING

Alexander, Elizabeth. 2008. "Prison Health Care, Political Choice, and the Accidental Death Penalty." *University of Pennsylvania Journal of Constitutional Law*, 11, 1.

Ball, David. 2011. "Normative Elements of Parole Risk." *Stanford Law & Policy Review*, 22, 395.

Barton, Gina. 2014. "Secretive System Keeps Parole-Eligible Inmates Behind Bars." *Milwaukee Journal Sentinel*, July 12. Retrieved from http://archive .jsonline.com/watchdog/watchdogreports/secretive-system-keeps-parole-eligible-inmates-behind-bars-b99307603z1-266891491.html.

Kaeble, Donald & Bonczar, Thomas. 2017. *Probation and Parole in the United States, 2015*. Washington, DC: U.S. Department of Justice.

O'Hear, Michael. 2012. "Solving the Good-Time Puzzle: Why Following the Rules Should Get You Out of Prison Early." *Wisconsin Law Review*, 2012, 195.

O'Hear, Michael. 2017. *The Failure of Sentencing Reform*. Santa Barbara, CA: Praeger.

Osler, Mark. 2017. "Clemency." In *Reforming Criminal Justice: Punishment, Incarceration, and Release*, 419. Edited by Erik Luna. Phoenix: Arizona State University.

Ruhland, Ebony, Rhine, Edward, Robey, Jason, & Mitchell, Kelly Lynn. 2016. *The Continuing Leverage of Releasing Authorities: Findings from a National Survey: Executive Summary*. Minneapolis, MN: Robina Institute of Criminal Law and Criminal Justice. Retrieved from https:// robinainstitute.umn.edu/publications/continuing-leverage-releasing-authorities-findings-national-survey-executive-summary.

Schwartzapfel, Beth. 2015. "Parole Boards: Problems and Promise." *Federal Sentencing Reporter*, 28, 80.

Sentencing Project. 2016. *Still Life: America's Increasing Use of Life and Long-Term Sentences*. Washington, DC: Sentencing Project.

Q23: GIVEN THE HIGH RECIDIVISM RATE OF RELEASED PRISONERS, SHOULDN'T THEY BE HELD BEHIND BARS AS LONG AS POSSIBLE?

Answer: Indiscriminately delaying prisoner releases for as long as possible would not be a cost-effective strategy for protecting public safety. Although most returning prisoners are rearrested within three years of release, few of these arrests are for major violent or sexual crimes. Indeed, if parole and similar forms of discretionary release authority were more consistently utilized to expedite the movement of lower-risk inmates out of prison, the research suggests that public safety might actually be *enhanced*.

The Facts: As discussed in Q22, parole, clemency, and other discretionary release opportunities remain at least theoretically available to most U.S. prisoners. This does not necessarily mean, however, that such releases *ought* to be routinely granted. Indeed, if fully crediting some of the arguments made for "truth in sentencing" (TIS) in the 1990s, then prisoners should only very rarely, if ever, be given their freedom before it is legally necessary to do so.

Much of the debate turns on considerations of public safety. Proponents of TIS point to the high recidivism rate of returning prisoners. Given how frequently the former prisoners commit new crimes, they argue, shouldn't they be held behind bars as long as possible?

Recidivism data must be interpreted with caution. For one thing, there is no single, generally accepted measure of reoffense rates. Different agencies in different states track and report recidivism numbers in different ways. Often, politicians and the media focus public attention on the worst figures available, even though this may create exaggerated perceptions about the dangerousness of returning prisoners.

One commonly repeated figure comes from national research conducted by the U.S. Department of Justice Bureau of Justice Statistics (BJS). In 2014, for instance, the BJS reported that, among prisoners released in thirty states in 2005, more than two-thirds were rearrested within three years (Durose, Cooper, & Snyder, 2014, 8). The figure was little changed from an earlier, much-cited BJS study of prisoners released in 1994 (2), suggesting a relatively stable—and dispiritingly high—recidivism rate for former prisoners.

In at least two respects, though, the reported reoffense rate of almost 68 percent may be misleading. First, this recidivism measure focuses exclusively on *arrests*, but arrest is not the same thing as proof of guilt. Police may arrest on "probable cause," a legal standard that requires relatively little evidentiary support. While precise data are not available, mistaken arrests are hardly unknown. Indeed, given stereotypes about the dangerous proclivities of former prisoners, it is probably somewhat more likely for ex-cons than others to be mistakenly arrested. In any event, the BJS reports a notably lower re-*conviction* rate of 45.2 percent (14).

Second, while there may be a tendency to assume that recidivism means that a released prisoner has committed a crime that is similar to the serious offense that originally put him behind bars, the most common offense category for rearrest is public order, a broad category of miscellaneous nonviolent offenses including DUI, disorderly conduct, illegal possession of a firearm, and violation of the conditions of parole (Durose, Cooper, & Snyder, 2016, 2). Rearrest is seldom for the most serious offenses that most concern the public. BJS data indicate that only 0.9 percent of prisoners are arrested for homicide within five years of release, and only 1.7 percent for rape. *Conviction* rates for these serious offenses are presumably lower still.

On the other hand, reported recidivism rates may in some respects *understate* the dangerousness of returning prisoners. Crimes committed by ex-cons do not show up in these statistics unless they are reported to the police and an arrest is made. However, there is doubtlessly some recidivism that slips between these cracks. For instance, survey research indicates that only about one-half of violent crimes, and only about one-third of property crimes, are reported to the police (Truman & Morgan, 2016, 6). That would leave about two and one-half million unreported violent crimes and ten million unreported property crimes annually. It is not known how many of these crimes are perpetrated by former prisoners, but the share may be substantial. Moreover, of the crimes that are reported to police, an arrest is made in fewer than one-half of the cases of violent crime, and fewer than one-fifth of the cases of property crime (Federal Bureau of Investigation, 2017).

Since officially reported recidivism figures suffer from various deficiencies, researchers have attempted to develop alternative methods to assess the risk posed by the release of incarcerated offenders. For instance, surveys of inmates themselves find remarkably high levels of self-reported crime, including an average of about fifteen to twenty serious violent or property crimes per prisoner per year (Bushway, 2017, 40). Taken at face value, this research suggests that a high volume of crime could indeed be avoided by keeping offenders behind bars for as long as possible. However, the data do not take into account "replacement effects." Since some share of the crime not committed by people behind bars would likely be committed anyway by someone else, we cannot assume that the crime-reducing effects of prolonged incapacitation would be fully fifteen to twenty serious offenses per prisoner per year. Additionally, this is an average figure that obscures wide variations in offense rates. Since a relatively few prisoners account for a greatly disproportionate share of the offenses, an indiscriminate extension of terms for all prisoners might not be a particularly efficient way to reduce crime.

Another research method attempts to measure the impact of changes to prisoner release policies on crime rates. If a given policy change results in a relatively rapid decrease or increase in the size of a jurisdiction's prison population, then it becomes possible to estimate the average number of crimes averted per prisoner held. Note that this approach does not suffer from the replacement effects problem of the earlier approach. Studies employing this method have found widely varying effects of different policy changes adopted in different places at different times (Bushway, 2017, 41–46). At the high end, some (mostly older) studies have reached conclusions that are similar to the survey research, finding that about fifteen to twenty serious offenses are averted per prisoner per year. Other studies find much smaller incapacitation effects, some on the order of only one or two crimes averted per prisoner per year.

Despite the numerical variation in results, the existing research seems to confirm that holding offenders behind bars for longer periods of time can reduce overall crime rates. Thus, for instance, crime rates might be expected to increase if prison sentences were reduced across the board by one year. Conversely, crime rates would be likely to drop if prison sentences were increased across the board by one year. Given a choice between a general increase or general decrease in sentence lengths, public safety might well support the increase.

Policy options, however, are not so limited. Again, the surveys of prisoners indicate that different inmates offend at dramatically different rates. If the high-rate offenders could be reliably identified and held behind bars for as long as possible, then the release of other prisoners might be expedited with little adverse impact on crime rates.

While human behavior cannot be predicted with 100 percent accuracy, researchers have identified several variables that are associated with recidivism in statistically significant ways, including, among others, criminal history, age, and gender (Monahan, 2017). Taking many—sometimes dozens—of such factors into account, various "tools" or algorithms have been developed to draw distinctions between offenders based on their likelihood of offending again. For instance, the Post Conviction Risk Assessment (PCRA) tool is used to assess convicted federal offenders as they begin a period of community supervision. The PCRA uses fifteen variables to divide offenders into four risk categories. In one recent study of the records of more than 33,000 individuals who were assessed under the PCRA, researchers determined that 21 percent of the high-risk offenders were later arrested for a violent offense, but only 2 percent of the low-risk offenders (Skeem & Lowenkamp, 2016, 691). Violent arrest rates for the in-between categories were 7 and 15 percent. Such results suggest that contemporary risk-assessment tools may indeed be of considerable value in identifying lower-risk inmates who could be released early with comparatively little risk to public safety.

Of course, "little" risk does not mean "zero" risk. Any system that regularly reduces the prison terms of even a carefully selected subset of the inmate population will eventually result in the commission of a serious crime that would not have occurred if all inmates were held for as long as possible. Given that reality, how can early release ever be squared with public safety?

Despite the high-profile crimes that are periodically committed by parolees, it is important to recognize that a well-designed, well-administered early-release programs is capable of generating a variety of public-safety benefits that may more than offset the public-safety costs. First, by reducing the size of the incarcerated population, early release saves money for the department of corrections—money that can be reinvested in improved programming and supervision for offenders both inside and outside prison. As seen in Q9 and Q16, research confirms the potential of adequately funded, evidence-based programming and supervision to reduce recidivism rates. Moreover, even without this sort of constructive reinvestment of cost savings, there may still be some reduction in the recidivism of returning inmates achieved simply by reducing prison overcrowding and diminishing the waiting lists for existing programs.

Second, early release programs can incentivize rehabilitative effort and program participation by inmates. In a rigid truth-in-sentencing system, many inmates perceive little reason to exert themselves to prepare for a distant release date, but that calculus may change if their efforts are capable of hastening the release date. Some indication of the potential societal benefit comes from the state of Washington, which expanded its "earned time" program in 2003. This program offers credits toward early release based on an inmate's good behavior and program participation. After comparing matched samples of inmates immediately pre- and post-reform, researchers from the Washington Institute for Public Policy concluded that the expansion of earned time reduced felony recidivism rates by 3.5 percent (Drake, Barnoski, & Aos, 2009).

Third, as explored in Q16, research increasingly bears out the long-standing suspicion that prison terms tend, on average, to *increase* recidivism risk, especially for those offenders with little prior criminal history. Fourth, and finally, as discussed in Q21, parental incarceration tends to have a multitude of adverse effects on children, including increasing *their* risk of offending.

The overall scale of long-term public-safety benefits from an early release program that reliably targets inmates with low to moderate risk, wisely reinvests the fiscal savings from reduced incarceration, and effectively incentivizes rehabilitative effort is not known. However, such benefits may quite plausibly exceed—even far exceed—the short-term crime-related costs of releasing some number of inmates to the streets a few months or years earlier than necessary. Again, the results of Washington's expansion of earned time may be instructive. Taking into account the recidivism reduction, and also factoring in fiscal savings from reduced incarceration and other benefits, the researchers from the Washington Institute for Public Policy found $1.88 in societal benefit from every $1.00 lost as a result of crimes committed by the participating offenders during their periods of early release.

FURTHER READING

Bushway, Shawn. 2017. "Incapacitation." In *Reforming Criminal Justice: Punishment, Incarceration, and Release*. Edited by Erik Luna. Phoenix: Arizona State University.

Drake, E. K., Barnoski, Robert, & Aos, Steve. 2009. *Increased Earned Release from Prison: Impacts of a 2003 Law on Recidivism and Crime Costs, Revised*. Olympia, WA: Washington Institute for Public Policy. Retrieved from http://www.wsipp.wa.gov/ReportFile/1039/Wsipp_Increased-Earned-Release-From-Prison-Impacts-of-a-2003-Law-on-Recidivism-and-Crime-Costs-Revised_Full-Report.pdf.

Durose, Matthew, Cooper, Alexia, & Snyder, Howard. 2014. *Recidivism of Prisoners Released in 30 States in 2005: Patterns from 2005 to 2010*. Washington, DC: U.S. Department of Justice.

Durose, Matthew, Cooper, Alexia, & Snyder, Howard. 2016. *Recidivism of Prisoners Released in 30 States in 2005: Patterns from 2005 to*

2010—*Supplemental Tables: Most Serious Commitment Offense and Types of Post-Release Arrest Charges of Prisoners Released in 30 States in 2005.* Washington, DC: U.S. Department of Justice.

Federal Bureau of Investigation. 2017. *Crime in the United States, 2016.* Washington, DC: U.S. Department of Justice.

Monahan, John. 2017. "Risk Assessment in Sentencing." In *Reforming Criminal Justice: Punishment, Incarceration, and Release,* 77. Edited by Erik Luna. Phoenix: Arizona State University.

Skeem, Jennifer & Lowenkamp, Christopher. 2016. "Risk, Race, and Recidivism: Predictive Bias and Disparate Impact." *Criminology*, 54, 680.

Truman, Jennifer & Morgan, Rachel. 2016. *Criminal Victimization, 2015.* Washington, DC: U.S. Department of Justice.

Q24: IS IT POSSIBLE FOR FORMER PRISONERS TO REINTEGRATE FULLY INTO SOCIETY AND LIVE A NORMAL LIFE?

Answer: Yes, but they face significant hurdles in doing so. About two-thirds of former prisoners find themselves in trouble with the law within the first three years of release, sometimes for committing new crimes and sometimes for violating one or more of the special conditions imposed for parole release. Such legal difficulties often result in a return to prison. Moreover, even among those former prisoners who manage to avoid new legal entanglements, it may take many months or even years to establish stable, satisfactory arrangements in such vital areas as employment, housing, and family relationships. The difficult life circumstances of ex-prisoners typically result from some combination of pre-imprisonment deficits in education, work history, and mental health; negative attitudes and life experiences acquired while behind bars; and the stigma and legal disabilities associated with a criminal conviction and prison term. Eventually, many former prisoners are able to overcome these challenges and become productive, law-abiding members of the community. However, few can expect ever to fully leave behind the stigma of their criminal history.

The Facts: For many "returning citizens," especially those who have served lengthy terms, the transition from prison to free society is psychologically bewildering and fraught with a host of unanticipated difficulties. Indeed, as discussed in Q23, the great majority—more than two-thirds—are rearrested within the first three years of release. Forty-five percent are convicted of a new crime within the same time frame, while 50 percent are returned to prison. (The return to prison number is larger because it includes parolees who are "revoked" and returned to prison for violating their conditions of release—a process that does not require a fresh criminal conviction.) Thus, even at the most basic level of avoiding reimprisonment, about half of newly released prisoners will fail to achieve a successful reintegration into free society.

The legal troubles of many recently released prisoners stem, at least in part, from the economic and psychological pressures associated with joblessness, homelessness, and other types of rootlessness. Indeed, even among the returning citizens who manage to remain out of prison, there are apt to be significant, long-term struggles with getting and holding onto one or more of the central features of what many Americans would consider to be a minimally satisfactory, "normal" adult life, including full-time employment paying a living wage; safe, stable housing; and healthy, supportive family relationships.

Consider the bleak employment picture for returning citizens. Multiple studies point to a joblessness rate of around 50 percent even a full year after release (Committee on Causes and Consequences of High Rates of Incarceration, 2014, 233). And for those who do find work, their earnings tend to be lower and slower-growing over the long run than similar workers who have not been incarcerated (242–47). Such patterns should be concerning not only for what they suggest about underutilized human potential and chronic marginalization and frustration in a rapidly growing segment of our nation's population but also because employment and job stability are associated (not surprisingly) with lower rates of recidivism (Pager, 2007, 25).

Why do former prisoners fare so poorly in the job market? Most explanations focus on one or more of four key considerations (Pager, 2007, 30–32). First, most ex-prisoners had significant pre-imprisonment deficits in various areas that tend to play an important role in getting and keeping a good job. For instance, about 40 percent of inmates lack a high school diploma or GED (Petersilia, 2011, 936). Moreover, learning disabilities and cognitive impairments are significantly more common among inmates than in the general population. Additionally, inmates' work histories tend to be limited and erratic, with one-third unemployed at the time of their most recent arrest. Three in four have a substance-abuse history, and one in six a mental illness (935). Simply put, many of the individuals in the returning citizen population would have poor employment prospects even without the burdens of a criminal conviction and prison term. To be sure, some prisoners do have good opportunities to address their employment-related deficits while they are behind bars, but, as discussed in Q17, there remain significant gaps in the quality and availability of programming in many institutions.

Second, for many inmates, the experience of imprisonment can add to or exacerbate whatever pre-imprisonment deficits they had. For instance, Q18 noted the prevalence of violence and sexual assault in American prisons; such traumatic incidents can have an adverse effect on mental health, as can a protracted stint in solitary confinement (Q19). A prison term may also create significant gaps in work history, leading to the erosion of regular work habits and of any specialized, marketable skills the inmate possessed beforehand (Q17). Incarceration may also disrupt family and other social relationships on the outside that can be vitally important to a successful job search (Pager, 2007, 31). Finally, as examined in Q16, the pressures and harsh realities of prison life may tend to instill in inmates certain kinds of attitudes (e.g., "hypermasculinity" or a reflexive distrust of authority) that are detrimental to effective functioning outside the institution.

Third, employment-seeking former prisoners must contend with a daunting array of legal restrictions on their ability to hold certain kinds of jobs. "Conviction can make one ineligible for public employment, such as in the military and law enforcement. It can preclude private employment, including working in regulated industries, with government contractors, or in fields requiring a security clearance" (Chin, 2017, 376–77). A conviction may also disqualify a person from various types of licenses or government permits, including in some cases a driver's license, that may be necessary for some jobs. Termed "collateral consequences" of a conviction, these sorts of rules have been adopted piecemeal over the course of decades in many states, adding up to a breathtakingly large and complex system of restrictions on careers and job holding. "For example, in Virginia there are 146 mandatory consequences affecting employment, ranging from ineligibility to work for the state lottery to ineligibility to hold a notary commission, and 345 mandatory consequences overall. In Ohio, there are at least 533 mandatory consequences, affecting areas ranging from contracting to child care to driving a truck" (National Association of Criminal Defense Lawyers, 2014, 32). Some collateral consequences last for only a certain period of time after the conviction, while others continue indefinitely. The law establishes procedures for relief from some consequences but not others. And, even when it is theoretically possible to gain relief, former prisoners with low educational attainment and no ability to hire a lawyer may find it difficult to take advantage of the opportunity.

In addition to all of the collateral consequences imposed by law, most returning citizens are also subject to some form of parole supervision for a term of years. Parolees may be subject to a dozen or more specific restrictions on their liberty that bear upon employability. For instance, some parolees are barred from using a computer or going on the Internet, which would put most office work beyond their reach. Others may be subject to a curfew that takes third-shift jobs off the table. Still others may find it harder to obtain work as a result of restrictions on their ability to change residences, to associate with other felons, or to be in a place in which alcohol is served. To be sure, it is often possible to have parole restrictions lifted or narrowed if there are good reasons for doing so. However, parole agents vary widely in their willingness to support changes in the rules of supervision.

Fourth, and finally, there is the stigma of a criminal conviction and prison term. Even when a former inmate identifies a job for which he or she is qualified and legally eligible, the prospective employer will often have to think long and hard before extending an offer. Of course, there are sound reasons to question the safety and trustworthiness of some convicted individuals. However, even when the risks are demonstrably low, an employer may be reluctant to take on an ex-con, fearing, for instance, negative reactions from customers or other employees. Exacerbating these concerns, if something goes wrong after a former prisoner has been brought aboard and a customer or coworker is harmed, the employer may face legal liability through a negligent hiring lawsuit.

Research tends to confirm the importance of these stigma effects. For instance, surveys of employers find that between 60 and 70 percent would not knowingly hire an ex-offender (Pager, 2007, 34). Employers indicate that they are especially resistant to hiring individuals with a violent or property crime conviction, but more open if the conviction is for a drug offense (124–25). One notable set of studies dispatched matched sets of pretend job applicants to apply for a variety of real entry-level positions in Milwaukee and New York City, giving each pair similar credentials except that one had a criminal conviction. The testers with a made-up criminal history received 30 to 60 percent fewer callback interviews in comparison with similarly qualified applicants who had no record. The negative effect of a conviction proved much greater for black than white applicants (Committee on Causes and Consequences of High Rates of Incarceration, 2014, 239–40).

Even beyond the difficulty of landing a decent job, similar dynamics—involving the interplay of pre-imprisonment deficits, the negative experiences of imprisonment, legal restrictions resulting from conviction and parole, and stigma—can present daunting challenges in other areas that are vital to reintegration and quality of life on the outside. For instance, it is thought that about 10 percent of former prisoners experience homelessness after release—a condition that is associated with increased recidivism risk (Turner, 2017, 355). For those who manage to avoid homelessness, living arrangements may nonetheless be problematic in a variety of ways—a couch in a family member's home; a room in a rough neighborhood that presents many vice temptations and risks of renewed criminal associations; or an overpriced, vermin-infested apartment with an unresponsive landlord, to suggest just a few of the possible unhappy outcomes. Simply put, returning citizens lack the range of good housing options that many Americans take for granted, reflecting the harsh realities of poor credit, low income, and a reluctance on the part of many landlords to rent to individuals with a criminal history (Logan, 2013, 1108). Ex-cons, moreover, may have little ability to take advantage of the federally supported programs that normally provide access to housing for low-income families in the United States. Federal law bans certain individuals with drug or sex convictions from public housing and permits local housing authorities to adopt even more stringent restrictions (National Association of Criminal Defense Lawyers, 2014, 40). Underscoring the importance of these programs to returning citizens, it is estimated that up to one-quarter lived in public housing before their imprisonment (Turner, 2017, 362–63).

The difficulties of finding decent housing are especially acute for returning sex offenders, who often confront a multitude of residency restrictions designed to keep them at a far remove from children—and also, of course, out of "good" neighborhoods where their presence may reduce property values. Once all of these restrictions are taken into account, returning sex offenders may find that there are very few, if any, areas that are legally open to them in their communities of origin. For some, homelessness seems almost unavoidable. Thus, for instance, before California moderated its restrictions in 2015, it was estimated that about one-third of registered sex offenders in the state were transients (Turner, 2017, 355).

Q21 examined the adverse impact of imprisonment on relationships with children and spouses. It is important, as well, to appreciate that difficulties in one area of life (employment, housing, family relationships) can exacerbate problems in other areas. The lack of a permanent address, for instance, can complicate a job search, while the breakdown of an intimate relationship may result in an ex-prisoner's expulsion from the partner's home and relegation to life on the street. Joblessness, meanwhile, may make it impossible for an ex-prisoner either to secure stable housing or to attract a mate. Moreover, chronic health conditions, mental illness, and habitual substance abuse can also become part of the complex stew of mutually reinforcing dysfunction.

In addition to legal restrictions that bear directly on the material conditions of life, such as limitations on employment and housing, former prisoners also face other sorts of restrictions that symbolically serve to reinforce their sense of exclusion from mainstream American life. Perhaps most notable is the disenfranchisement—the loss of the right to vote—that often accompanies a felony conviction. The rules vary considerably from state to state, but in thirty-four states disenfranchisement continues after release from prison and through any subsequent term of parole (Uggen, Larson, & Shannon, 2016, 4). In twelve of these states, disenfranchisement continues even past the end of the parole term. Returning prisoners also commonly face restrictions on their ability to serve on a jury, to hold public office, and to possess a firearm.

Given these rules and all of the other formal and informal ways that society signals its mistrust of former inmates, there are concerns that the apparent expectations of maladjustment and renewed criminal activity can become a sort of self-fulfilling prophecy. "[R]esearch makes clear that stigma can have a self-fulfilling criminogenic effect, predisposing individuals to become the deviants they were branded to be" (Logan, 2013, 1107). Consider the employment context again. The evidence that former prisoners are much less successful than other job-seekers in getting callback interviews suggests that the ex-cons are apt to experience much longer, confidence-sapping delays between interviews, which may impair interview performance (Pager, 2007, 147–48). Then, as more time passes since release, gaps in work history grow longer and more troubling for prospective employers. Eventually, after repeated rejections, the frustrated former prisoner becomes increasingly likely to drop out of the search for legitimate work entirely. A job search that may have begun with the best of intentions can thus end in seeming confirmation of negative expectations about the willingness and ability of convicted individuals to live productive, law-abiding lives.

To be sure, these are only general tendencies and not the inevitable fate of all former inmates. It is easy enough through an Internet search to identify quite a few ex-prisoners who have achieved impressive degrees of success after release. The comedian and actor Tim Allen built his career after serving time on a drug charge. Already remarkably successful before incarceration, both Martha Stewart and Robert Downey Jr. succeeded in rebuilding their careers after release. Chuck Colson, an aide to President Nixon who was ensnared in the Watergate scandal, later established a much-admired prison ministry program. Shon Hopwood, a bank robber, served more than a decade in federal prison but then earned a law degree after his release and now teaches as a member of the prestigious faculty of Georgetown Law School.

Still, the number of such high-visibility success stories amounts to only a tiny fraction of the 600,000+ individuals exiting prison each year. More modest, but still very meaningful, successes—a job obtained, an addiction beaten, a promotion earned, a comfortable apartment in a safe neighborhood rented—are more common, but still elusive for most returning citizens in the first months and even years following release. With persistence and support, such markers of reintegration are likely to be achieved eventually. Yet, even then, some of the stigma and collateral consequences of a conviction and prison term will persist. It is not only the records of celebrities that are easy to find online. For many years, or even decades, after release, a former prisoner may encounter conviction-related difficulties in getting a job, promotion, loan, license, or permit, or even simply in feeling an accepted, trusted member of a community.

As the number of former prisoners in the United States continues to swell, policy makers increasingly appreciate that the levels of stigma and exclusion they experience may be unnecessary and even counterproductive to the societal goals of reducing crime and recidivism. In recent years, the most popular reform has probably been "ban the box" laws, which prohibit employers from asking about criminal records on job application forms. More than 100 cities have adopted such rules (Turner, 2017, 359). There has also been a push in recent years to reduce the number and severity of collateral consequences and to provide better avenues for relief when consequences do more harm than good in individual cases (National Association of Criminal Defense Lawyers, 2014, 32–35). Governors and presidents might ease some of the problems if they would use their pardon power more frequently and systematically in support of offenders who can demonstrate rehabilitation; pardons generally erase all legal significance from a conviction. However, as noted in Q22, there tends to be a great deal of politically minded reluctance to exercise such clemency powers. Alternatively, more states might establish procedures for individuals to earn certificates of rehabilitation and restoration of rights, as is already done in a handful of states (45). Additionally, states might adopt expungement laws, which limit public access to some criminal records. Twenty-two states currently provide for the expungement of some criminal convictions (58). Even where they are already on the books, though, expungement laws could be improved if policy makers expanded the number of eligible offenses, lifted age restrictions, and reduced post-sentence waiting periods. Despite some recent successes by reformers, there remain good reasons to think that the law erects many unnecessary barriers to full reintegration of former prisoners into free society.

FURTHER READING

Chin, Gabriel. 2017. "Collateral Consequences." In *Reforming Criminal Justice: Punishment, Incarceration, and Release*, 371. Edited by Erik Luna. Phoenix: Arizona State University.

Committee on Causes and Consequences of High Rates of Incarceration, National Research Council of the National Academies. 2014. *The Growth of Incarceration in the United States*. Washington, DC: The National Academies Press.

Logan, Wayne. 2013. "Informal Collateral Consequences." *Washington Law Review*, 88, 1103.

National Association of Criminal Defense Lawyers. 2014. *Collateral Damage: America's Failure to Forgive or Forget in the War on Crime*. Washington, DC: National Association of Criminal Defense Lawyer.

Pager, Devah. 2007. *Marked: Race, Crime, and Finding Work in an Era of Mass Incarceration*. Chicago, IL: University of Chicago Press.

Petersilia, Joan. 2011. "Parole and Prisoner Reentry." In *The Oxford Handbook of Crime and Criminal Justice*, 925. Edited by Michael Tonry. New York: Oxford University Press.

Turner, Susan. 2017. "Reentry." In *Reforming Criminal Justice: Punishment, Incarceration, and Release*, 341. Edited by Erik Luna. Phoenix: Arizona State University.

Uggen, Christopher, Larson, Ryan, & Shannon, Sarah. 2016. *6 Million Lost Voters: State-Level Estimates of Felony Disenfranchisement, 2016*. Washington, DC: The Sentencing Project.

Q25: ARE MOST PAROLEES RETURNED TO PRISON FOR TECHNICAL VIOLATIONS?

Answer: About half of all former prisoners are returned to prison within three years of release, some for the commission of new crimes and some for violating parole conditions. If a parole violation does not involve fresh criminal conduct, it is sometimes characterized as merely "technical." Many states have made efforts in recent years to reduce the number of parolees returned to prison for purely technical violations. While there is a growing consensus that re-imprisonment should generally not be employed as a response to low-level violations, good national data are not available regarding the precise frequency of this practice. Based on the available figures, it appears that states vary widely in their willingness to revoke parole in the absence of a new crime. In some states, it is possible that many, if not most, of the parolees sent back to prison are technical violators only.

The Facts: Of those inmates leaving American prisons in any given year, more than two-thirds are subject to a term of supervised release in the community (Carson & Anderson, 2016, 11). These former prisoners on supervised release are commonly referred to as "parolees" in order to distinguish them from probationers, who serve time on supervised release not *after*, but *instead of*, a prison term. The "parolee" label is a holdover from the time when most prisoners were released through the discretionary act of a parole board (see Q22). Since then, many states have abolished discretionary parole, leaving the sentencing judge to set a term of post-prison community supervision. Still, it remains conventional to say that an ex-prisoner who lives in the community in a special status of conditional liberty is "on parole." Each year, more than 400,000 state and federal prisoners are released to this status.

In many respects, parole supervision functions just like probation supervision. As explained in Q8, probationers are subject to a variety of restrictions on their liberty, with some imposed as a matter of course on most or all probationers (meet periodically with an agent, report all changes of residence and employment in advance, submit to drug tests, do not associate with convicted felons, etc.) and some more customized to the offense or the offender (do not use a computer, avoid contact with children, do not consume alcohol, etc.). Field agents normally have a great deal of discretion in deciding how to respond to violations. If there is a major violation, or a series of minor violations, the agent may choose to initiate the process for revocation of supervised release, which would result in the probationer's incarceration. All of this normally works the same with parole. Perhaps the most notable difference in the handling of probation and parole violations is that probation revocation normally involves a return trip to court, while parole revocation is typically handled as an administrative matter by the parole board, the department of corrections, or some other agency (Klingele, 2013, 1040).

In recent years, the rate at which parolees are put back behind bars has remained consistently at fourteen per one hundred parolees per year (Kaeble & Bonczar, 2017, 6). Probationers, by contrast, fare somewhat better, with incarceration ordered for only eight per one hundred (4). The return-to-prison rate has fallen sharply since 2005, when twenty-five parolees per one hundred exited community supervision to incarceration (6). This may reflect the efforts by many states to make prisoner reentry more successful, reduce recidivism rates, and develop better alternatives to revocation.

Barely one-quarter of the parolees returned to prison have a new sentence (Kaeble & Bonczar, 2017, 24). By contrast, more than 60 percent are categorized as revoked without a new sentence. If we exclude the cases for which the reason for return is unknown, then the "no-new-sentence" revocations account for about 70 percent of the returns. At first blush, it would appear that these revocations should be counted as "technical"; that is, it appears they are based on violations of release conditions that do not involve fresh criminal conduct. The possibility that most returns to prison result from technical violations raises concerns that parole agents may be exercising their discretion in an overly strict manner, routinely sending individuals back to prison for minor misconduct that does not truly implicate public safety.

But the 60 (and 70) percent figures likely overstate the importance of purely technical revocations. There are at least two significant ways in which the figure may be misleading. First, some individuals who are revoked do eventually pick up a conviction and new sentence for their violation conduct. For instance, a parolee who is arrested for selling cocaine may be revoked because drug distribution violates the standard condition that parolees not commit any new crimes. As the revocation process moves forward, a prosecutor may decide to file a new charge on the basis of the same cocaine sale. However, because revocations are typically handled administratively with relatively informal procedures, the revocation may be finalized many weeks or even months before the criminal case. Additionally, prosecutors may hold up the criminal case in order to gain the assistance of the defendant in building a case against the defendant's confederates. And, even after the criminal case is resolved, there may be further delays in adding the new sentence to corrections records. As a result, there are likely many returns to prison that are misclassified as revocation-only. For example, in its publicly reported data, the Wisconsin Department of Corrections indicates that about three-quarters of the state's revocations do not involve a new sentence; it appears, however, that in reality about one-third of the "no-new-sentence" revocations are eventually associated with a new sentence (O'Hear, 2017).

Second, even for those revocations that never do draw an overlapping conviction, it is important to realize that the revocation may nonetheless rest on fresh criminal conduct. Due to resource constraints, prosecutors routinely decline to file charges even when they believe they could readily prove a crime and obtain a conviction. Often, when a prospective defendant has already been revoked, or seems on track for revocation, a prosecutor will think that to be adequate as punishment. Initiating a new criminal case on top of the revocation may seem a waste of time. In such cases, there may be no new crime formally proven in court, but it would still not be entirely accurate to characterize the revocation as merely technical in nature. How often this scenario occurs in practice is simply not known.

Overall, even if we could account more precisely for time-lag and data-reporting problems, it is plausible that half or more of the parolee returns to prison are based on conduct for which there will never be a new conviction and prison sentence. However, if we were somehow to factor out the revocations that were motivated by uncharged criminal conduct on the part of the parolee, the proportion of truly technical revocations would likely be considerably lower.

Whatever their import, national figures on revocation may mask wide state-to-state variation. In at least five states (Arizona, Arkansas, Hawai'i, New Hampshire, and New Jersey), no-new-sentence returns to prison outnumber new-sentence returns by a ratio of more than ten to one. Meanwhile, in at least three other states (Kansas, Mississippi, and Ohio), the reverse is true—the vast majority of returns to prison involve a new sentence.

Some of the variation may reflect the impact of reforms adopted in some states in order to reduce the frequency of revocations based solely on technical violations. For instance, in 2011, North Carolina adopted legislation that generally prohibits revocation based on noncriminal conduct (Klingele, 2013). At least a handful of other states have passed similar, albeit more narrowly focused, reforms that restrict the permissible grounds for revocation. In still other states, corrections departments have adopted new guidelines for parole agents that are intended to encourage greater use of alternatives to revocation for low-level violations.

The national reform movement in this area reflects an emerging consensus among experts that revocations are often both costly and unhelpful—if not downright counterproductive—to the goal of public safety. Parole revocations have contributed substantially to prison overcrowding and burgeoning corrections budgets. In 2015, for instance, revocations accounted for about one-quarter of prison admissions nationally (Carson & Anderson, 2016)—this even after a decade of significant reductions in the rate of revocations. Yet, there are reasons to doubt whether strict supervision of parolees contributes much to crime control. Of particular concern are short returns to prison, which may prove extremely detrimental to the offender's ability to maintain employment, housing, mental health treatment, and family relationships on the outside—all vital to long-term reintegration and risk reduction—while failing to provide the offender with enough time in the institution to benefit from any available rehabilitative programming.

How to handle low-level parole violations—whether criminal in nature or not—presents a difficult policy problem. The problem could be substantially alleviated if greater care were taken to minimize the number of conditions to which parolees are subjected to, imposing only those that demonstrably bear on public safety—fewer conditions necessarily means fewer violations. Beyond that, rigorous risk-assessment has an important role to play in decisions about whom to return to prison, just as it does in decisions about whom to release from prison (see Q23). Additionally, the whole business of parole supervision should be informed by an appreciation of the profound challenges former prisoners face as they attempt to establish new lives for themselves in the community (see Q24). The system should strive to make reentry more manageable, which, among other things, requires a minimization of the disruptions of reincarceration. Parole supervision remains an area urgently in need of rethinking and reform, regardless of precisely how many revocations are purely technical in nature.

FURTHER READING

Carson, E. Ann & Anderson, Elizabeth. 2016. *Prisoners in 2015*. Washington, DC: U.S. Department of Justice.

Kaeble, Donald & Bonczar, Thomas. 2017. *Probation and Parole in the United States, 2015*. Washington, DC: U.S. Department of Justice.

Klingele, Cecelia. 2013. "Rethinking the Use of Community Supervision." *Journal of Criminal Law & Criminology*, 103, 1015.

O'Hear, Michael. 2017. "Wisconsin Sentencing in the Walker Era: Mass Incarceration as the New Normal." *Federal Sentencing Reporter*, 30, 125.

5

❖

Women, Juveniles, and Other Special Offender Populations

When people think of prisoners in the United States, they normally imagine a young or middle-aged adult male. This stereotype is not unreasonable, given that more than 90 percent of prisoners are male and nearly 80 percent are between the ages of twenty and fifty. However, the experiences of other demographic groups in the criminal justice system also have important ramifications for the system's fairness, cost, and effectiveness. This chapter considers the system's treatment of female and juvenile offenders, and of prisoners who are elderly or disabled. It also examines how the system responds to mental illness and to the particular recidivism risks that are commonly thought to be posed by sexual offenders.

Q26: DO FEMALE OFFENDERS RECEIVE PREFERENTIAL TREATMENT WHEN IT COMES TO SENTENCING AND CORRECTIONS?

Answer: On average, women receive somewhat more lenient sentences than men convicted of the same offenses. It is not entirely clear why the disparity exists and whether it is justifiable. The female offender population differs from the male offender population in various ways that may arguably be relevant to sentencing. For instance, a woman is more likely than a man to be the sole caregiver for a young child, which may explain some of the male-female sentencing disparity—judges are less likely to send a defendant to prison if that would result in the displacement of a child. In any event, if a female defendant is sent to prison, she will normally be held in a separate facility from male prisoners. The general practice of segregating prisoners by sex means that male and female experiences of imprisonment will tend to differ in some respects. On the whole, though, it is hard to say that the female experience embodies preferential treatment. Although certain types of hardship seem less common in women's prisons, such as nonsexual assaults by fellow inmates, other types of hardship are more common, such as sexual assaults.

The Facts: Women exhibit markedly different patterns of criminal offending than men, which complicates efforts to compare their treatment by the criminal justice system. Men commit a much greater share of crime—and especially violent crime—than women. About 90 percent of the individuals arrested for homicide are male, as are about 80 percent of the perpetrators of less serious violent crime (Gartner, 2011, 352–53). Men also account for about two-thirds of property offenses (354). As a result of such patterns, there are many fewer women than men involved in the criminal justice system, and those who are in the system tend to have less serious charges and convictions. Thus, for instance, in 2015, about 1.4 million of the 1.5 million prisoners in the United States were men (Carson & Anderson, 2016, 3). Moreover, only 32 percent of the female inmates were incarcerated for violent crimes, as compared to 48 percent of the male inmates (30–31). Drug and property offenses accounted for correspondingly higher percentages of the female prison population.

It is true that the female prison population has for a full generation been growing more quickly than the male. The female imprisonment rate increased almost exactly six-fold between 1980 and 2005—a time period during which the male rate "only" tripled (Kruttschnitt, 2011, 901). Moreover, since 2005, the female prison population has continued to grow, even as the male has stabilized (Carson & Anderson, 2016, 4). Still, the female imprisonment rate was so much lower than the male rate in 1980 that there remains a very wide gap today. As of the end of 2015, the male imprisonment rate was more than thirteen times greater than the female (8). Although the rapid growth in female imprisonment has not come close to ending the gender gap, it has generated more public attention on questions regarding the treatment of women in the criminal justice system.

Any attempt to determine whether women are unfairly advantaged (or, for that matter, unfairly disadvantaged) in the system must take into account different gender patterns of criminal offending. At the sentencing stage, several studies with appropriate controls do find more lenient judgments for female than male defendants (Gartner, 2011, 369). For instance, one researcher studied federal sentencing data from 1992 to 2001 and concluded that women's sentences were on average 5.4 months shorter than those of similar male defendants (Schanzenbach, 2005). The overall sentence length in the sample was 48.2 months, which suggests that female defendants might often receive a sentence around 10 percent shorter than similarly situated males. Interestingly, sex disparities tended to be smaller in the districts with the highest proportion of female judges—to the point that measurable sex disparities might plausibly disappear if all judges were female. This finding suggests that the more lenient sentences of women largely resulted from the attitudes of male judges, either a generalized sense of "chivalry" toward females (perhaps limited to those who seem to conform to certain ideals of femininity) or a tendency to give greater weight to various mitigating circumstances that are more common among female than male defendants.

These mitigating circumstances might arguably provide a good justification for the pattern of more lenient sentences for women. Although researchers can control for key measures of offense severity and criminal history, it is much harder to take into account certain other variables that tend to differentiate male and female defendants. Perhaps, most important, female defendants are more likely to play a critical role as parent and caregiver to a child. For instance, among state prison inmates, 62 percent of women, but only 54 percent of men, report having a minor child (Glaze & Maruschak, 2010, 3). Moreover, 55 percent of the female inmates indicate that they lived with at least one of their minor children in the month before their arrest, as opposed to only 36 percent of the male inmates (4). Additionally, of the women who had a child at home pre-arrest, more than three-quarters were living in a single-parent household. By contrast, most of the men with a child at home were part of a two-parent household. Not surprisingly, then, the vast majority of the children of male inmates were able to live with their mothers during the period of paternal incarceration (5). However, a period of maternal incarceration normally means that a nonparent ends up taking care of the child, most commonly a grandparent. For 11 percent of imprisoned mothers, though, the children are in foster care. The corresponding figure for men is only 2 percent. In sum, a prison sentence for a female defendant is more likely to have a significant effect on the day-to-day life of a child than would be the case for a male defendant, including a greater likelihood that the child will be placed into foster care. It is possible that many judges take such considerations into account in sentencing women who have minor children, potentially explaining much of the overall sex disparity. After all, it seems intuitively unfair to punish the innocent child for the misdeeds of a parent.

Female defendants are also more likely than male to present a variety of other mitigating circumstances. About two-thirds of women in jail report having a chronic health condition, as opposed to only half of male inmates (Swavola, Riley, & Subramanian, 2016, 9). Nearly one-third of women in jail suffer from a serious mental illness, which is more than twice the rate for jailed men (10). Among jail and prison inmates, women are seven times more likely than men to have experienced sexual abuse before their incarceration and four times more likely to have experienced physical abuse (National Center on Addiction and Substance Abuse, 2010, 30–31). Female inmates are also more likely to have a substance use disorder, to have experienced homelessness, to have been placed in foster care when a child, and to have had a parent or guardian who abused alcohol or drugs. Such life experiences and vulnerabilities on the part of a defendant may elicit sympathy from the sentencing judge and support claims that the defendant was not entirely to blame for her offense—for instance, that an abusive partner may have pressured her to break the law. Moreover, such mitigating circumstances may dovetail with the paternalistic attitudes of some judges, that is, tendencies to assume "that women are the weaker sex, in need of protection from themselves as well as others, and not fully responsible for their actions" (Gartner, 2011, 372).

Whether for legitimate reasons or otherwise, the evidence suggests that a convicted woman is somewhat less likely to receive a prison sentence than a man with the same criminal history who has been convicted of the same offense. It should be stressed, though, that this is only a general tendency. There are concerns, for instance, that some women may be treated *more* harshly than similarly situated men if they fail to demonstrate "appropriate feminine characteristics, such as deference, vulnerability, and sobriety" (Gartner, 2011, 370).

If a woman *is* incarcerated, her experience behind bars may also differ in some important respects from that of her male counterparts. These differences stem in part from the strict sex segregation of inmates that is the norm in American correctional systems.

The separation of female from male inmate populations may offer some benefits to the women. We have already seen, for instance, that a much higher proportion of the male population is serving time for violence. We should not be surprised, then, that female inmates are less likely than male to be assaulted by a fellow prisoner (see Q18).

However, women's prisons are hardly immune from the general harshness of American penal institutions, and their inmates may, in fact, face distinctive difficulties that are no less severe than those of male inmates.

As discussed in Q18, for instance, women prisoners report a higher incidence of sexual assault than men. Indeed, some research suggests that upwards of three-quarters of staff sexual misconduct in prisons involves female inmates as victims (Committee on Causes and Consequences of High Rates of Incarceration, 2014, 171).

Additionally, pregnancy and childbirth during incarceration involve particular challenges that are unique to female inmates. In both the courts and the media, there has been an apparent surge of claims in recent years that corrections officials fail to make appropriate pregnancy-related accommodations (Goldstein, 2017). For instance, female inmates may be required to wear shackles during labor and delivery, even though this practice increases the risk of harm to both mother and child—and despite the lack of any documented escape attempt by an unshackled woman during childbirth (Swavola, Riley, & Subramanian, 2016, 17). Additionally, most mothers are required to separate from their newborns within forty-eight hours after birth, which can be detrimental to both. More generally, some research suggests that the pain of being cut off from family relationships is felt more acutely by female than male prisoners (Committee on Causes and Consequences of High Rates of Incarceration, 2014, 171).

There are also concerns that various standard correctional management techniques developed for male inmates may be harmful if not adapted to the particular circumstances of female inmates. For instance, many of the risk-assessment tools used to classify inmates were based primarily or exclusively on experience in dealing with men; their use with women may result in systematic "over-classification," that is, the placement of women in higher security classifications (and hence more tightly controlled environments) than is truly warranted by their risk level (Swavola, Riley, & Subramanian, 2016, 13–14). Similarly, routine strip searches may be ill-advised for an inmate population that has experienced such a high level of sexual victimization; PTSD symptoms may result from a search that is perceived to be sexually degrading (14).

In sum, while women are apt to experience incarceration differently than men, there is little basis for concluding that women benefit in a generalized way from preferential treatment by corrections officials.

FURTHER READING

Carson, E. Ann & Anderson, Elizabeth. 2016. *Prisoners in 2015*. Washington, DC: U.S. Department of Justice.

Committee on Causes and Consequences of High Rates of Incarceration, National Research Council of the National Academies. 2014.

The Growth of Incarceration in the United States. Washington, DC: The National Academies Press.

Gartner, Rosemary. 2011. "Sex, Gender, and Crime." In *The Oxford Handbook of Crime and Criminal Justice*, 348. Edited by Michael Tonry. New York: Oxford University Press.

Glaze, Lauren & Maruschak, Laura. 2010. *Parents in Prison and Their Minor Children (Revised 3/30/10)*. Washington, DC: U.S. Department of Justice.

Goldstein, Joseph. 2017. "Pregnant Inmates Say a Federal Jail Is No Place for Them, and Some Judges Agree." *New York Times*, March 14. Retrieved from https://www.nytimes.com/2017/03/14/nyregion/pregnant-inmates-federal-jail-in-brooklyn.html.

Kruttschnitt, Candace. 2011. "Women's Prisons." In *The Oxford Handbook of Crime and Criminal Justice*, 897. Edited by Michael Tonry. New York: Oxford University Press.

National Center on Addiction and Substance Abuse. 2010. *Behind Bars II: Substance Abuse and America's Prison Population*. New York: Columbia University.

Schanzenbach, Max. 2005. "Racial and Sex Disparities in Prison Sentences: The Effect of District-Level Judicial Demographics." *Journal of Legal Studies*, 34, 57.

Swavola, Elizabeth, Riley, Kristi, & Subramanian, Ram. 2016. *Overlooked: Women and Jails in an Era of Reform*. New York: Vera Institute of Justice.

Q27: DOES THE SYSTEM REALLY HOLD JUVENILES ACCOUNTABLE FOR THEIR CRIMES?

Answer: Juvenile offenders have traditionally been handled in a separate court and corrections system. The special emphasis within the juvenile system on rehabilitation has given the system a reputation for being "soft" on crime. Reflecting such perceptions, many states reformed their laws in the 1990s so as to push more young offenders into the regular adult system. For those still handled in the juvenile system today, punishment may tend to be less severe in some respects than in the adult system. It is far from clear, however, that these differences are unwarranted. Rather, distinctive aspects of youth experience and capacity seem to support distinctive approaches to holding juvenile offenders accountable.

The Facts: When Cook County, Illinois, developed the nation's first juvenile court in 1899, reformers hoped that a separate justice system for young people would more effectively promote rehabilitation than the adult system, in which impressionable juveniles would inevitably be corrupted through contact with more hardened criminals (Nellis, 2016). Juvenile court officials were seen as stand-ins for ineffective or absent parents, administering discipline in the same restrained, benevolent fashion as would a good parent. Criminal behavior might land a child in juvenile court but so might a broad range of lesser misconduct. Consistent with their distinctive mission, early juvenile courts developed unique procedures, involving less formality and greater confidentiality than adult courts. Even the terminology was different: a juvenile was "adjudicated delinquent," instead of "convicted of a crime."

One important similarity between the early juvenile systems and their adult counterparts lay in the use of confinement as a basic response to criminal offending. Although juveniles were kept in their own detention facilities, the conditions were not necessarily much better than what prevailed in adult prisons. "Youth continued to be held in large, overcrowded, and poorly maintained institutions with minimal programming and where corporal punishment was condoned" (Nellis, 2016, 16).

Despite the gaps that often existed between its rehabilitative ideals and the harsh realities of its practice, the juvenile court model spread quickly across the United States and soon became the nation's dominant approach to dealing with youth crime—defined in most states as offenses committed before the offender's eighteenth birthday (Chester & Schiraldi, 2016, 9). However, the juvenile system was buffeted by two major reform waves in the second half of the twentieth century. First, between the 1960s and 1980s, came a wave of progressive reform that increased professionalism in juvenile courts, strengthened procedural rights for juvenile defendants, and implemented new, community-based alternatives to confinement (Nellis, 2016, 27–32). But then, in the 1990s, the pendulum swung back toward more punitive, less rehabilitative responses to youth crime. Among other things, this shift reflected an explosion in youth violence between the mid-1980s and mid-1990s, reinforcing perceptions that the juvenile justice system was unduly soft and ineffectual (49). Adopted under the slogan of "adult crime, adult time," popular reforms of the era included lowering the age cutoff for the juvenile system (e.g., from seventeen to sixteen in some states); requiring that certain serious offenses be transferred automatically from juvenile to adult court; easing the discretionary transfer of cases to adult court; implementing military-style boot camps for juvenile offenders; and extending capital punishment and mandatory minimums to some juveniles. The result was a surge of juveniles into adult courts. For instance, in 1991, an estimated 176,000 young defendants were channeled into adult courts as a result of reduced age cutoffs (56). Other sorts of reforms likely pushed many thousands more each year into adult courts.

Although talk of remorseless juvenile "superpredators"—a prominent feature of public discussions of youth crime in the 1990s—has died out, many of the punitive reforms of the late twentieth century remain in place. Thus, in considering whether juveniles are truly held accountable for their criminal offenses today, the first point to appreciate is that many young people, especially those accused of the most serious offenses, are convicted and sentenced through precisely the same system as adult offenders.

Once in the adult system, it is not clear whether juvenile offenders tend to receive different treatment than their older peers. On the one hand, youth is often recognized as a mitigating factor that supports relatively lenient treatment (more about this later in the text). On the other hand, many juvenile offenders may actually appear *more* dangerous to judges and prosecutors for their age-related tendencies to act impulsively and without due respect for authority.

Several studies have attempted to determine whether transferred juveniles are sentenced differently from adults convicted of similar offenses, but the results have not been consistent. Some studies find harsher treatment, while others find lenience or no statistically significant difference in either direction. For instance, one recent study of sentencing in Florida found indications of *both* greater *and* lesser severity for juveniles: juveniles were less likely to be sentenced to prison than similarly situated adults, but, if sent to prison, they tended to receive longer terms (Lehmann, Chiricos, & Bales, 2017). While such results may point to a complex calculus in the way that juvenile status is handled in the adult system, they also belie any suggestion that young people convicted of serious crimes can count on nothing worse than the proverbial slap on the wrist. Indeed, other studies find that three-quarters of juveniles convicted of violent felonies in adult court are sent to prison, while juveniles convicted of murder are more likely to be sentenced to life without the possibility of parole than are adult murderers (Feld, 2017, 378–79).

Even for the young offenders prosecuted in juvenile court, it should not be assumed that the system fails to deliver meaningful accountability.

For instance, more than 20 percent of defendants in the juvenile system are held in detention facilities while their cases are pending in court (National Center for Juvenile Justice, 2017, 34). Moreover, while many juvenile cases are resolved informally, most of the cases that are referred to juvenile court based on alleged criminal conduct (56 percent) are "petitioned," that is, a prosecutor or other government official recommends a formal adjudication of delinquency or a transfer of the case to adult court (38). Indeed, when serious violent crime is alleged, nearly 80 percent of cases are petitioned. Among the petitioned cases, more than half (54 percent) result in a delinquency adjudication (46). And for the juveniles found delinquent, judges order commitment to an institution or some other form of out-of-home placement more than one-quarter of the time (49).

To be sure, juvenile-court outcomes tend to be more lenient than adult-court outcomes, at least as these things are typically measured (Kurlychek & Johnson, 2010, 725). For instance, of the juveniles adjudicated delinquent in connection with serious violent crimes, only about 37 percent receive an out-of-home placement (National Center for Juvenile Justice, 2017, 62). By comparison, in urban adult courts, more than 80 percent of defendants convicted of serious violent crimes receive an incarceration sentence (Reaves, 2013, 29). Additionally, juvenile commitments can normally last only until the young offender reaches a particular age, either the age cutoff for the juvenile court's jurisdiction or in some states a few years beyond that. This limitation can make it hard for a juvenile court judge to impose a term of confinement that is comparable to what would be imposed on an older offender convicted of a similar crime, especially in cases involving the most serious offenses. Of course, in many such cases, transfer to adult court is available as an alternative route to an appropriately severe punishment.

Still, since most young offenders continue to be prosecuted in juvenile court, and since juvenile court outcomes generally appear more lenient than adult court outcomes, one might question whether young people face sufficient accountability for their criminal behavior. If the goal is "adult crime, adult time," it is doubtful that the objective is reliably met in practice.

But should that actually be the yardstick? For one thing, as indicated in Q16 and Q23, there are reasons to suspect that "adult time" is often excessive or even counterproductive from the standpoint of public safety. For another, juvenile offenders tend to differ from adult offenders in a variety of ways that are arguably quite relevant to punishment.

A large body of research amply documents these differences. Key findings have been summarized as follows:

> Youths differ from adults in risk perception, appreciation of consequences, impulsivity and self-control, sensation-seeking, and compliance with peers. The regions of the brain that control reward-seeking and emotional arousal develop earlier than those that regulate executive functions and impulse control. Adolescents underestimate the amount and likelihood of risks, emphasize immediate outcomes, focus on anticipated gains rather than possible losses to a greater extent than adults, and consider fewer options. . . . Researchers attribute youths' impetuous decisions to a heightened appetite for emotional arousal and intense experiences, which peaks around 16 or 17. (Feld, 2017, 385–86)

A recognition of these tendencies of youth may cause juvenile crime to be seen as less blameworthy than adult crime, and hence less suitable for harshly punitive treatment. Moreover, these tendencies also suggest that extended periods of criminal justice supervision are apt to be unnecessary for young offenders—as a natural part of the aging process, most will find risky behaviors less appealing and destructive impulses more readily contained.

Any assessment of the sufficiency of juvenile punishment must also take into account at least three additional considerations. First, responses to juvenile crime have long been marked by troubling racial disparities. Among those young people referred to juvenile court, blacks are more likely than whites to be petitioned, to be sent to adult court, and to be given an out-of-home commitment (National Center for Juvenile Justice, 2017, 60). Black youths are also more likely than white to be detained while their cases are being considered, even holding type of offense constant (Feld, 2017, 333). In some states, the disparities are particularly striking. For instance, in New York, it was recently observed that blacks and Latinos account for 80 percent of the placements in juvenile facilities, but only 44 percent of the state's overall youth population (Nellis, 2016, 109). Although some of the disparities can be explained by racial differences in offending, researchers have also concluded that differential treatment by justice system officials also likely plays a role (109–10). The data thus suggest that accountability in the juvenile system may work differently for white offenders than for people of color.

Second, despite their purported rehabilitative mission, some juvenile facilities are marked by a harshness and austerity that can be hard to distinguish from even some of the toughest adult institutions. Overcrowding is the norm (Feld, 2017, 341), and solitary confinement is utilized as a punishment in nearly one-quarter of juvenile facilities (Nellis, 2016, 113). Sexual victimization levels are not much lower in juvenile than in adult institutions, with about 2 percent of juvenile inmates reporting victimization by a fellow inmate and about 5 percent reporting sexual misconduct by staff (Heaton et al., 2016, 7). In some facilities, fights among inmates, suicide attempts, disciplinary segregation, and excessive uses of force by staff seem to be common aspects of institutional life (Marley, 2016). Researchers have also raised concerns regarding both the quantity and the quality of educational opportunities, mental health treatment, and other rehabilitative programs in juvenile facilities, with at least one study suggesting that some young offenders might find better programming in adult institutions (Ng, Sarri, Shook, & Stoffregen, 2012). At the same time—lest the deficiencies of juvenile facilities be seen as an argument for handling more young offenders in the adult system—it is also important to note that some studies suggest that juveniles in adult prisons are more likely than their older fellow inmates to experience physical assault, sexual victimization, and disciplinary sanctions for rules violations (Kurlychek & Johnson, 2010).

Third, while juvenile courts have traditionally employed special procedures intended to prevent the public exposure of offenders' identities and to give them an opportunity to enter adulthood with a clean slate, juveniles are increasingly subject to long-term adverse consequences from their youthful mistakes—consequences that may prove to be no less severe and life-altering than the formal sanctions imposed for a delinquency adjudication. (These trends overlap with the phenomenon of "collateral consequences" for adult convictions, which we considered in Q24.) Importantly, during the get-tough 1990s, many states relaxed the confidentiality protections for juvenile court records. Seven states now permit full public access to juvenile court records, while thirty-three others provide for partial access (McMullen, 2018). Additionally, even information that is not available to the general public can typically be shared with schools, law enforcement personnel, and other government agencies, which can lead to discrimination by those agencies, as well as "leakage" to prospective employers and other private parties. Of course, in the Internet age, whatever information gets out today may remain readily available to the public in perpetuity. Juveniles who commit sexual offenses—which might include consensual relations with a boyfriend or girlfriend of about the juvenile's same age—have been particularly affected by the erosion of confidentiality protections, with many now required to register as sex offenders and abide by the many legal restrictions that go along with that status (Nellis, 2016, 69–71).

Policy makers and court officials seem increasingly to appreciate that harshly punitive responses to juvenile crime are often unwarranted and that rehabilitative interventions are apt to prove better over the long run at protecting public safety and putting the juvenile offender on the path to a productive, law-abiding adulthood. Indeed, a growing body of research concludes that "states can handle most delinquents safely in community settings with cognitive-behavioral models of change" (Feld, 2017, 340). In any event, reformers have achieved their most notable legislative successes in the handful of states that have recently increased the cutoff age for their juvenile courts, reversing the trend of the 1990s. Preliminary research suggests that these reforms are not leading to increases in youth crime (Loeffler & Chalfin, 2017). A few states are even considering further increases to age twenty or twenty-one (Chester & Schiraldi, 2016, 13). Elsewhere, state- and local-level reformers have focused on developing, improving, and expanding diversion and community-based treatment options for juvenile offenders (Nellis, 2016, 83–92). A notable and surprising counterpart to such reform efforts has been a pair of decisions by the U.S. Supreme Court in *Graham v. Florida* (2010) and *Miller v. Alabama* (2012), which imposed new constitutional restrictions on the practice of sentencing juveniles to life without the possibility of parole.

To some extent, the impact of evolving policies and practices may be seen in a sharp decline in the number of juveniles confined in secure facilities, including a 44 percent drop between 1999 and 2011 (Nellis, 2016, 78). Much of the drop, though, simply reflects a reduction in youth crime and juvenile arrests, with the latter falling by 31 percent between 2002 and 2011. Still, the decline in delinquency adjudications (48 percent between 2005 and 2014) and out-of-home placements (50 percent) has been somewhat greater than the drop in referrals to juvenile court (42 percent), suggesting that there have been changes not only in the patterns of youth offending but also in the system's responses to juvenile crime (National Center for Juvenile Justice, 2017, 6, 45, 48).

FURTHER READING

Chester, Lael & Schiraldi, Vincent. 2016. *Public Safety and Emerging Adults in Connecticut: Providing Effective and Developmentally Appropriate Responses for Youth under Age 21*. Cambridge, MA: Malcolm Wiener Center for Social Policy, Harvard University.

Feld, Barry. 2017. "Juvenile Justice." In *Reforming Criminal Justice: Punishment, Incarceration, and Release*, 329. Edited by Erik Luna. Phoenix: Arizona State University.

Heaton, Leanne et al. 2016. *Facility-Level and Individual-Level Correlates of Sexual Victimization in Juvenile Facilities, 2012*. Washington, DC: U.S. Department of Justice.

Kolivoski, Karen & Shook, Jeffrey. 2016. "Incarcerating Juveniles in Adult Prisons: Examining the Relationship between Age and Prison Behavior in Transferred Juveniles." *Criminal Justice and Behavior*, 43, 1242.

Kurlychek, Megan & Johnson, Brian. 2010. "Juvenility and Punishment: Sentencing Juveniles in Adult Criminal Court." *Criminology*, 48, 725.

Lehmann, Peter, Chiricos, Ted, & Bales, William. "Juveniles on Trial: Mode of Conviction and the Adult Court Sentencing of Transferred Juveniles." *Crime & Delinquency*. Prepublished June 14, 2017.

Loeffler, Charles & Chalfin, Aaron. 2017. "Estimating the Crime Effects of Raising the Age of Majority: Evidence from Connecticut." *Criminology & Public Policy*, 16, 45.

Marley, Patrick. 2016. "Crisis at Lincoln Hills Juvenile Prison Years in Making." *Milwaukee Journal Sentinel*, December 17. Retrieved from https://www.jsonline.com/story/news/investigations/2016/12/17/crisis-lincoln-hills-juvenile-prison-years-making/95383518/.

McMullen, Judi. 2018. "Invisible Stripes: The Problem of Youth Criminal Records." *Southern California Review of Law and Social Justice*, 27, 1.

National Center for Juvenile Justice. 2017. *Juvenile Court Statistics: 2014*. Pittsburgh, PA: National Council of Juvenile and Family Court Judges.

Nellis, Ashley. 2016. *A Return to Justice: Rethinking Our Approach to Juveniles in the System*. New York: Rowman & Littlefield.

Ng, Irene, Sarri, Rosemary, Shook, Jeffrey, & Stoffregen, Elizabeth. 2012. "Comparison of Correctional Services for Youth Incarcerated in Adult and Juvenile Facilities in Michigan." *Prison Journal*, 92, 460.

Reaves, Brian. 2013. *Felony Defendants in Large Urban Counties, 2009—Statistical Tables*. Washington, DC: U.S. Department of Justice.

Q28: ARE MENTALLY ILL OFFENDERS ABLE TO GET THE TREATMENT THEY NEED THROUGH THE CRIMINAL JUSTICE SYSTEM?

Answer: Prisons and jails are legally obligated to provide at least some minimal level of treatment to mentally ill inmates who are in need of it, but treatment resources are notoriously spread thin. While some mentally ill inmates are able to receive effective care behind bars, others have little or no access to individualized treatment from which they might benefit. Additionally, there are concerns that certain aspects of institutional life, including the use of special housing units for "problem" inmates, may tend to exacerbate mental illness. Moreover, whatever treatment is received behind bars, there are apt to be difficulties with maintaining continuity of care after release. In light of skepticism that the system manages mental illness effectively during and after incarceration, there is growing interest in diversion programs that put mentally ill offenders into supervised treatment in the community.

The Facts: Mental illness is common among the inmates of America's jails and prisons. By some measures, a majority of inmates may be afflicted. For instance, in a 2011–2012 survey, slightly more than one-half of prisoners, and fully 64 percent of jail inmates, reported either current symptoms of serious psychological distress or a mental illness diagnosis at some time in the past (Bronson & Berzofsky, 2017). The most common diagnosis was for a major depressive disorder. Serious psychological distress was about three times more prevalent among prison inmates, and about five times more prevalent among jail inmates, than in the general adult population. Female inmates were significantly more likely to report indicators of mental illness than male. For instance, the percentage of female prisoners with a past diagnosis (66 percent) was almost twice as high as that of male prisoners (35 percent).

Other studies using different criteria find varying results, but the research consistently points to higher rates of mental illness among inmates than in the general population. Not surprisingly, similar trends are apparent among offenders on community supervision. In one survey, for instance, individuals who had been on probation or parole in the past twelve months were more than twice as likely to report symptoms of serious psychological distress as were adults in the general population (Bronson & Berzofsky, 2017). Another study found that individuals currently or recently on probation suffered from elevated rates of psychosis, mania, and posttraumatic stress disorder (PTSD) when compared with the general population (Crilly et al., 2009). These figures on the prevalence of mental illness do not even include substance use (addiction) disorders, which will be considered separately later.

The well-established correlation between mental illness and justice system involvement reflects a complicated and uncertain web of causal connections. In some cases, mental disorders may contribute to criminal behavior. Perhaps, most important, the efforts of mentally ill individuals to "self-medicate" may lead to illegal drug use. On the other hand, and despite stereotypes to the contrary, it is not clear that the mentally ill are any more prone to commit serious violent crime than others, especially when the effects of substance abuse are factored out. As one researcher has put it, "Most people with mental disorder do not engage in serious criminal behavior and are more likely to be victims of violence than perpetrators. . . . The strongest association between mental disorder and violent conduct is self-harm, especially suicide by gun" (Morse, 2017, 260).

If elevated rates of offending do not fully account for the correlation between mental illness and justice system involvement, a variety of other explanations are available. For instance, mental illness and related behaviors, deficits, and stereotypes may increase the likelihood of apprehension and conviction after the commission of an offense, the risk of *wrongful* conviction, and the severity of sentences. Additionally, some—but not all—studies suggest that prisoners with mental illness are less likely than other inmates to receive favorable parole decisions (Matejkowski, Caplan, & Cullen, 2010, 1020–21). It is also likely that the stresses of justice system involvement cause or exacerbate mental illness in some individuals. For instance, as we noted in Q19, the use of solitary confinement in prisons may contribute to mental disorder among inmates.

At least one additional aspect of the mental illness/justice system relationship merits attention. In the first half of the twentieth century, the United States relied heavily on involuntary institutional commitments as a response to mental health problems, with hundreds of thousands of "patients" held, often in wretched conditions, in large state mental hospitals (Harcourt, 2011). However, for a variety of practical and humanitarian reasons, these institutions fell out of favor by the century's middle decades. As the preferred model of care shifted from institutional to community based, the old mental hospitals did empty and close, but the hoped-for new system of neighborhood clinics and other local treatment centers was never adequately funded. By default, police, courts, and corrections departments often became the agencies primarily responsible for managing both mental health crises and the lower-level behavioral problems that can make some mentally ill individuals community irritants. Naturally, these agencies tended to employ the basic tools of criminal justice coercion that were most familiar to them. Ironically, then, many of the individuals who would have been institutionalized in the old system also wound up institutionalized in the new system, but in jails or prisons instead of mental hospitals. Labeled "transinstitutionalization," this phenomenon is sometimes identified as a major contributor to the great imprisonment boom of the late twentieth century. While some of these claims are overstated (Schlanger, 2017, 297), it is probably true that many individuals are regularly cycling through the jails in some jurisdictions as a result of repeated low-level criminal misconduct that is related to an untreated or poorly treated mental illness.

Whatever the specific numbers and the underlying causes, American correctional institutions find themselves in custody of a large population of mentally ill individuals, and there are several good reasons why they should want to provide effective treatment for this group. For one thing, all inmates with known, treatable health care needs, including *mental* health care needs, have a constitutional right to treatment. On the other hand, the constitutional standards for quality of care are not necessarily very high (Morse, 2017, 264), and, as we saw in Q15, it can be very difficult for prisoners to enforce their constitutional rights in court. Federal disabilities statutes (the Rehabilitation Act and the Americans with Disabilities Act) arguably set a higher standard of care, but the law in this area remains poorly developed (Schlanger, 2017, 315–17).

Yet, even if not legally required to provide much by way of treatment, corrections officials might still find it in their interest to try to alleviate mental illness. Inmates with mental health problems seem more likely to get into trouble behind bars. For instance, in the 2011–2012 survey of prison and jail inmates, those who indicated a mental health problem were two to three times more likely to be written up or charged with assault (Bronson & Berzofsky, 2017, 9). Similarly, a review of corrections records in at least one state has confirmed a statistically significant correlation between having a severe, diagnosed mental illness and being disciplined for institutional misconduct (Matejkowski, Caplan, & Cullen, 2010). Indeed, not surprisingly, mentally ill inmates were identified in one survey of jail administrators as the group most responsible for institutionally disruptive behavior (Ruddell, 2006). The study found that "inmates with mental illness were perceived to be involved in problematic behaviors at nearly twice the rate of the next nearest group, gang members."

From a broader societal perspective, treatment may also seem important insofar as it reduces recidivism risk. Mental illness is correlated in some studies with repeat offending and returns to prison, although it is not clear whether and to what extent mental illness functions as a risk factor independently of other variables (Osterman & Matejkowski, 2014). Because it is correlated with other risk factors, such as unemployment and homelessness, mental illness in and of itself may not contribute much to recidivism. Still, the treatment of mental illness may carry crime-reduction benefits by mitigating or reducing other risk factors. For instance, mentally ill homeless offenders may not recidivate any more frequently than other homeless offenders, but treatment of the mentally ill may nonetheless reduce overall recidivism if that means that some of the treated are able to avoid or escape homelessness.

Of course, beyond such instrumental arguments, many people believe that there exists an ethical imperative for society to aid individuals who are in deep psychological distress, especially if society has rendered them unable to procure help on their own by putting them behind bars. The imperative may be even greater still to the extent that various common corrections practices, such as chronic institutional overcrowding and the routine use of solitary confinement, tend to exacerbate mental disorders. It is also well documented that mentally ill inmates are particularly vulnerable to exploitation and abuse behind bars (see Q18; Schlanger, 2017, 298–300). Elevated suicide rates offer a particularly stark demonstration of the desperate circumstances in which some of these inmates find themselves.

However, despite such considerations, mental health treatment, like so many other potentially beneficial services for inmates, remains underfunded. For instance, in the 2011–2012 survey, only about one-third of prison and jail inmates reporting symptoms of serious psychological distress were currently receiving treatment (Bronson & Berzofsky, 2017, 8). The gaps in care are especially acute in jails. Among inmates in serious psychological distress in these local institutions, fewer than 13 percent reported that they were receiving counseling or therapy from a trained professional. Meanwhile, in a survey of 134 jails in 39 states, one-half reported no mental health unit, one-quarter reported no mental health case managers, and nearly one-tenth reported no mental health training for officers (Ruddell, 2006, 125). Some research suggests that deficiencies in both the availability and the quality of mental health care may be most acute for African American inmates (Thompson, Newell, & Carlson, 2016).

In prisons and jails, the treatment of first resort is apt to be medication, sometimes with little or no counseling to go along with the drugs. Prison inmates report somewhat higher, and jail inmates *much* higher, rates of medication than counseling (Bronson & Berzofsky, 2017, 8). These patterns reflect the fiscal pressures that limit treatment resources, but they may not embody the most effective therapeutic strategy. For many psychiatric patients, drugs provide little or no relief (Morse, 2017, 258). Moreover, achieving optimal effectiveness with these medications often requires more labor-intensive, individualized care than is available in many institutions (264). Similarly, counseling for inmates tends to be in the form of group sessions, which are less costly, but also potentially less effective, than individual sessions (266).

Concerns have also been raised about the quality and dedication of some correctional treatment providers. Clinicians tend not to regard prisons and jails as the most desirable practice settings. Critics charge that correctional institutions sometimes "become the employers of last resort for subpar clinicians" (Schlanger, 2017, 320). There is also research suggesting that prison-based treatment providers "tend to be more jaded and less empathetic toward their patients when compared with their civilian counterparts."

Additional treatment issues arise after release—"when prisoners usually leave with only a few days' worth, if that, of any medication, without a doctor's appointment to get a refill, and often far from their families without transportation home" (Schlanger, 2017, 318). The Affordable Care Act ("Obamacare") has eased matters a bit in the thirty-plus states that agreed to expand their Medicaid systems (321). In these states, nearly all inmates are now eligible for Medicaid, which can facilitate the transition from institutional to community care for mental illnesses. Still, the affected former inmates "carry the double stigma of a mental illness and a criminal history," which may further exacerbate the normal challenges faced by returning citizens in finding housing, getting a job, and reestablishing family and other social relationships (Fisher et al., 2014, 813–14). Such difficulties may have important implications for mental health, recidivism risk, and the likelihood of a return to prison (see Q24). Criminal history stigma may also create obstacles to finding a willing care provider in the community, as may a lack of private insurance and difficulties in navigating the public assistance bureaucracies. Additionally, some researchers have raised concerns about the capacity and willingness of parole officers to identify the mental health needs of their clients and to provide help for the mentally ill in accessing treatment resources (Thompson, Newell, & Carlson, 2016).

While there are good reasons to wish for improvements in the quality and quantity of treatment programs available to mentally ill offenders, both inside and outside correctional institutions, it is important to note that even the highest quality of care cannot always ensure either a prompt, durable alleviation of symptoms or a cessation of unlawful activities. Although mental illnesses are often casually analogized to physical ailments, their diagnosis and treatment may present much deeper challenges than is the case with some familiar infectious diseases. Individuals who report similar problematic moods, attitudes, and behaviors may receive the same mental health diagnosis on that basis, but the underlying causes may be quite different, as may the responsivity of symptoms to varying treatments (Morse, 2017, 255). We have already noted the difficulties with pharmaceutical approaches. "There is essentially no marker to guide clinicians in the choice of which drug from within an appropriate class will work best. There are general guidelines, but therapy is empirically guided in individual cases" (258). Prescribing physicians must carefully follow up with their patients to determine whether medications are having the desired effects and to address sometimes-serious problems with side effects. Similarly, there are also important gaps in the research about what works best in the area of non-pharmaceutical treatment (counseling) (266).

Even as it is important to have realistic expectations about what treatment can accomplish, many studies do suggest that therapeutic programs can benefit a sizeable share of mentally ill offenders. Indeed, recent meta-analyses of dozens of studies conclude that therapeutic interventions have been associated with statistically significant reductions in both symptoms and recidivism (Martin et al., 2011; Morgan et al., 2011).

Thus far, we have not considered substance use disorders in our assessment of mental illness. It is clear that the use of alcohol, marijuana, and other psychoactive substances is common among justice-involved individuals. It is also clear that some mentally ill individuals turn to such substances as a sort of nonprescription self-medication. Less clear is whether and under what circumstances the use of these substances should be considered as a mental illness in its own right (Morse, 2017, 257). Nonetheless, it now seems widely accepted that offenders with substance-use problems should normally be offered treatment, either in lieu of or in addition to conventional criminal sanctions. Research provides moderate, albeit not unmixed, support for this view, with numerous studies finding that treatment is able to reduce drug use and/or recidivism more generally (Thompson, Newell, & Carlson, 2016; Welsh & Zajac, 2013). Much of the research has focused on one particular intervention, the drug treatment court, which was discussed in some detail in Q10. However, as with mental health treatment more generally, drug treatment resources in the criminal justice system are not sufficient to satisfy demand. For instance, while about half of prisoners meet diagnostic criteria for drug dependence or abuse, only about one-fifth of the inmates thought to be in need of treatment receive it (Welsh & Zajac, 2013).

Given the success of drug treatment courts, as well as concerns that incarceration may tend to exacerbate mental health problems, there has been growing interest in developing community-based diversion programs for mentally ill offenders, including specialized mental health courts that are closely modeled on drug courts. There are more than 400 mental health courts in operation, and studies find that at least some of them seem successful in reducing recidivism (Johnston & Flynn, 2017, 686–87). On the other hand, less work has been done to assess the impact of these courts on mental health symptoms and quality of life, and, as with drug courts, there are substantial risks that some participants may end up spending more time behind bars than they would have if processed through the conventional court system (686–87, 693). Other promising community-based initiatives include specially trained probation supervision teams and specialized day-reporting centers that offer psychiatric and other services for mentally ill offenders (Heilbrun et al., 2012; Carr, Baker, & Cassidy, 2016).

FURTHER READING

Bronson, Jennifer & Berzofsky, Marcus. 2017. *Indicators of Mental Health Problems Reported by Prison and Jail Inmates, 2011–2012*. Washington, DC: U.S. Department of Justice.

Carr, W. Amory, Baker, Amy, & Cassidy, James. 2016. "Reducing Criminal Recidivism with an Enhanced Day Reporting Center for Probationers with Mental Illness." *Journal of Offender Rehabilitation*, 55, 95.

Crilly, John et al. 2009. "Mental Health Services Use and Symptom Prevalence in a Cohort of Adults on Probation." *Psychiatric Services*, 60, 542.

Fisher, William et al. "Recidivism among Released State Prison Inmates Who Received Mental Health Treatment While Incarcerated." *Crime & Delinquency*, 60, 811.

Harcourt, Bernard. 2011. "Reducing Mass Incarceration: Lessons from the Deinstitutionalization of Mental Hospitals in the 1960s." *Ohio State Journal of Criminal Law*, 9, 53.

Heilbrun, Kirk et al. 2012. "Community-Based Alternatives for Justice-Involved Individuals with Severe Mental Illness: Review of the Relevant Research." *Criminal Justice & Behavior*, 39, 351.

Johnston, E. Lea & Flynn, Conor. 2017. "Mental Health Courts and Sentencing Disparities." *Villanova Law Review*, 62, 685.

Martin, Michael et al. 2011. "Stopping the Revolving Door: A Meta-Analysis on the Effectiveness of Interventions for Criminally Involved Individuals with Major Mental Disorders." *Law & Human Behavior*, 36, 1.

Matejkowski, Jason, Caplan, Joel, & Cullen, Sara Wiesel. 2010. "The Impact of Severe Mental Illness on Parole Decisions: Social Integration within a Prison Setting." *Criminal Justice and Behavior*, 37, 1005.

Morgan, Robert et al. 2011. "Treating Offenders with Mental Illness: A Research Synthesis." *Law & Human Behavior*, 36, 37.

Morse, Stephen. 2017. "Mental Disorder and Criminal Justice." In *Reforming Criminal Justice: Introduction and Criminalization*, 251. Edited by Erik Luna. Phoenix: Arizona State University.

Osterman, Michael & Matejkowski, Jason. 2014. "Exploring the Intersection of Mental Health and Release Status with Recidivism." *Justice Quarterly*, 31, 746.

Ruddell, Rick. 2006. "Jail Interventions for Inmates with Mental Illness." *Journal of Correctional Health Care*, 12, 118.

Schlanger, Margo. 2017. "Prisoners with Disabilities." In *Reforming Criminal Justice: Punishment, Incarceration, and Release*, 295. Edited by Erik Luna. Phoenix: Arizona State University.

Thompson, Melissa, Newell, Summer, & Carlson, Matthew. 2016. "Race and Access to Mental Health and Substance Abuse Treatment in the Criminal Justice System." *Journal of Offender Rehabilitation*, 55, 69.

Welsh, W. & Zajac, G. 2013. "A Multisite Evaluation of Prison-Based Drug Treatment: Four-Year Follow-Up Results." *Prison Journal*, 93, 251.

Q29: DO REGISTRATION, COMMUNITY NOTIFICATION, RESIDENCY RESTRICTION, AND CIVIL COMMITMENT LAWS HELP TO REDUCE THE THREAT POSED BY SEX OFFENDERS AFTER THEIR PRISON TERMS ARE COMPLETED?

Answer: Research indicates that sex-offender registration, community notification, and residency restrictions laws offer low, if any, net public-safety benefits. Laws that provide for indefinite "civil" commitment may help to prevent recidivism by the very small percentage of sexual offenders who engage in serial, predatory assaults. However, there remain substantial concerns that civil commitment laws do not represent the most cost-effective strategy for dealing with the risk posed by these offenders, and that, as implemented in some states, civil commitment may violate constitutional and ethical norms.

The Facts: The problem of child sex abuse became a matter of growing public concern in the United States in the 1970s and 1980s. In the light of several highly publicized stories of child abduction and molestation, perpetrators came to be seen as irredeemable deviants, who would continue to prey on young victims indefinitely in the absence of forceful state intervention. By the early 1990s, many states were adopting new laws that were intended to supplement conventional criminal justice responses and establish greater control over sex offenders, typically without making much distinction between those with child and adult victims (Petrunik, Murphy, & Federoff, 2008). Most widely and swiftly established were sex offender registries. Registration laws require offenders to provide the authorities with certain personal information, including home address, and to update the information on a regular basis. Community notification provisions then make much of this information available to members of the public, including through Internet databases. In addition to the public shaming inherent in community notification, registered sex offenders may also be subject to a range of legal disabilities, including restrictions on where they can live. Finally, many states also adopted new civil commitment laws, which authorize the indefinite confinement of some sex offenders, potentially lasting many years or even decades after they have completed the prison terms to which they were formally sentenced.

A substantial body of research is now available to assess the effectiveness of these various enactments. The best known measures in this regard are sex offender registration and notification (SORN) laws. Adopted in all fifty states, SORN laws vary in their details from place to place, although uniformity is mandated in some respects by federal law. Proponents assert that SORN laws may reduce sex offending in at least three different ways. First, law enforcement agencies can make use of the registration information in order to more quickly identify and apprehend registered individuals when they commit new crimes. Second, the notification component of SORN laws may help vulnerable members of the public to take protective measures. For instance, if the parents of a child know that a sex offender lives in their neighborhood, they may warn the child to avoid that person. Finally, the stigma of appearing on a registry may serve as a deterrent to future would-be sexual offenders.

Despite these potential benefits, SORN laws have been criticized on several grounds (Logan, 2017, 398–99). First, registration is based on conviction of certain crimes, and not dangerousness as determined by an empirically validated risk-assessment instrument. Although having a particular conviction may be a relevant consideration, the most effective risk-assessment tools also take into account a number of additional variables, as we will see in the discussion of civil commitment laws below. The comparatively crude approach taken by SORN laws can cause many low-risk individuals to be caught in the registration net, including juveniles.

Second, SORN laws may exacerbate risk for many offenders, especially those who were not high-risk to begin with. In particular, the stigma of registration and the associated difficulties in securing stable housing, employment, and social relationships may leave some offenders more, rather than less, likely to offend. Third, SORN laws may create a false sense of security for the public and lead to a misdirection of attention and resources; while SORN laws are premised on the assumption that sexual assaults are normally perpetrated by predatory strangers and recidivists, the research instead indicates that the great majority of sex offenses are committed by someone who is known to the victim and who does not have a prior conviction. Finally, SORN laws encourage and facilitate vigilante actions against registrants. There are numerous documented instances, including "murders, assaults, and acts of vandalism and arson against registered offenders and their property" (Wright, 2008, 130).

Careful statistical analyses provide greater support for the critics than the proponents, with numerous studies finding very little or no statistically significant reduction in sex offense rates after the adoption of SORN laws. For instance, one study focused on Harris County in Texas (Houston) and sought to assess the impact of the initial implementation of the state's SORN law in 1991 and subsequent expansions of the law in 1997 and 2005 (Bouffard & Askew, 2017). The researchers found no statistically significant reduction in sex offense case filings after any of these three legal developments. Nor did they find any evidence of an impact when they looked more specifically at sex offenses against children, repeat offending, or first-time offending. Studies in other states have mostly reached similar conclusions (Levenson & Zgoba, 2016). Notably, two states that did experience drops in sex offender recidivism after implementing SORN laws, Minnesota and Washington, integrated empirically based risk assessment into their management of these offenders.

The debate over residency restrictions echoes the debate over SORN laws. In at least thirty states and thousands of municipalities, registered sex offenders are prohibited from living within a certain distance of various sensitive locations where children are often present, such as schools, parks, and day care centers (Levenson & Zgoba, 2016). As with SORN laws, residency restrictions seem premised on the (mistaken) belief that the threat of sexual crime comes mostly from predatory strangers who serially assault multiple victims. Also as with SORN laws, critics argue that residency restrictions may prove counterproductive to the extent that they further marginalize and stigmatize those with sexual convictions and impede their reintegration into society. In particular, with affordable housing in very short supply in many cities, restrictions may leave many

sex offenders without viable residence options, leading to a greater incidence of homelessness and transience. Of course, among other problems,
this tendency cuts against the objective of SORN laws to ensure that law
enforcement agencies always have up-to-date information regarding registrants' whereabouts.

Residence restrictions have not been examined as extensively as
SORN laws, but the existing research casts considerable doubt on their
effectiveness (Stucky & Ottensmann, 2016). For instance, one multistate
study found that the number of reported rapes tended to *increase* after the
adoption of residence restrictions (Socia, 2015). Another study focused
on Jacksonville, Florida, and found that the expansion of a residence
restriction resulted in no statistically significant reduction in either sex
crime arrests or sex offender recidivism (Nobles, Levenson, & Youstin,
2012). Yet another study concerned New York State, where some counties have residence restrictions and others do not (Socia, 2012). The presence of a restriction was not associated with reduced rates of either sexual
repeat offending or sexual offending against children. Curiously, however,
counties with restrictions did have a lower rate of sex crimes against adults
committed by first-timers, suggesting that a fear of becoming subject to
residence restrictions may have a modest deterrent effect on prospective
offenders. Still, even if this result were generalizable to other jurisdictions,
there would be reason to question whether the limited deterrence benefits
outweigh the adverse and potentially risk-*increasing* effects of residence
restrictions on registrants.

Civil commitment presents a more complicated picture. While SORN
laws and residence restrictions can be quite harmful to the welfare of registered offenders, the impact of indefinite confinement—potentially lasting the rest of the offender's life—must be regarded as far more severe, and
hence as requiring a far more compelling justification.

Modern civil commitment laws, which have been adopted by twenty
states and the federal government, generally permit the continued confinement of a sex offender beyond his or her term of imprisonment if four
conditions are satisfied: (1) the person has a history of sexual offending,
(2) the person has a mental disorder or abnormality, (3) the person's ability to control his or her behavior is impaired, and (4) there is a likelihood of future sexual offending (Knighton et al., 2014). With about 5,400
individuals now confined under such laws, there have been substantial
challenges raised as to their constitutionality (Harris, 2017). While the
Supreme Court has upheld the concept of civil commitment, it has also
indicated that efforts must be made to treat the confined individuals and
provide them with some hope of eventual release. Indeed, in a few states,

courts have insisted on modifications to civil commitment programs so as to ensure better opportunities for "graduation." However, the need for treatment programs contributes to the extraordinarily high cost of civil commitment, which is estimated to exceed $100,000 per inmate per year, or about triple the cost of conventional imprisonment.

Are civil commitment laws helping to protect Americans from the threat of sexual victimization? High costs have kept, and will likely continue to keep, the civil commitment population quite small relative to the overall number of sexual offenses. In 2016, for instance, there were more than 320,000 sexual assaults nationally (Morgan & Kena, 2017, 5). Against that backdrop, the 5,400 committed individuals would have had to have been rather prolific offenders for their presence in the community to have made much difference in the overall risk of sexual victimization. It becomes important to know, then, how successfully civil commitment laws target only the most dangerous serial sex offenders. Before turning to that question, though, we might recall the research, noted earlier, indicating that the great majority—two-third or more—of sexual offenses are committed by first-timers (Bouffard & Askew, 2017; Levenson & Zgoba, 2016). The relatively modest role of recidivism as a driver of sexual offending casts further doubt on the ability of long-term confinement of a relatively small number of recidivists to make a substantial difference in the incidence of sex crime.

Civil commitment laws, unlike their SORN counterparts, expressly confine their regulatory reach to offenders who have been individually identified as dangerous. If the standard criteria for civil commitment were rigorously applied, there would be good reason to think that only the highest-risk offenders were being held past the end of their sentences. Whether this is actually the case, though, is hard to know. On the one hand, civil commitment decisions are aided by increasingly sophisticated, empirically based risk-assessment tools, which have some demonstrable ability to predict the likelihood that a given person will reoffend. For instance, the Static-99 tool, which has been widely used with sex offenders, gives individuals a score based on ten factors, including number of prior convictions, age, and victim characteristics. Users can then ascertain the recidivism rate of other offenders who have had the same score in the past. Researchers have confirmed in multiple studies involving different sex offender populations that higher scores on this and similar tools are indeed correlated with higher rates of repeat offending (Hanson & Morton-Bourgon, 2009).

But, on the other hand, the scientific aspects of risk assessment are considered within a legal decision-making process that leaves much room for discretion, politics, and subjective value judgments. Ultimately, it will be a lay jury or judge that determines whether the requisite dangerousness threshold is met. States vary in how precisely the legal standard is defined (Knighton et al., 2014). In many states, the civil commitment decision turns on whether the offender is "likely" to reoffend sexually, with no particular probability specified. In such states, judges and jurors are essentially free to decide on a case-by-case basis "how safe is safe," creating a possibility that highly risk-averse decision makers might order confinement for offenders who most likely would not have committed new crimes after release. In other states, the law places the requisite likelihood of reoffense above 50 percent. Since the overall rate of sexual recidivism is only in the range of 10–15 percent (Hanson & Morton-Bourgon, 2009), the 50-percent-plus standard would, in principle, seem to reserve civil commitment for only a small proportion of the highest-risk offenders. However, there remain concerns about the ability of lay jurors, and to some extent also judges, to properly interpret the scientific data on risk, especially when it is filtered through competing expert witnesses in an adversarial legal proceeding. Moreover, since those for whom commitment is sought already have sexual convictions, and thus belong to a particularly stigmatized class of offenders, they are unlikely to get much benefit of the doubt in any aspect of their cases.

A study of jurors in Texas highlights the difficulties (Knighton et al., 2014). The researchers submitted questionnaires to individuals who actually served on civil commitment juries in 2009 and 2010 in order to ascertain their interpretation of the Texas civil commitment standards, "likely to engage in a predatory act of sexual violence." More than 90 percent of the jurors (153 in all) returned their questionnaires, with the majority indicating that even very low recidivism risks would satisfy the legal standard. For instance, nearly 54 percent of the jurors said that even a 1 percent chance of recidivism would be sufficient to support indefinite civil commitment. Similarly, nearly 82 percent of the jurors felt that a 15 percent risk of reoffense would suffice. As the researchers observed, "[I]t appears that most jurors would find the vast majority of sexual offenders eligible for civil commitment. . . . However, if most jurors find most sex offenders eligible for civil commitment, the civil commitment laws no longer serve their original purpose of intervening only with the most high-risk offenders" (302).

Two safeguards may to some extent mitigate this concern. First, jurors do not independently decide whom to target for civil commitment, but, rather, only become involved after a screening process involving various professionals in the fields of criminal justice and mental health. The specifics of this process differ a great deal from state to state. Initial screening may be performed by a mental health agency, a corrections department, or a law enforcement agency. The ultimate decision to file a civil commitment petition may be made by a local prosecutor or by a state attorney general. However, these screening processes are structured; the professionals in the system may help to ensure that jurors never have an opportunity to commit run-of-the-mill, low-risk sex offenders. A recent study in New York suggests that this safeguard may indeed contribute to the proper deployment of civil commitment laws (Sandler & Freeman, 2017). New York has a multistage, multiagency screening process. When the researchers studied the recidivism of individuals screened out at each stage of the process, they found steadily higher sexual rearrest rates, suggesting that the process worked as intended to remove more of the relatively low-risk offenders from the civil commitment pool each step of the way. Still, a couple of caveats are in order. For one thing, other states with simpler, more decentralized screening processes might not necessarily achieve the same results as New York. For another, at only about 11 percent, the recidivism rate of even those who were recommended for civil commitment at the end of the screening process was not especially high, suggesting that some of the sex offenders considered for commitment by the courts were hardly among the most dangerous.

A second safeguard is the requirement of a mental abnormality or disorder. Risk alone is not enough to trigger civil commitment but must be accompanied by and related to some diagnosed mental condition. In principle, this requirement might help to protect many of the run-of-the-mill sex offenders from confinement. However, in practice, there are concerns that this requirement is often applied in scientifically unsound ways that do not really accomplish much narrowing of the class of eligible offenders. For instance, one common diagnosis in civil commitment proceedings is "paraphilia not otherwise specified—nonconsent" (Prentky et al., 2006). This diagnosis purports to cover individuals who are sexually aroused by the resistance of a prospective sexual partner, which might indicate a predisposition to commit rape. However, there is little research to support the validity of this diagnosis or establish criteria for its application. Critics thus characterize it as a "wastebasket" diagnosis, so amorphous that it could be applied to "all sexual offenders with multiple offenses (spanning at least 6 months)" (367). If diagnoses like this are accepted, then the requirement of a mental abnormality or disorder adds very little in practice to the (perhaps no less amorphous) "likely to reoffend" requirement.

None of this is to suggest a complete absence of selectivity in applying civil commitment laws. Indeed, given how proportionately few sexual offenders are civilly committed, there is obviously in some sense a high degree of selectivity. Rather, the concern is that the selection processes are unsystematic, only loosely based on empirically derived risk-assessment tools, and liable to be influenced by questionable considerations— including the desire of elected prosecutors and judges to appear tough in dealing with the most feared and despised offenders moving through the criminal justice system.

Moreover, even to the extent that initial admission to civil commit-ment is limited to the highest-risk offenders, there are also serious ques-tions about the ability of these offenders to secure release after their dangerousness has diminished. To be sure, the effectiveness of treatment for sex offenders, in and of itself, seems limited (Morse, 2017, 258–59), albeit not entirely hopeless (Olver & Wong, 2009). However, whatever the efficacy of treatment, the simple passage of time normally reduces risk. For all violent offenses, prevalence rates peak in the teen years and then tail off in adulthood (Prentky et al., 2006). With respect to sexual offend-ing in particular, much research points to steadily declining sexual desire and activity in middle age and thereafter, which likely complements the normal tendency for individuals to desist from crime as they age. Over-all, it has been estimated that a person's risk of sexual reoffense can be expected to drop by about 2 percent each year after age forty (377). Such aging dynamics are especially important to bear in mind in the present context since those who are in civil confinement tend to be an older offender group—after all, they are normally not considered for this status until they have reached the end of a prison term that was imposed for a serious offense. Thus, taking age and treatment effects into account, we might expect that many of the civilly committed would "graduate" from the highest risk categories within a few years of admission.

Despite such expectations, it has proven extremely difficult to obtain release in some states. For instance, over the first two decades of Minneso-ta's civil commitment law, not one of the 700 offenders committed under the law was permitted to return home—even though more than thirty of them were in their seventies (Davey, 2015). Similarly, over the first 15 years of its program, Missouri released only 7 of 250 committed offenders.

Low release rates reflect a combination of practical and political con-siderations. Ideally, the release process would include a transitional period of close supervision in a special facility in the community (Prentky et al., 2006). However, no neighborhood wants to host such a facility. If it is even possible to create a transitional program, public concerns demand extensive (and expensive) precautions. Thus, some states have found the per offender costs of transitional housing to be twice the cost of regular civil confinement (Harris, 2017). Such costs discourage release from regular confinement—as more generally does the reluctance of politically accountable officials to approve the release of individuals bearing the "sexual predator" label that typically accompanies civil commitment.

In short, the picture that emerges of civil commitment in practice includes the confinement of some individuals who most likely were not going to reoffend sexually after their release from prison, and the prolonged confinement of many other individuals past the point at which reoffense can be expected. At the same time, civil commitment does surely succeed in incapacitating *some* genuinely dangerous individuals. Does the prevention of horrific crimes by a few individuals justify taking away the freedom of a number of other individuals who would do nothing wrong if released? The question presents a difficult and troubling philosophical dilemma. At a minimum, ethical considerations—and, for that matter, a due regard for individual constitutional rights—may demand the implementation of more rigorous safeguards to ensure that civil commitment is truly reserved for only those offenders who present a demonstrably high level of present danger.

Better still might be the replacement of the current institutionalization model of civil commitment with a community-based alternative. "Civil commitment" in the community would involve intensive supervision by corrections agents, often including electronic monitoring. As discussed in Q9, recent research has been supportive of GPS-based electronic monitoring as a recidivism-reduction tool. Although more expensive than conventional parole, the intensive community supervision model of civil commitment would nonetheless cost far less than the institutionalization model. It could thus be used with a larger number of offenders and potentially have a greater impact on overall rates of sexual victimization. Additionally, while there might continue to be significant ethical and constitutional concerns with indefinite community supervision beyond sentence completion, the restrictions on liberty would at least be somewhat less than with institutionalization. New York already makes intensive community supervision available as a civil commitment option, and other states have developed their own variations on this theme (Rydberg, 2017, 942). However, more research is necessary to determine the costs and benefits of this approach.

FURTHER READING

Bouffard, Jeff & Askew, LaQuana. 2017. "Time-Series Analyses of the Impact of Sex Offender Registration and Notification Law Implementation and Subsequent Modifications on Rates of Sexual Offenses." *Crime & Delinquency*. Prepublished July 27, 2017.

Davey, Monica. 2015. "States Struggle with What to Do with Sex Offenders after Prison." *New York Times*, October 29. Retrieved from https://www.nytimes.com/2015/10/30/us/states-struggle-with-what-to-do-with-sex-offenders-after-prison.html.

Hanson, R. Karl & Morton-Bourgon, Kelly. 2009. "The Accuracy of Recidivism Risk Assessment for Sexual Offenders: A Meta-Analysis of 118 Prediction Studies." *Psychological Assessment*, 21, 1.

Harris, Andrew. 2017. "Policy Implications of New York's Sex Offender Civil Management Assessment Process." *Criminology & Public Policy*, 16, 949.

Knighton, Jefferson et al. 2014. "How Likely Is 'Likely to Reoffend' in Sex Offender Civil Commitment Trials?" *Law and Human Behavior*, 38, 293.

Levenson, Jill & Zgoba, Kristen. 2016. "Community Protection Policies and Repeat Sexual Offenses in Florida." *International Journal of Offender Therapy and Comparative Criminology*, 60, 1140.

Logan, Wayne. 2017. "Sex Offender Registration and Notification." In *Reforming Criminal Justice: Punishment, Incarceration, and Release*, 397. Edited by Erik Luna. Phoenix: Arizona State University.

Morgan, Rachel & Kena, Grace. 2017. *Criminal Victimization, 2016*. Washington, DC: U.S. Department of Justice.

Morse, Stephen. 2017. "Mental Disorder and Criminal Justice." In *Reforming Criminal Justice: Introduction and Criminalization*, 251. Edited by Erik Luna. Phoenix: Arizona State University.

Nobles, Matt, Levenson, Jill, & Youstin, Tasha. 2012. "Effectiveness of Residence Restrictions in Preventing Sex Offense Recidivism." *Crime & Delinquency*, 58, 491.

Olver, Mark & Wong, Stephen. 2009. "Therapeutic Responses of Psychopathic Sexual Offenders: Treatment Attrition, Therapeutic Change, and Long-Term Recidivism." *Journal of Consulting and Clinical Psychology*, 77. 328.

Petrunik, Michael, Murphy, Lisa, & Federoff, J. Paul. 2008. "American and Canadian Approaches to Sex Offenders: A Study of the Politics of Dangerousness." *Federal Sentencing Reporter*, 21, 111.

Prentky, Robert et al. 2006. "Sexually Violent Predators in the Courtroom: Science on Trial." *Psychology, Public Policy, and Law*, 12, 357.

Rydberg, Jason. 2017. "Civil Commitment and Risk Assessment in Perspective." *Criminology & Public Policy*, 16, 937.

Sandler, Jeffrey & Freeman, Naomi. 2017. "Evaluation of New York's Sex Offender Civil Management Assessment Process Recidivism Outcomes." *Criminology & Public Policy*, 16, 913.

Socia, Kelly. 2012. "The Efficacy of County-Level Sex Offender Residence Restrictions in New York." *Crime & Delinquency*, 58, 612.

Socia, Kelly. 2015. "State Residence Restrictions and Forcible Rape Rates: A Multistate Quasi-Experimental Analysis of UCR Data." *Sexual Abuse: A Journal of Research and Treatment*, 27, 205.

Stucky, Thomas & Ottensmann, John. 2016. "Registered Sex Offenders and Reported Sex Offenses." *Crime & Delinquency*, 62, 1026.

Wright, Richard. 2008. "From Wetterling to Walsh: The Growth of Federalization in Sex Offender Policy." *Federal Sentencing Reporter*, 21, 124.

Q30: SHOULD ELDERLY, DISABLED, AND CHRONICALLY ILL PRISONERS BE GIVEN "COMPASSIONATE RELEASE"?

Answer: One important legacy of the tougher sentencing laws and practices of the late twentieth century has been a rapid increase in the number of Americans who serve such long prison terms that they reach old age behind bars. Many of these inmates suffer from a wide range of debilitating health conditions. Nearly all states have established procedures—sometimes called "compassionate release"—to move inmates who are elderly, disabled, or terminally ill out of prison. However, the standards tend to be restrictive and the procedures slow and cumbersome. Some prison reform advocates favor making compassionate release more generous, based chiefly on the low recidivism risk and high cost of caring for inmates who are aged or infirm, as well as humanitarian considerations.

The Facts: Compassionate release provides an early-release opportunity to prisoners for whom continued incarceration presents special hardships, including those who are terminally ill, physically or mentally disabled, or simply very old. Compassionate release is structured quite differently in different jurisdictions, and goes by a variety of different names, including medical parole, medical furlough, and geriatric release. Programs of these sorts date back at least to the 1970s (Maschi et al., 2015). However, they have been expanded in many states since 2000 as a way to deal with growing prison populations and the unusually high expenses associated with ill and disabled inmates. At least forty-six states now offer some type of compassionate release (O'Hear, 2017, 60).

In principle, there seems a strong fiscal case for compassionate release. America's elderly inmate population has grown even more explosively since the 1970s than has the national prison population as a whole. There are now about a quarter-million inmates who are age fifty or older (American Civil Liberties Union, 2012, i). These prisoners are unusually expensive to incarcerate. While the average inmate costs about $34,000 per year, the average older inmate (fifty plus) costs $68,000—fully twice as much (ii). Much of the additional cost results from the disabilities and chronic illnesses that often afflict the elderly. About half of older prisoners suffer from diabetes, hypertension, arthritis, dementia, asthma, or other chronic conditions (28). While many elderly individuals on the outside also have such conditions, the particular circumstances of incarceration complicate treatment and tend to make illness and disability even more expensive to manage behind bars. For instance, specialized treatment needs may require a trip from the correctional institution to a hospital, with staff members needed to provide transportation and security—often paid at overtime rates. Consider the experience of one older female inmate:

> The shrunken 82-year-old wakes up every morning to change into her prison uniform. Then guards must outfit her with ankle chains, belly chains, and handcuffs. Next, she is transported 40 minutes for dialysis. She suffers from chronic renal failure, a condition that she figures costs the state $436,000 a year, not counting the two $24.75-an-hour armed corrections officers who guard her, all five feet and 90 pounds, for up to 8 hours a day three times a week. (Hillerman, 2007)

Even beyond medical treatment needs, older inmates may consume a disproportionate share of staff time to the extent that they require extra help with hygiene, eating, and other daily activities, as well as special accommodations in living arrangements (e.g., no upper bunks) and movement around the institution (e.g., extra time to reach dining facilities).

If the costs of imprisoning older inmates are exceptionally high, the public-safety benefits are exceptionally low. As we have noted before, recidivism risks fall as individuals age. For instance, in one national study, researchers found that prisoners released at age forty-five or later were returned to prison for a new crime within three years only about 17 percent of the time (American Civil Liberties Union, 2012, 22). By contrast, the rate for prisoners in the range of eighteen to twenty-four years was almost twice as high at 30 percent. Other studies focused on older inmate groups find even lower recidivism rates. In New York, for instance, only 4 percent of the inmates released at age sixty-five or older were returned to prison for a new crime, while in Virginia the rate for inmates released at age fifty-five or older was an even smaller 1.3 percent (23–24).

In light of such figures, it should not be surprising that so many states have adopted compassionate release laws. At the same time, however, the laws have not been designed in particularly generous ways. The modest pace of change doubtlessly reflects the fear of a public backlash if a notorious criminal were able to secure early release or if a seemingly harmless inmate defied expectations and committed a major violent crime after being let out.

By way of illustration, consider how the Wisconsin law operates. Inmates may seek a sentence modification on the basis of age or an "extraordinary healthy condition." Age-based release requires either that the inmate be at least sixty-five and have served at least five years behind bars, or be at least sixty and have served at least ten years. Individuals convicted of Class A or B felonies, that is, the most serious offenses, are excluded entirely. Of course, these tend to be the prisoners with the longest sentences—precisely those who could most benefit from compassionate release. Moreover, even for those inmates who meet the basic criteria for compassionate release, the process is slow and seemingly tilted against the petitioning prisoner. The inmate must first get approval from corrections officials, with no right to appeal if they refuse. Then, the inmate must file his or her petition with the original sentencing judge. Prosecutors and victims must also be given notice and an opportunity to oppose the petition. The burden is on the inmate to show that early release would be in the public interest. This vague legal standard leaves the judge with wide discretion to refuse release no matter how low the petitioner's recidivism risk. Thus, only about a handful of inmates receive compassionate release in Wisconsin each year, even though more than 1,200 of the state's prisoners are age 60 or older, and dozens of inmates die in prison annually (O'Hear, 2017, 61–62).

Wisconsin's experience is hardly unique. New York released only 371 prisoners through its medical parole program between 1992 and 2014—fewer than 17 per year (Bedard, 2015). Yet, the state averages about 100 inmate deaths from natural causes annually. Pennsylvania appears even more restrictive, with inmates required to prove that they are terminally ill and could receive better care outside of prison (Benzing, 2015). As a result, only nine prisoners obtained compassionate release between 2010 and mid-2015. Meanwhile, Virginia's geriatric parole program has more flexible criteria, but the outcomes are not much different: only forty-six releases between 2002 and 2013 (Hansen, 2013). In one year, even as

84 prisoners passed away behind bars in Virginia, fewer than 1 percent of the state's 800 eligible inmates received geriatric release.

If the legal standards and procedures for compassionate release were eased, many states would likely achieve substantial fiscal savings in their corrections budgets. To be sure, some of the costs of caring for elderly and disabled former inmates would simply be passed onto other government programs, such as Medicaid and Medicare. However, because care can often be provided more conveniently, effectively, and inexpensively in the community, especially to individuals who have supportive family members or others who are willing and able to assist with caregiving, there are good reasons to expect significant net cost savings for taxpayers. And, of course, compassionate release might also be favored out of a sense of mercy—a recognition that the indignities of old age and disability are apt to be greatly amplified in the prison setting, where privacy is almost nonexistent and any vulnerabilities are prone to exploitation by others.

At the same time, compassionate release does raise at least two sets of concerns, which come from quite different directions. From one side, there is fear that more robust release programs will lead to prisons simply "dumping" expensive older inmates who have no support on the outside and who may fare even worse than if they remained behind bars. It is thus important to ensure that inmates have viable reentry plans in place before they are given compassionate release.

From the other side, there is the objection that compassionate release constitutes unwarranted lenience. Purely age-based release seems particularly open to challenge on this basis. When a judge imposes a sentence that is likely to keep the defendant behind bars into old age, that will normally be perfectly clear at the time. We can presume that the judge deliberately chose to include old-age incarceration as an appropriate component of the defendant's punishment. It is not clear what would justify revisiting such choices on a routine basis. If there are concerns that judges are not sufficiently knowledgeable about the high costs and low risks of elderly inmates, then those concerns might be better addressed through a judicial education campaign than through an expansion of compassionate release. If, instead, the concern is that sentencing judges do not have sufficient incentives to take seriously the inefficiency (or indignity) of old-age imprisonment, a more straightforward policy response would be to eliminate life-without-parole sentences (an important contributor to the explosion in the number of elderly inmates) and impose tighter restrictions on the use of other multidecade sentences.

Compassionate release for illness or disability presents a different picture. While some decline in health behind bars may be foreseeable when a long sentence is imposed, a judge cannot know the precise pace or extent of decline. The appearance or aggravation of a serious health condition during a prison term may well be a fact that would have led to a different sentence if it had been anticipated by the judge. For instance, the judge who imposes a twenty-year prison term on a forty-year-old will not normally think of that as a life sentence, but cancer or heart disease can effectively bring about that result. Whatever purposes the judge hoped to serve through the twenty-year term might no longer appear so well served when the prisoner receives his or her terminal diagnosis. Major, unexpected health developments like this do seem a reasonable basis for reconsidering punishment.

Yet, several difficult questions remain as to how compassionate release ought to be conceived and structured. For instance, should the petition go for final decision to the sentencing judge, as in Wisconsin, or to a parole board or other executive agency, as in New York and Virginia? The judge would be in the best position to answer whether the sentence would have been different if the current health condition had been foreseen, while an executive agency would best ensure statewide consistency in the way that new information about health conditions is assessed. An appropriate state agency might also have some expertise in the practical realities of managing various disabilities and chronic illnesses behind bars, including the costs and availability of care.

Additionally, there may be particular difficulties in states that purport to practice "truth in sentencing," with no or very minimal opportunities for conventional parole release (see Q23). In such states, many victims of major crimes have the expectation that the offender will fully serve whatever prison term is imposed by the judge. Compassionate release might then feel like a slap in the face. It seems only fair to give victims advance notice and an opportunity to be heard on compassionate release decisions. It is less clear, though, how much weight ought to be given to victim views. Should victim opposition alone be enough to keep behind bars an inmate who is terribly expensive to incarcerate and who would pose virtually no risk in the community? Critics contend that such an elevation of private interests may not be appropriate for a criminal justice system that purports to punish in the name of the public interest.

FURTHER READING

American Civil Liberties Union. 2012. *At America's Expense: The Mass Incarceration of the Elderly*. New York: American Civil Liberties Union.

Bedard, Rachael. 2015. "When Dying Alone in Prison Is Too Harsh a Sentence." *New York Times*, December 28. Retrieved from https://www.nytimes.com/2015/12/28/opinion/when-dying-alone-in-prison-is-too-harsh-a-sentence.html.

Benzing, Jeffrey. 2015. "Prison Release Rarely an Option for Dying State Inmates." *PublicSource*, June 14. Retrieved from http://publicsource.org/investigations/prison-release-rarely-option-for-dying-state-inmates#.VubeH_krIdU.

Hansen, Louis. 2013. "Uncommon Freedom: Geriatric Release from Prison Rare." *The Virginian-Pilot*, December 28. Retrieved from http://pilotonline.com/news/local/crime/uncommon-freedom-geriatric-release-from-prison-rare/article_e41dd00b-bfb9-5478-9e1c-ff77f84ad732.html.

Hillerman, Ron. 2007. "Older Prisoners: Is There Life after 'Life' Sentencing? A White Paper." In *Policy and Program Planning for Older Adults*, 351. Edited by E. Jurkowski. New York: Springer.

Maschi, Tina et al. 2015. *An Analysis of United States Compassionate and Geriatric Release Laws: Towards a Rights-Based Response for Diverse Elders and Their Families and Communities.* New York: Fordham University Be the Evidence Press. Retrieved from https://www.researchgate.net/publication/275652571_An_Analysis_of_United_States_Compassionate_and_Geriatric_Release_Laws_Towards_a_Rights-Based_Response_for_Diverse_Elders_and_Their_Families_and_Communities 2/14/16.

O'Hear, Michael. 2017. *The Failure of Sentencing Reform.* Santa Barbara, CA: Praeger.

6

❖❖❖

Causes and Significance of
"Mass Incarceration"

It is often said that the United States has entered an era of "mass incarceration." It is certainly true that current U.S. incarceration rates are near all-time historical highs, and that the United States stands out internationally for its exceptionally heavy use of imprisonment. There is less consensus as to the cause of high-incarceration rates in the United States. High rates of crime, and especially violent crime, in the late twentieth century were likely an important driver, as were the increasingly tough-on-crime tendencies of American policy makers, prosecutors, and judges. Eventually, as incarceration rates reached record levels, crime rates did come down. However, the recent association between high incarceration and low crime does not necessarily mean that incarceration rates must remain high in order to prevent a return to the much higher crime rates of the late 1980s and early 1990s.

Q31: HOW DOES THE U.S. INCARCERATION
RATE COMPARE TO INTERNATIONAL
AND HISTORICAL NORMS?

Answer: During a three-decade era of sustained growth beginning in the 1970s, the American imprisonment rate (i.e., the number of prisoners per 100,000 residents) reached new highs that were unprecedented in the nation's history. The rate has dipped a little since the peak but remains far above the nation's historical norms. Similarly, the American imprisonment rate is far higher than that of virtually any other nation.

The Facts: After a long period of stability, the American imprisonment rate began to rise sharply and consistently in the early 1970s, as depicted in Figure 6.1. Between 1925, when the federal government began to systematically collect national data, and 1972, the rate floated between 79 and 138 prisoners per 100,000 U.S. residents. In the three decades prior to 1972, the rate remained even more narrowly between 90 and 120. However, over the next three decades, the number increased almost every single year. Between 1972 and the peak year of 2007, the American imprisonment rate more than quintupled to 527 per 100,000. Since 2007, the rate has steadily declined but remains far above mid-twentieth-century norms. The 2016 rate of 464 per 100,000 stands about four-and-a-half times higher than the prevailing rates of the 1940s through the early 1970s.

"Imprisonment rate" can be contrasted with "incarceration rate." While the former counts only the individuals who are held under the jurisdiction of state and federal prison systems, the latter also includes those held in local jails. Because jail data were not systematically collected prior to the

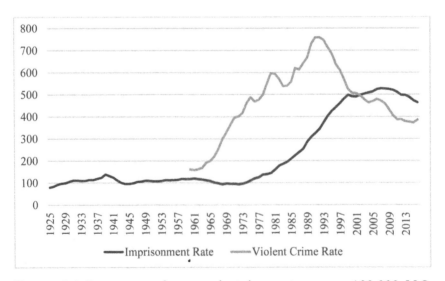

Figure 6.1 Prisoners and reported violent crimes, per 100,000 U.S. residents.

Source: United States Bureau of Justice Statistics; Federal Bureau of Investigation.

1970s, it is much harder to track incarceration rate trends over extended periods of time. However, since the 1970s, it is clear that incarceration rates have generally followed the same path as imprisonment rates. Jail populations are consistently about half the size of prison populations. Thus, the overall incarceration rate grew from 161 per 100,000 in 1972 to 767 per 100,000 in 2007—mirroring the quintupling of the imprisonment rate over the same time period (Committee on Causes and Consequences of High Rates of Incarceration, 2014, 33). As with the imprisonment rate, the incarceration rate has since dropped but remains more than four times higher than its 1972 level. This ongoing phenomenon of historically high rates of prison and jail confinement is often referred to as "mass incarceration."

Other sorts of criminal justice supervision also stand at relatively high levels. The probation rate rose from 423 per 100,000 in 1976 to 1,274 per 100,000 in 2010 (Committee on Causes and Consequences of High Rates of Incarceration, 2014, 40). Likewise, the post-prison supervision rate rose from 66 per 100,000 in 1975 to 271 per 100,000 in 2012. Overall, at the end of 2015, one out of every thirty-seven U.S. adults was subject to some form of incarceration or supervision (Kaeble & Glaze, 2016, 4).

Such national averages mask wide state-to-state variations. Table 6.1 reveals the wide gap between the top and bottom three imprisoning states in 2016. Still, even the lowest-imprisoning states have imprisonment rates today that are two to three times higher than they were four decades earlier. National averages also mask sharp racial differences. These racial disparities will be considered in Chapter 7.

Table 6.1 Prisoners per 100,000 adult residents

Top Three	
Louisiana	997
Oklahoma	891
Mississippi	822
Bottom Three	
Maine	169
Massachusetts	195
Rhode Island	239

Source: Carson (2018).

Incarceration rates are usefully compared with crime rates. Figure 6.1 includes data on major violent crimes (nonnegligent homicide, rape, robbery, and aggravated assault) reported to the police since 1960. The violent crime rate rose swiftly after 1961, eventually peaking three decades later at a point nearly five times higher—a level of increase that corresponds remarkably closely to the quintupling of national incarceration rates. In short, if crime prevalence is taken into account, then late twentieth-century incarceration rates do not seem so out of step with historical norms. On the other hand, violent crime rates fell precipitously after 1991, and now stand at only about half their peak. Incarceration rates have dropped far more modestly. Seen in this light, current incarceration rates remain historically anomalous.

U.S. incarceration rates are high not only by historical norms but also relative to other nations. Table 6.2 depicts incarceration rates in the G8, a group of leading industrialized nations. The rate in the United States stands far above that in any of the other nations, including nearly five times higher than that in the United Kingdom (here, England and Wales) and more than six times higher than that in Canada—the two nations of the world that are perhaps closest to the United States politically and culturally. The gap with other Western European nations and Japan is greater. The United States even far outpaces Russia. Indeed, according to data compiled by the International Centre for Prison Studies regarding 223 prison systems around the globe, only tiny Seychelles has a higher incarceration rate than the United States, with no other country even close.

These differences can be partly explained by reference to crime rates. The United States has unusually high rates of lethal violence among

Table 6.2 Prison and jail inmates per 100,000 residents

United States	698
Russia	445
United Kingdom	148
Canada	106
France	95
Italy	86
Germany	78
Japan	48

Source: International Centre for Prison Studies (2016).

Western-style industrialized democracies. For instance, the United States has more—in some cases *many* more—intentional homicides per capita than Canada, France, Germany, Italy, and the United Kingdom (Malby, 2010, 14). Yet, in other respects, crime patterns in the United States do not stand out so much in comparison with these peer nations. Canada has a higher rate of reported rapes than the United States, and the United Kingdom is not much behind the United States (Hesikanen, 2010, 38–39). The United Kingdom reports a much higher assault rate than the United States, while Canada and Germany are in the same range as the United States (36–37). Similarly, the United Kingdom reports a higher robbery rate than the United States, and Italy is not far behind the United States (41). Likewise, the United Kingdom has a much higher burglary rate than the United States, while Canada, France, and Germany are in the same range (43). Across all of these categories of serious crime, the American-European disparities in offense rates tend to be much smaller than the disparities in incarceration rates.

Thus, disparate incarceration reflects not merely disparities in crime but also in sentencing policies and practices. No other Western nation adopted the sorts of extreme tough-on-crime sentencing laws that the United States did in the late twentieth century, such as mandatory life-without-parole and three-strikes-and-you-are-out laws (Tonry, 2016a, 462). While life-without-parole sentences are authorized in a few other countries, they are only very rarely imposed in practice. In most Western nations, the longest permissible sentence for any crime short of murder is in the range of twelve to twenty-one years—normally subject to a one-third reduction for good behavior in prison. By contrast, in American jurisdictions, life (with or without parole) and other multidecade sentences are often authorized for a variety of nonhomicide, and even nonviolent, offenses (Nellis, 2017, 12).

In many other Western nations, including Germany and England, fewer than 10 percent of offenders are sentenced to incarceration (Tonry, 2016a, 484–85). Comparable national-level data are not available for the United States, but the percent-incarcerated figure here is without a doubt far higher. For instance, in Pennsylvania, 45 percent of offenders (felony and misdemeanor) are put behind bars. In the federal system, the figure is 93 percent. And among felony defendants in large urban counties, 73 percent are sentenced to jail or prison.

There are a variety of different theories to account for the relative harshness of American sentencing. For instance, the U.S. culture of prosecuting and judging is quite distinctive. While American state-court judges and head prosecutors are typically elected and thus subject to tough-on-crime political dynamics, judges and prosecutors throughout the rest of the Western world are normally apolitical career civil servants (Tonry, 2016b, 3). Moreover, prosecutors outside the United States are not thought of as partisans in an adversarial system of justice, but rather as impartial judicial or quasi-judicial officials. In any event, prosecutors elsewhere do not exercise the degree of control over sentencing outcomes that has become common in the United States (see Q2).

Yet, while these differences in the roles of prosecutors and judges may play an important role in determining sentencing severity, they also beg the question, why have politically accountable legislators in Europe caused or permitted their national court processes to operate in so politically insulated and lenient a fashion? By contrast, faced with, say, Finland's 3 percent incarceration rate in criminal cases (Tonry, 2016a, 485), one imagines that many American legislators would be quick to demand the adoption of mandatory minimum prison terms. The question raises many complicated issues of political culture and social values that lie beyond the scope of this book, but one particularly influential theory offered by the legal historian James Q. Whitman in 2005 is worthy of note. Whitman traces the roots of the European-American punishment divide back more than two centuries. From early in their history, Americans developed distinctively egalitarian values and a deep suspicion of government, which proved at odds with both the exercise of official mercy in criminal cases and a European-style bureaucratization of the justice system. These long-standing tendencies, Whitman contends, have contributed to the harsher sentencing and corrections practices of the United States today.

FURTHER READING

Carson, E. Ann. 2018. *Prisoners in 2016*. Washington, DC: U.S. Department of Justice.

Committee on Causes and Consequences of High Rates of Incarceration, National Research Council of the National Academies. 2014. *The Growth of Incarceration in the United States*. Washington, DC: The National Academies Press.

Hesikanen, Markku. 2010. "Trends in Police-Recorded Crime." In *International Statistics on Crime and Justice*. Edited by Stefan Harrendorf, Marrku Hesikanen, & Steven Malby. Helsinki: European Institute for Crime Prevention and Control.

International Centre for Prison Studies. 2016. *World Prison Population List*. London: International Centre for Prison Studies.

Kaeble, Donald & Glaze, Lauren. 2016. *Correctional Populations in the United States, 2015*. Washington, DC: U.S. Department of Justice.

Malby, Steven. 2010. "Homicide." In *International Statistics on Crime and Justice*. Edited by Stefan Harrendorf, Markku Hesikanen, & Steven Malby. Helsinki: European Institute for Crime Prevention and Control.

Nellis, Ashley. 2017. *Still Life: America's Increasing Use of Life and Long-Term Sentences*. Washington, DC: Sentencing Project.

Tonry, Michael. 2016a. "Equality and Human Dignity: The Missing Ingredients in American Sentencing." *Crime & Justice*, 45, 459.

Tonry, Michael. 2016b. "Differences in National Sentencing Systems and the Differences They Make." *Crime & Justice*, 45, 1.

Whitman, James Q. 2005. *Harsh Justice: Criminal Punishment and the Widening Divide between America and Europe*. New York: Oxford University Press.

Q32: DID THE WAR ON DRUGS CAUSE MASS INCARCERATION?

Answer: The great imprisonment boom of the late twentieth century coincided with a surge in drug enforcement activity and a sharp increase in penalties for drug offenses. However, the so-called War on Drugs cannot be regarded as the exclusive or dominant cause of mass incarceration. Indeed, throughout the mass incarceration era, a far greater share of America's prisoners has been serving time for violence than for drug offenses.

The Facts: When President Richard Nixon declared a "war" on drugs in 1969, he set the tone for a tough new approach to drug control that would prevail through the end of the twentieth century (O'Hear, 2017, 21–22). Four years later, New York adopted its draconian Rockefeller Drug Laws, which proved to be just the start of a national wave of new mandatory minimum sentencing laws for drug offenses (see Q1). These were not just symbolic enactments but complemented a dramatic intensification of drug enforcement activity by police and prosecutors. The number of drug arrests in the United States almost tripled between 1980 and 2000. Prison admissions for drug offenses spiked similarly. For instance, in 2002, in large urban counties, drug offenders accounted for about 28 percent of the felony defendants who were sentenced to jail or prison (Cohen & Reaves, 2006, 32–33).

Historically speaking, the advent and escalation of the War on Drugs closely coincided with the imprisonment boom of the late twentieth century, giving rise to perceptions that the former was the primary driver of the latter. For instance, Professor Michelle Alexander, in her best-selling book *The New Jim Crow: Mass Incarceration in the Age of Colorblind-ness*, asserts, "The uncomfortable reality is that arrests and convictions for drug offenses—not violent crime—have propelled mass incarceration" (Alexander, 2012, 102). However, such claims likely overstate the impor-tance of the War on Drugs as a direct cause of the imprisonment boom.

While the number of defendants sentenced to prison for drug crimes climbed sharply in the decades following Nixon's declaration of "war," so, too, did the number of defendants sentenced for violent offenses. More-over, the violent-crime sentences tended to be longer, giving them a much greater impact on overall imprisonment rates. For instance, while drug offenders may have accounted for 28 percent of the defendants sentenced to incarceration in 2002, they were only 14 percent of the defendants who got more than twenty years in prison (Cohen & Reaves, 2006, 32). In all, drug sentences were responsible for only about one-quarter of the growth in state prison populations between 1985 and 2000 (Mauer, 2006, 21–23)—a significant contribution, to be sure, but probably not enough to qualify as a dominant cause.

The federal story is a bit different, with drug enforcement playing a more prominent role in the swelling tide of prisoners. Between 1982 and 2007, drug offenders accounted for 42 percent of the increase in federal defendants annually sentenced to incarceration (Bureau of Justice Sta-tistics, 1993, 15; Bureau of Justice Statistics, 2010, Table 5.1). Over the same time period, the proportion of federal drug defendants receiving an incarceration sentence increased from 74 to 93 percent, with the aver-age term growing from 55 months (with the possibility of parole) to 88 months (without the possibility of parole)—a much steeper increase than occurred with federal sentences overall. By 2007, 53 percent of federal prisoners were serving time primarily for a drug offense, in comparison to 20 percent of state prisoners (West & Sabol, 2008, 21). However, while the War on Drugs was a major part of the federal imprisonment boom, the federal system accounts for only about 12 percent of the national prison population. It would thus be inappropriate to generalize from the federal experience to draw conclusions about the importance of drug enforce-ment to the larger national phenomenon of mass incarceration.

Whatever the impact of the War on Drugs through 2007, that year proved to be the high-water mark for drug imprisonment in the United States. The number of prisoners serving time primarily for a drug sen-tence dropped by 12 percent over the next eight years, reflecting a similar, contemporaneous decline in drug trafficking arrests by police, as well as a softening of drug sentencing laws in many states—including the legalization of marijuana in a handful (O'Hear, 2017, 41–54). By 2015, the drug portion of the federal prison population had dipped below 50 percent and of state prison populations to just 15 percent. Over time, it is becoming even less credible to characterize the War on Drugs as the primary driver of mass incarceration.

Instead, it is violent crime that stands out as the most important source of American imprisonment. Nearly 55 percent of state prisoners are serving time for a violent offense, and more than 49 percent of all prisoners (Carson, 2018, 19–20). No other offense category is even close. Indeed, the violent portion might be even higher if more expansive definitions of violent crime are used. For instance, burglary (accounting for 5 percent of all prisoners), weapons offenses (also 5 percent), and DUI (2 percent) are sometimes characterized as violent crimes because of the risks of physical injury associated with them. If these offenses are added, then about 60 percent of American prisoners are serving time for violent crimes— more than three times larger than the drug-offender portion.

The number of violent-offense prisoners has climbed sharply during the mass-incarceration era, more than doubling from about 314,000 state prisoners in 1990 to 708,000 in 2015 (using the narrower definition of violence). This increase is all the more remarkable when one considers that the number of violent crimes reported to the police *fell* by more than one-third over the same time period. A burgeoning number of violent offenders in prison during a time of declining violent crime strongly suggests that the criminal justice system is now responding to violence with an intensified toughness. And, indeed, the data do indicate that prosecutors are charging violence cases more aggressively and judges imposing longer prison terms (O'Hear, 2017, 9–10, 11–13). For instance, over the 1990s, the average sentence in murder cases in large urban counties jumped from 233 to 282 months—an increase of more than four years (12).

The raw prison-population figures may, if anything, understate the importance of fear and anger regarding violent crime as a driver of mass incarceration. This is because the War on Drugs *itself* may have been as much, if not more, about violence than it was about controlled substances *per se*. Linkages between drugs and violence, both real and imagined, have been regularly invoked as justifications for tougher drug enforcement policies. In the U.S. Supreme Court's 1991 decision in *Harmelin v. Michigan*, for example, Justice Anthony Kennedy's key opinion refused to treat a drug offense as nonviolent. Kennedy noted the use of violence by drug traffickers, as well as the potential that drug users might commit nondrug crimes as a result of intoxication or addiction.

Moreover, such drug-violence associations have not only fueled the adoption of new tough-on-drugs policies, but they also support the "pretextual" use of drug laws by police and prosecutors to target individuals who are suspected of violent crime (see Q4). For instance, if a violent gang is being targeted, a standard law enforcement strategy is to build strong drug cases against a few underlings, often through sting operations, and then put pressure on those low-level defendants to cut a deal and testify against the higher-ups. In such an operation, most or all of the resulting prison sentences may be formally classified as drug-related, but the true motive for the law-enforcement action would be to address violence.

Pretextual prosecutions help to explain two curious features of the War on Drugs. First, there is the much greater prevalence of drug prosecutions in federal than in state court. Since the federal government does not generally have jurisdiction over routine, street-level violent crime, federal authorities must often rely on pretextual drug prosecutions in order to address violence. By contrast, state authorities normally have an array of broad, flexible violent crime charging options available to them. In some state cases, to be sure, a drug crime may seem the best charging strategy for taking a particular violent offender out of circulation, but state authorities are not as reliant on drug charges as their federal counterparts.

Second, there is the remarkable racial disparity in drug arrests and prosecutions. Given that blacks and whites use and distribute drugs at about equal rates, one might expect that the black share of drug cases would correspond to the black share of the overall population. However, blacks are imprisoned on drug charges at about nine times the rate of whites (Stuntz, 2011, 272). The disparity cannot be explained by reference to different rates of involvement in drug crime, but it does roughly correspond with the demographics of violent crime. In other words, the racial disparities in drug enforcement are in line with what would be expected if drug enforcement were being done largely as an indirect strategy for getting individuals suspected of criminal violence off the street.

In sum, mass incarceration is probably more reflective of a War on Violence than a War on Drugs. This does not necessarily mean, however, that mass incarceration represents a sound policy choice. When critics attribute mass incarceration to the War on Drugs, they normally mean to delegitimize mass incarceration, recognizing that public opinion has shifted in favor of treatment and against imprisonment as the preferred strategy for addressing drug abuse in our society (O'Hear, 2017, 36, 56). However, long prison terms may not be much more productive in cases of violent crime than they are in cases of drug crime. Indeed, on average, violent offenders actually have *lower* recidivism rates than drug offenders

(Durose, Cooper, & Snyder, 2014, 3). More generally, as discussed in Q23, prison terms are not always beneficial to public safety, and they can even make some offenders more dangerous after their release. This is no less true of violent offenders than others. In the next question, we will consider in more detail what the research shows about the effectiveness of the great imprisonment boom in reducing crime.

FURTHER READING

Alexander, Michelle. 2012. *The New Jim Crow: Mass Incarceration in the Age of Colorblindness*. New York: New Press.

Bureau of Justice Statistics. 1993. *Federal Criminal Case Processing, 1982–91*. Washington, DC: U.S. Department of Justice.

Bureau of Justice Statistics. 2010. *Federal Justice Statistics, 2007—Statistical Tables*. Washington, DC: U.S. Department of Justice.

Cohen, Thomas & Reaves, Brian. 2006. *Felony Defendants in Large Urban Counties, 2002*. Washington, DC: U.S. Department of Justice.

Durose, Matthew, Cooper, Aaron, & Snyder, Howard. 2014. *Recidivism of Prisoners Released in 30 States in 2005: Patterns from 2005 to 2010*. Washington, DC: U.S. Department of Justice.

Mauer, Marc. 2006. *Race to Incarcerate*. New York: New Press.

O'Hear, Michael. 2017. *The Failure of Sentencing Reform*. Santa Barbara, CA: Praeger.

Stuntz, William. 2011. *The Collapse of American Criminal Justice*. Cambridge, MA: Belknap Press.

West, Heather & Sabol, William. 2008. *Prisoners in 2007*. Washington, DC: U.S. Department of Justice.

Q33: HAS MASS INCARCERATION HELPED TO REDUCE CRIME?

Answer: Swelling U.S. incarceration rates in the late twentieth century likely had an overall positive effect in reducing crime, although quantifying the benefit has proven a difficult and contentious matter. Moreover, whatever the crime-control effects of the first half of the imprisonment boom (1972–1989), the benefits of the second half (1990–2007) were likely much smaller, and perhaps even nonexistent. In other words, past some point, there appear to be diminishing marginal returns to America's prolonged escalation of its incarceration rate. Thus, the continued toughening of the American criminal justice system past 1990 likely made no more than a quite modest contribution to the sharp, durable drop in U.S. crime rates that followed. A growing body of evidence now suggests many American states could substantially reduce their incarceration rates without experiencing any increases in crime.

The Facts: As a purely theoretical matter, historically high incarceration rates might be expected to reduce crime through two distinct mechanisms. First, there are the *incapacitation* effects of incarceration: holding a person behind bars makes it much harder (albeit certainly not impossible) for the person to commit new crimes. As Q23 explained, research provides support for the hypothesis that, *on average*, each offender-year of incarceration in the United States results in at least one or two victimizing crimes avoided outside of prison. On the other hand, as also discussed in Q23, there are good reasons to think that large incapacitation benefits may be limited to the incarceration of a relatively small number of high-frequency offenders. Second, there are the *deterrent* effects of incarceration. To the extent that high rates of incarceration are indicative of greater certainty or severity of punishment, society is sending a stronger deterrent message to prospective offenders. Still, there are significant questions about the extent to which prospective offenders accurately assess their risk of punishment and take that risk into account in deciding whether to break the law.

An expert panel of the National Academy of Sciences recently summarized the research on the deterrence and incapacitation effects of imprisonment this way: "The incremental deterrent effect of increases in the length of prison sentences is modest at best. Because recidivism rates decline markedly with age, lengthy prison sentences, unless they specifically target high-rate or extremely dangerous offenders, are an inefficient approach in preventing crime by incapacitation" (Committee on Causes and Consequences of High Rates of Incarceration, 2014, 5).

As against the crime-*reducing* effects of mass incarceration, there may be a number of countervailing crime-*increasing* effects over the long run. For instance, while imprisonment may reduce risk during the time that the offender is behind bars, it can increase risk post-release (see Q16). Additionally, the incarceration of a parent may increase the likelihood that children will later become involved in criminal activity (see Q21). There are also concerns, albeit less well established in the existing research, that high rates of incarceration in socioeconomically disadvantaged urban neighborhoods can contribute to social instability, undermine mechanisms of informal social control, diminish respect for law, and ultimately lead to further increases in crime rates (Committee on Causes and Consequences of High Rates of Incarceration, 2014, 282, 288–302). Finally, the fiscal burdens of mass incarceration likely reduce the money that is available for other types of government spending that might help to reduce crime, such as drug treatment, larger police forces, improved public schools, economic development, and evidence-based rehabilitative interventions for juvenile offenders.

As a matter of theory, it is far from clear whether the positive or negative effects of incarceration are stronger. Indeed, it is likely that the answer varies at different levels of incarceration. This is because incapacitation benefits are expected to diminish as a society increases its incarceration rate. If a society incarcerates very few offenders, we would expect those offenders to be among the most dangerous. However, as a society's incarceration rate grows, it will run out of identifiably high-danger individuals who can be put behind bars, meaning that further efforts to incapacitate will mostly sweep up people who would have committed very few or no crimes if left in the community. Once incarceration levels reach a point where the marginal incapacitation benefits are very low or nonexistent, then the crime-*increasing* effects of further incarceration are more likely to predominate.

Many researchers have attempted to quantify more precisely the impact of high incarceration rates on crime. This has proven quite analytically challenging as a result of all the "moving parts" implicated in crime trends. Considered as a broad social phenomenon, crime seems dauntingly complex, driven by a multitude of factors, many of which remain poorly understood. Researchers must attempt to control for all of the pertinent variables as fully as they can. Additionally, disentangling the effect of incarceration rates on crime rates presents a special difficulty since the causal relationship between these variables runs in both directions: while incarceration may affect crime through incapacitation effects and the like, crime also affects incarceration—more crime normally means more offenders, more arrests, more convictions, and ultimately more prisoners.

One notable recent study was sponsored by the Brennan Center for Justice at New York University School of Law (Roeder, Eisen, & Bowling, 2015). The researchers gathered data regarding reported crime, imprisonment, age and race demographics, number of police officers, unemployment rate, median income, and other variables from all fifty states and the District of Columbia for each year from 1980 to 2013. In the years near the start of this time period, the researchers calculated that each 1 percent increase in imprisonment in the United States was associated with a reduction in the crime rate of about 0.6 percent, controlling for the other variables that were tracked (23). However, they found steadily declining marginal returns from imprisonment between 1980 and 2000. Indeed, for the period between 1990 and 2013, there was no statistically significant effect from increased imprisonment on crime rates. The study thus suggests that the first half of the imprisonment boom may have generated substantial crime-reduction benefits, but the second half accomplished far less—perhaps even nothing at all. Moreover, to the extent there were continued gains after 1990, it appears that these were almost entirely in the area of property crime, not violent crime.

Older studies cover earlier time periods, control for different variables, and use different regression models. Not surprisingly, they have reached a range of different conclusions, with some finding a substantially greater positive impact from elevated incarceration rates, but at least one finding that in the 1990s the imprisonment boom actually tended to make crime worse (22; Committee on Causes and Consequences of High Rates of Incarceration, 2014, 147–48). The phenomenon of diminishing marginal returns has been found in several of these studies.

Much of the public debate over mass incarceration has centered on the 1990s. On the face of things, the American experience in that decade—the national crime rate fell sharply as the incarceration rate spiked—seems to provide powerful ammunition for defenders of the high-incarceration status quo. If getting tough on crime did not make us safer in the 1990s, they challenge the critics, then what did?

Several different theories have been advanced to explain the "great American crime decline," as it has been labeled by criminologist Franklin Zimring (2007). For instance, the aging of the U.S. population likely played a role. We have already noted that crime is mostly a young person's game (Q30). By the start of the 1990s, the baby boomers had already passed their peak crime-committing years, and, by the decade's end, most had reached middle age. However, aging can only account for a modest share of the 1990s crime decline. For one thing, the proportion of the U.S. population in the high-risk age range of fifteen to twenty-four had already been falling for a decade before the crime decline began (61); if that demographic trend were a major driver of crime rates, then the decline should have begun earlier than it did. For another, the drop in young people ended during the 1990s, but the crime decline just kept going. Based on its regression analyses, the Brennan Center researchers estimate that aging accounted for no more than 5 percent of the crime drop in the 1990s (Roeder, Eisen, & Bowling, 2015, 5).

The economy provides another obvious explanation. In comparison with the 1980s, the 1990s was a decade of remarkably sustained, consistent economic growth that raised employment and wage rates across the income spectrum. Economic prosperity tends to reduce the incentives for people to engage in crime for financial gain, while good jobs may help to pull at-risk individuals out of criminogenic behaviors and relationships. The Brennan Center researchers found that low rates of unemployment in the 1990s may be credited with as much as 5 percent of the crime decline, while growth in income may account for as much as 7 percent (5).

The Brennan Center study identified several other notable contributors to the crime decline, including decreased alcohol consumption (accounting for up to 10 percent of the decline) and higher numbers of police officers (also up to 10 percent). Through a complementary city-level analysis, the researchers also found a significant benefit from the adoption of "CompStat"—a policing innovation of the 1990s that involves the systematic collection of crime data, swift responses to emerging crime patterns, and enhanced accountability for officers and units (67–68). By the end of the 1990s, CompStat had been implemented in about a dozen large cities, including New York City—a national leader in the great crime decline.

Researchers have pointed to a variety of other potential contributing factors; although plausible, further research is necessary to confirm and quantify their significance. For instance, the phasing out of lead from gasoline in the 1970s resulted in reduced lead exposure for the cohort of young people reaching their peak crime-committing years in the 1990s. Since childhood lead exposure has been linked to various behavioral and development problems, one might expect stronger regulation of lead to produce a crime-reduction dividend about two decades later. A growing body of research now lends support to this hypothesis (Mielke & Zahran, 2012).

Another, and potentially related, cause of the crime drop may have been the decline of urban crack cocaine markets (Zimring, 2007, 82–85). Crack's arrival in American cities in the 1980s was associated with a surge in youth gun violence as distribution organizations competed for position in the lucrative new drug market. However, in the 1990s, decreased demand and stabilization in the market likely contributed—perhaps quite substantially—to the drop in violence among urban youth. It is far from clear, though, that crack had anything much to do with other aspects of the crime decline.

Yet another, far more controversial, hypothesis is that the legalization of abortion in the 1970s meant that fewer unwanted children were around to reach their peak crime-committing years in the 1990s. It does seem plausible that the children of unwanted pregnancies would tend to grow up in circumstances of disadvantage, and that such circumstances would increase the risk of involvement in crime in the teen years and thereafter. However, whether abortion is legal or not is only one of many factors that might determine how many unwanted pregnancies are carried to term. While some research does suggest that abortion may have contributed to the crime decline, the analysis has been sharply criticized by other scholars (Zimring, 2007, 85–103).

Apart from all of the multivariate regression studies, perhaps the most compelling response to the claim that mass incarceration caused the great crime decline comes from a cross-border comparison. No less than the United States, Canada experienced steep reductions in reported crime in the 1990s, including drops in aggravated assault and theft that were even greater than in the United States (Zimring, 2007, 108). Yet, across the decade, Canada's imprisonment rate *declined* by 6 percent—even as the American rate jumped by 57 percent (121). The Canadian example thus strongly suggests that the great American crime decline had less to do with mass incarceration—a uniquely American phenomenon—than with broader demographic, economic, and cultural trends that were not confined to a single nation.

Further support for this view comes from the more recent experience of a handful of American states that have achieved substantial reductions in imprisonment without experiencing any corresponding increase in crime. For instance, between 2005 and 2014, California reduced its imprisonment rate by 26 percent, while its violent crime rate dropped by 25 percent. Similarly, over the same time period, New Jersey's imprisonment rate declined by 24 percent, while its violent crime rate tumbled 26 percent. In New York, imprisonment fell by 18 percent and violent crime by 14 percent. And, in Michigan, imprisonment dropped by 11 percent and violent crime by 23 percent. To be sure, we have identified here only crude associations between reductions in imprisonment and violence; it is conceivable that violence would have dropped even more in these states if imprisonment had held steady. (More sophisticated statistical analyses of certain key policy changes in California find no indication of an impact on violent crime rates but a small adverse effect on property crime [Lofstrom & Raphael, 2016].) However, the experiences of these decarcerating states seem to belie any suggestion that current, historically high rates of incarceration are necessary to prevent a return to the high rates of crime that prevailed through much of the late twentieth century. In Chapter 8, we will explore in more detail the prospects for a large-scale reduction in American imprisonment rates.

FURTHER READING

Committee on Causes and Consequences of High Rates of Incarceration, National Research Council of the National Academies. 2014. *The Growth of Incarceration in the United States.* Washington, DC: The National Academies Press.

Lofstrom, Magnus & Raphael, Steven. 2016. "Incarceration and Crime: Evidence from California's Public Safety Realignment Reform." *Annals of the American Academy of Political and Social Science*, 664, 196.

Mielke, Howard & Zahran, Sammy. 2012. "The Urban Rise and Fall of Air Lead (Pb) and the Latent Surge and Retreat of Societal Violence." *Environment International*, 43, 48.

Roeder, Oliver, Eisen, Lauren-Brooke, & Bowling, Julia. 2015. *What Caused the Crime Decline?* New York: Brennan Center for Justice at New York University School of Law.

Zimring, Franklin. 2007. *The Great American Crime Decline.* New York: Oxford University Press.

7

❖

Race, Ethnicity, and Punishment

In recent years, the single most politically divisive aspect of public discussions regarding criminal justice policies has likely been the charge of racial discrimination in policing and punishment. Although wide racial disparities in the American criminal justice system have been noted critically for decades, the emergence of a nationally prominent, broad-based "Black Lives Matter" movement in 2014 gave a new urgency to questions about the disparate impact of so many criminal justice policies and practices in the United States. While the existence of disparities in the system is beyond dispute, the cause and significance of those disparities has been hotly contested.

Before considering the evidence in more detail, a few words about terminology are in order. Inconsistent uses of key terms make constructive conversations about race all the more difficult to achieve. In this chapter, except where the context makes a different meaning clear, the terms "racially disparate" or "racially disproportionate" incarceration indicate that some racial group is overrepresented in the incarcerated population, that is, the group's share of the incarcerated population is larger than its share of the general population. These terms are meant to be purely descriptive, not critical. A disparity, as I use the term, may be either warranted or unwarranted. A group's overrepresentation in the incarcerated population might be warranted if, for instance, the group was responsible for a disproportionate share of serious crime. However, to the extent that disparate incarceration cannot be explained by reference to disparate offending or other appropriate, race-neutral considerations, the disparity is unwarranted and indicates that some form of unfair racial bias may be influencing some of the decisions being made by police, prosecutors, judges, and/or corrections officials. "Bias," however, need not be a matter of deliberate racial discrimination but may instead operate at a subconscious level.

This chapter focuses particularly, but not exclusively, on one type of racial disparity: the disproportionate incarceration of African Americans. Other social groups also experience disproportionate incarceration, but most of the public conversation (and, for that matter, most of the academic research) has centered on black-white disparities, which is why they get the most attention here. The disproportionate incarceration of Native Americans (American Indians) and Hispanics (Latinos) will also be briefly considered.

By the standard conventions of researchers and government agencies, "Native American," like "African American," is treated as a racial category, while "Hispanic" is treated as an ethnic category. At some level, of course, all racial and ethnic categories are artificial constructs and arguably serve to divide and aggregate individual human beings in ways that do more harm than good. Still, these categories can hardly be ignored in a book on prisons and punishment. The historical development of criminal justice policies and practices in the United States has been profoundly shaped by public attitudes regarding the individuals seen as belonging to various disfavored racial and ethnic categories. Given this history, it is perhaps inevitable that these categories should continue to play a central role in criminal justice policy debates today.

Q34: ARE AFRICAN AMERICANS INCARCERATED DISPROPORTIONATELY IN THE UNITED STATES?

Answer: African Americans are incarcerated at a rate more than two and half times greater than would be expected based on their share of the U.S. population. To some extent, this disproportionality reflects different patterns and rates of criminal offending, but, even taking this into account, there are still substantial disparities in black incarceration.

The Facts: At year-end 2016, African Americans accounted for almost exactly one-third of the U.S. prison population, including both state and federal inmates (Carson, 2018, 5). Following current federal data-reporting conventions, this figure excludes individuals of Hispanic

(Latino) origin and individuals of two or more races. By way of comparison, the U.S. Census Bureau reports that African Americans constituted just 13.3 percent of the overall population in 2016. Thus, the black share of the prison population is two and half times greater than would be the case if black and non-black imprisonment rates were equal. Put differently, if black imprisonment rates were the same as non-black, there would be nearly 300,000 fewer African Americans in prison.

Similar disparities are apparent with respect to other forms of criminal justice supervision. At year-end 2015, African Americans accounted for 35 percent of jail inmates, 30 percent of probationers, and 38 percent of parolees (Zeng, 2018, 4; Kaeble & Bonczar, 2016, 7). We have already noted wide racial disparities in the juvenile system (see Q27).

A strikingly large portion of the African American *male* population, in particular, bears the stigma of contact with the criminal justice system. For instance, 33 percent of African American adult males have a felony conviction, as compared to only 8 percent of all adults (Shannon et al., 2017). Similarly, 15 percent of African American adult males have spent time in prison, as compared to only 3 percent of all adults.

As is often the case with criminal justice data, national averages mask substantial variation from state to state. Black and white imprisonment rates for selected states are indicated in Table 7.1, including the states with the four highest rates of black imprisonment. Some states with very high rates of black imprisonment, such as Oklahoma, also have exceptionally high rates of white imprisonment. In other states, black and white imprisonment rates diverge dramatically. The largest gaps are found in New Jersey, Wisconsin, Iowa, and Minnesota. Focusing more

Table 7.1 Prisoners per 100,000 residents, by race

State	Black Rate	White Rate
Oklahoma	2,625	580
Wisconsin	2,542	221
Vermont	2,357	225
Iowa	2,349	211
Minnesota	1,219	111
New Jersey	1,140	94
Hawai'i	585	246

Source: Nellis (2016).

particularly on the rate of black male imprisonment, states range from one in sixty-one on the low end (Hawaii) to one in fourteen on the high end (Vermont).

The numbers can look quite different still at the city or neighborhood level. Black male imprisonment can reach shocking proportions in some communities marked by concentrated socioeconomic disadvantage. The area of Milwaukee covered by zip code 53206—said to be the most incarcerated zip code in the United States—provides a striking illustration. Based on Census data, this 95 percent African American community displays multiple signs of disadvantage, including a 22 percent unemployment rate and a poverty rate of 45 percent in 2016. Out of an adult male population of about 7,260, more than 4,000 have either served time in a state prison or are currently incarcerated in a state institution. The incarceration rate would be even higher if residents held in local jails were included. After mapping the home addresses of the former prisoners in 53206, two researchers observed that "nearly every residential block in the neighborhood had multiple numbers of ex-offenders with prison records" (Pawasarat & Quinn, 2013, 25). In Milwaukee as a whole, the researchers determined that more than half of the African American males between the ages of thirty and forty-four were either in a state prison or had been held in such an institution in the past (13).

Although the national black imprisonment rate remains much higher than the white rate, the gap has narrowed considerably since 2002. Between that year and 2016, the African American prison population dropped by 22 percent, while the non-Hispanic white prison population fell by only 7 percent. The cause for this trend is not clear, but several factors may be playing a role (Hager, 2017). First, black drug imprisonment has fallen, while white has increased—likely reflecting a shift of drug enforcement effort from crack cocaine, a drug particularly associated with blacks, to meth and opioids, which are associated more with whites. Second, a decline in the economic prospects of whites without college degrees has created or exacerbated circumstances of concentrated disadvantage in some white communities. Third, post-2000, criminal justice reforms intended to reduce incarceration have occurred primarily in cities, missing the rural communities that tend to be more white and that have been experiencing rising incarceration rates in recent years.

Notwithstanding these recent trends, there is no question that African Americans are incarcerated disproportionately to their share of the general population. But are they incarcerated disproportionately to their share of crime-committing? This latter form of disproportionality is much more important to measure if the ultimate objective is to assess the racial fairness of the criminal justice system. Unfortunately, there is no entirely satisfactory way to determine which racial groups are responsible for what percentage of crime.

Victimization surveys supply one tool. Representative samples of crime victims are regularly asked to identify the race of their victimizers. For instance, a leading survey conducted by the federal government finds that 27 percent of violent offenders are black (Morgan, 2017, 3). (This figure does not include the nearly 14 percent of violent offenses in which there were multiple offenders from different racial groups or the victim was otherwise unable to identify a single racial category for the offender.) To the extent this data accurately indicates the black share of serious crime in the United States, it would go a long way—albeit not necessarily all the way—toward accounting for the black share of incarceration. However, the victimization survey includes some important gaps, including a failure to include homicide offenses, which account for a sizeable share (about 15 percent) of state prisoners; a failure to include property offenses; and a failure to include important categories of "victimless" crimes (drugs, DUI, illegal weapons possession, immigration, and others). Additionally, there are concerns about the ability of victims to make reliable determinations of race, especially in cases involving only a brief (and normally highly stressful) interaction with a stranger assailant.

Arrest data can help to fill in these gaps but suffer from difficulties of their own. Most fundamentally, if the goal is to assess the racial fairness of the criminal justice system, police decisions to arrest are themselves part of that system. To the extent that arrest figures may include unwarranted racial disparities, they need to be used with caution as an indicator of relative rates of crime-committing. The arrest data are thought to be reasonably reliable with respect to serious violent crimes, as to which police face the greatest pressure to apprehend the culprit, but less so with respect to other types of crimes, as to which police responses are more selective (Committee on Causes and Consequences of High Rates of Incarceration, 2014, 95–96).

Table 7.2 indicates the black share of those who were arrested in 2016, including a breakdown for various offense categories that contribute in significant ways to state prison populations. Black overrepresentation is pronounced across the board.

More sophisticated statistical analyses of the arrest and imprisonment data in the 1980s and 1990s have found that racial differences in arrest rates explained three-quarters or more of the imprisonment disparities

Table 7.2 Black share of population, prisoners, and arrests

Prison Population	33%
General Population	13%
Arrests	
All Offenses	27%
Major Violent Crimes	38%
Burglary	29%
Drugs	27%
Fraud	31%
Weapons	42%

Source: Federal Bureau of Investigation (2017).

(Committee on Causes and Consequences of High Rates of Incarceration, 2014, 95–96). However, studies covering more recent years find a greater share of "unexplained" disparity. The gap may be most pronounced in the drug area, with one study of the 2008 data finding that 66 percent of the racial disparity in drug imprisonment was left unexplained by arrest patterns.

Drugs are also an area in which there are particularly strong reasons to suspect that the arrest rates themselves do not mirror underlying rates of criminal activity. Surveys indicate that the black share of the drug user population corresponds closely to the black share of the general population (O'Hear, 2009, 467); yet, the black share of the drug arrest population is about twice as high. To be sure, some portion of the black drug arrests are likely "pretextual," that is, motivated by the desire to pick up an individual who is thought to present a risk of violence (see Q32). If drug arrests commonly target violence, not drug use or distribution *per se*, then it would not be surprising that blacks were "overrepresented" among drug arrestees. Even at that, we might wonder whether unfair racial stereotypes could be affecting police judgments about which drug offenders are the dangerous ones who ought to be pretextually arrested. This stereotyping issue will be further discussed in Q35.

Weapons offenses (mostly illegal firearms possession) stand out as another area of concern. African Americans account for 45 percent of those held in state prisons on weapons convictions—nearly three and a half times their share of the general population (Carson, 2018, 19). While African Americans have elevated arrest rates for weapons offenses, these crimes are similar to drug offenses in lying outside that sphere of major violent crime as to which arrest rates are thought most reliably to mirror offending rates. Notably, survey research indicates that rates of gun ownership are 50 percent higher among whites than blacks (Parker et al., 2017, 7).

In sum, while it is not possible to say with complete certainty whether and to what extent African Americans are incarcerated disproportionately to their rate of criminal offending, the evidence tends to indicate that such a disparity does exist and may be especially pronounced with respect to drug and other nonviolent offenses.

FURTHER READING

Carson, E. Ann. 2018. *Prisoners in 2016*. Washington, DC: U.S. Department of Justice.

Committee on Causes and Consequences of High Rates of Incarceration, National Research Council of the National Academies. 2014. *The Growth of Incarceration in the United States*. Washington, DC: The National Academies Press.

Federal Bureau of Investigation. 2017. *Crime in the United States, 2016*. Washington, DC: U.S. Department of Justice.

Hager, Eli. 2017. "A Mass Incarceration Mystery." *Washington Post Wonkblog*, December 15.

Kaeble, Donald & Bonczar, Thomas. 2016. *Probation and Parole in the United States, 2015*. Washington, DC: U.S. Department of Justice.

Morgan, Rachel. 2017. *Race and Hispanic Origin of Victims and Offenders, 2012–15*. Washington, DC: U.S. Department of Justice.

Nellis, Ashley. 2016. *The Color of Justice: Racial and Ethnic Disparity in State Prisons*. Washington, DC: The Sentencing Project.

O'Hear, Michael. 2009. "Rethinking Drug Courts: Restorative Justice as a Response to Racial Injustice." *Stanford Law & Policy Review*, 20, 463.

Parker, Kim et al. 2017. *America's Complex Relationship with Guns: An In-Depth Look at the Attitudes and Experiences of U.S. Adults*. Washington, DC: Pew Research Center.

Pawasarat, John & Quinn, Lois. 2013. *Wisconsin's Mass Incarceration of African American Males: Workforce Challenges for 2013*. Milwaukee: University of Wisconsin-Milwaukee.

Shannon, Sarah et al. 2017. "The Growth, Scope, and Spatial Distribution of People with Felony Records in the United States, 1948–2010." *Demography*, 54, 1795.

Zeng, Zhen. 2018. *Jail Inmates in 2016*. Washington, DC: U.S. Department of Justice.

Q35: WHAT CAUSES THE DISPROPORTIONATE IMPRISONMENT OF AFRICAN AMERICANS?

Answer: Disproportionate black imprisonment results from the interplay of multiple factors. These likely include disproportionate involvement in crime, particularly violent crime; policing practices in predominantly African American neighborhoods; disparate treatment in the court and corrections systems; and harsh sentencing laws that disproportionately affect black defendants.

The Facts: The American criminal justice system has been marked by stark racial disparities for at least a century and half. Most horrific was likely the use of a vicious and transparently biased "justice" system by southern whites after the Civil War in order to force the newly freed blacks into conditions of bondage that closely resembled slavery (Oshinsky, 1996). The era's most notorious practice may have been routinely sending black convicts (and only rarely white) into chain-gang labor involving conditions of extreme (and frequently lethal) privation. Later, as the nineteenth century shifted to the twentieth, a new system of "Jim Crow" justice developed that may have been less brutal in some respects but that continued to treat black defendants unequally, especially in cases in which a black person was alleged to have assaulted or raped a white victim (Klarman, 2009).

Yet, while southern justice remained notoriously racist through the middle of the twentieth century, it should also be appreciated that northern justice was hardly a model of racial enlightenment. Northern prejudice became increasingly salient as the so-called Great Migration of the early and middle decades of the twentieth century brought a flood of southern blacks into northern and western cities. Through a combination of formal and informal housing restrictions, the new arrivals found themselves crowded into segregated, run-down "ghetto" neighborhoods. Heavy-handed policing of these neighborhoods led to a series of major urban race riots in the 1960s.

During the Civil Rights Era, overtly racist laws and government practices were finally overturned across the United States, but racial disparities in the criminal justice have persisted to the present day. Thoughtful commentators now debate whether the present system is appropriately labeled "the new Jim Crow," which would imply that contemporary mass incarceration reflects an agenda of legally enforced racial subordination reminiscent of the pre-Civil Rights South (Alexander, 2012; Forman, 2012).

It has proven difficult to fully and precisely delineate the causes of disproportionate African American incarceration. Q34, for example, examined how much of the disproportionality can be explained by reference to different rates and severity of criminal activity? Based on the victim survey and arrest data, it seems reasonably clear that African Americans are disproportionately the perpetrators (and, for that matter, also disproportionately the victims) of major violent crime. At the same time, the available evidence also suggests that disproportionate black crime cannot fully account for disproportionate black incarceration. Put differently, it seems likely that differential treatment by various actors in the criminal justice system likely amplifies the impact of differential crime patterns.

Before considering more specifically how disparity arises in the criminal justice system, one further point about crime patterns should be emphasized: to say that disproportionate incarceration is *caused* by disproportionate crime is not to say that disproportionate incarceration is *excused* by disproportionate crime. In other words, even if the mass incarceration of African Americans represented a good faith, unbiased response by criminal justice officials to serious crime problems in black communities, disparate incarceration should still be regarded as a matter of public policy concern. As Q33 detailed, mass incarceration does not likely represent the most cost-effective response to crime. When it is further appreciated that mass incarceration is experienced disproportionately by individuals who live in deeply disadvantaged African American neighborhoods, such as "53206" in Milwaukee (see Q34), it becomes clear that the social costs of mass incarceration are borne largely by individuals, families, and communities that already exist in a highly precarious position—a position that to some extent reflects the legacy of generations of racial discrimination. Arguably, a due regard for this legacy creates an even greater responsibility for policy makers to implement more effective crime-control measures that impose fewer collateral costs on disadvantaged communities.

Police activity stands out as a major driver of disparate incarceration. Officers arrest African Americans at greatly disproportionate rates for serious crimes that often result in incarceration (see Q34). Moreover, the arrest disparities correspond fairly closely to the overall incarceration disparities, which suggest that the police may be the single most important institutional player in causing racial disproportionality in the criminal justice system.

Based on victimization surveys, the disproportionality in arrests for major violent crimes may very roughly mirror underlying patterns in offending. In other crime categories, disproportionate arrests are more likely to result from selective enforcement practices by the police (Q34).

Researchers studying drug enforcement in Seattle provide a striking illustration (Becket, Nyrop, & Pfingst, 2006, 129–30). They found far more police activity targeting one racially diverse open-air drug market than an overwhelmingly white open-air market operating elsewhere in the city—a disparity that could not be explained based on either crime rates or citizen complaints. The researchers "were able to observe hundreds of outdoor heroin transactions in [the white] area in a fairly short period, the vast majority of which involved white users and dealers" and that seemed "largely invisible to law enforcement" (130). Even in the racially diverse drug market, interviews with police officers suggested that they paid little heed to "a significant and overwhelmingly white market for illegal prescription drugs" that operated alongside the black-dominated distribution of crack cocaine on which officers focused. The researchers concluded that there was likely an "unconscious impact of race on official perceptions of who and what constitutes Seattle's drug problem."

Disproportionate drug arrests are sometimes defended as "pretextual," that is, as reflecting an appropriate, opportunistic use of drug laws as a tool to nab individuals who are suspected of violent or other serious non-drug crimes (see Q32). The defense often goes like this: if police resources are concentrated as they should be in high-crime neighborhoods, and if officers in those neighborhoods proactively stop and investigate individuals who fit a "profile" for likely involvement in nondrug crimes, then resources will be concentrated disproportionately in African American neighborhoods and the residents of those neighborhoods will be disproportionately stopped by the police, with some percentage of those stops inevitably turning up contraband (drugs or guns) and leading to an arrest. In this way, a race-neutral policing strategy that properly seeks to disrupt nondrug crime may lead to racially disparate arrest numbers for drug and gun offenses.

Yet, there remain concerns about the extent to which disproportionate arrests may reflect unfair racial biases. Consider three bodies of evidence. First, research indicates that police have a higher "hit" rate when they stop whites than blacks, that is, they are more likely to find contraband or otherwise establish a basis for making an arrest (Harris, 2017, 138–39). This suggests that officers tend to be less accurate when they determine that a black person may be involved in criminal activity. Second, research indicates that predominantly African American neighborhoods are stigmatized, which includes being perceived as crime-ridden without regard to the actual crime rate (Hannon, 2017). Such racially biased perceptions can affect police behavior. For instance, a recent study in Philadelphia found elevated rates of police frisking pedestrians for weapons in black neighborhoods regardless of neighborhood violent crime rate. The study also found that frisks in black neighborhoods tended to have a lower hit rate, suggesting that police were unduly quick to decide that residents of those neighborhoods might pose a threat.

Third, and finally, a quite large body of research finds that negative stereotypes about African Americans are widespread, often operating at a subconscious level (Ghandoosh, 2014, 13–16). The term "implicit racial bias" is used for these subconscious racial views. One set of studies makes use of the online Implicit Association Test (IAT), which draws out the negative and positive associations that people have with different groups. About 75 percent of test-takers seem to exhibit a bias in favor of whites over blacks. This sort of bias has also been found when the IAT has been administered to criminal justice professionals, including judges and even defense lawyers. Other studies have found that Americans tend to overestimate the proportion of crime committed by blacks, and to believe that blacks are more violence-prone than whites. Video-simulated shooter studies, including studies involving police officers, find that blacks are more quickly perceived to be armed and dangerous than whites.

Collectively, all of this evidence lends support to suspicions that some black neighborhoods may be unjustifiably targeted for high-intensity policing, and that many police stops of black pedestrians and motorists may be tainted by racial biases. Through such mechanisms, police bias could conceivably play a significant role in the racial disparities that exist in the arrest data, and hence also the disparities that exist in the imprisonment data.

Although prosecutors are the recipient of a racially disparate arrestee population, they may in some respects exacerbate the disparities. Particularly important are their charging and plea-bargaining decisions. There is no reason to assume that prosecutors are immune from the problems of stereotyping and implicit racial bias that seem so widespread in American society. However, the prosecutor's role in relation to disparate incarceration has been studied much less extensively than the roles of the police and sentencing judges. Still, the available research, while limited, tends to find that race does affect charging and plea bargaining (Committee on Causes and Consequences of High Rates of Incarceration, 2014, 97). For instance, a recent study of court records in Madison, Wisconsin, found that white defendants were 25 percent more likely than black to have a charge dropped or reduced by the prosecutor (Berdejo, 2018). Notably, this disparity did not exist in higher-level felony cases or as to defendants with prior convictions. The patterns suggest that first-time white defendants facing misdemeanor or low-level felony charges benefit more than their black counterparts from a presumption that the criminal conduct was aberrational and is unlikely to be repeated.

Research on the judicial role similarly finds measurable, but generally modest, contributions to incarceration disparities. Most studies focus on sentencing, although there is also some research on other judicial decisions. For instance, judges are more likely to order black defendants than white defendants jailed while awaiting trial (Committee on Causes and Consequences of High Rates of Incarceration, 2014, 93). This tendency is important in its own right but may have even greater significance than first appears since pretrial detention is associated with less favorable plea deals, higher conviction rates, and a greater likelihood of an incarcerative sentence.

When it comes to sentencing, much evidence suggests that black defendants tend to receive harsher punishment than whites. For instance, in federal court, sentences are on average nine months longer for black than white males (Schmitt, Reedt, & Blackwell, 2017, 3). Nationally, blacks account for more than 48 percent of life-sentenced prisoners (Nellis, 2017, 15). In Florida, blacks convicted of felony drug offenses receive sentences two-thirds longer than whites (Salman, Lee, & Braga, 2016). In Madison, Wisconsin, 52 percent of black defendants are sentenced to incarceration, as opposed to only 35 percent of whites (Berdejo, 2018).

However, such gross comparisons do not necessarily indicate that judges are exercising their sentencing discretion in disparate ways. For one thing, some racial sentencing differences result from the application of mandatory minimums. For instance, in the federal system, more black than white drug defendants are subject to a mandatory minimum (U.S. Sentencing Commission, 2011, D-39). Indeed, blacks account for 54 percent of mandatory sentences of twenty years or more, and nearly two-thirds of mandatory life terms. In Florida, blacks account for two-thirds of the defendants subject to a sentence enhancement for carrying drugs in one of the protected zones around churches, parks, and housing projects (Salman, Lee, & Braga, 2016). Such sentencing laws have a disproportionate impact on African Americans in other states, too; the high-density urban neighborhoods where many African Americans live tend to be blanketed by protected zones (Ghandoosh, 2015, 15). "Three strikes and you are out" and other recidivism-based mandatory minimums may also disproportionately affect African Americans. Meanwhile, under the Minnesota sentencing guidelines, many more black defendants are recommended for imprisonment than would be expected based only on racial differences in arrest or conviction rates (Frase & Mitchell, 2017).

Yet, even apart from the impact of minimums and guidelines, there appear to be racial disparities in sentencing that cannot readily be accounted for by reference to legally permissible sentencing factors, such as offense severity and criminal history. For instance, the U.S. Sentencing Commission has concluded that on average black male defendants receive sentences that are 19 percent longer than similarly situated white male defendants (Schmitt, Reedt, & Blackwell, 2017, 2). Dozens of other studies on federal and state sentencing systems find similar results (Spohn, 2017). Controlling for a range of different variables, blacks are in general more likely than whites to be sentenced to incarceration, and when incarcerated to receive longer terms behind bars. It is not clear why race has this impact, but it seems quite plausible that implicit racial bias plays a role, as well as some aspects of African American socioeconomic disadvantage that are not controlled for in the research.

Similar factors may also affect decision making at the "back end" of the criminal justice system. While racial disparities in corrections and parole have not been studied as much as disparities at the sentencing stage, some studies do find that black offenders tend to receive less favorable outcomes as to, for instance, discretionary parole release from prison and revocations of community supervision (Huebner & Bynum, 2008; Steinmetz & Anderson, 2015).

In sum, while African Americans are already dramatically overrepresented relative to their share of the general population at the very first (arrest) stage of the criminal process, racial disparities are likely amplified at later stages from charging and pretrial release through parole release and community supervision. Moreover, it does not appear that disparate outcomes in the court and corrections systems can be entirely accounted for by reference to offense severity or criminal history. However, in appropriately controlled studies, the unexplained racial disparities are not necessarily large at any given stage of the process and are often confined to particular offense categories. Yet, as a committee of the National Research Council recently concluded, the "cumulative effect [of modest unwarranted disparities at each stage] is significant" (Committee on Causes and Consequences of High Rates of Incarceration, 2014, 93).

FURTHER READING

Alexander, Michelle. 2012. *The New Jim Crow: Mass Incarceration in the Age of Colorblindness*. New York: New Press.

Becket, Katherine, Nyrop, Kris, & Pfingst, Lori. 2006. "Race, Drugs, and Policing: Understanding Disparities in Drug Delivery Arrests." *Criminology*, 44, 105.

Berdejo, Carlos. 2018. "Criminalizing Race: Racial Disparities in Plea Bargaining." *Boston College Law Review*, 59, 1187.

Committee on Causes and Consequences of High Rates of Incarceration, National Research Council of the National Academies. 2014. *The Growth of Incarceration in the United States*. Washington, DC: The National Academies Press.

Federal Bureau of Investigation. 2017. *Crime in the United States, 2016*. Washington, DC: U.S. Department of Justice.

Forman, James. 2012. "Racial Critiques of Mass Incarceration: Beyond the New Jim Crow." *New York University Law Review*, 87, 21.

Frase, Richard & Mitchell, Kelly Lyn. 2017. "Why Are Minnesota's Prison Populations Continuing to Rise in an Era of Decarceration?" *Federal Sentencing Reporter*, 30, 114.

Ghandoosh, Nazgol. 2014. *Race and Punishment: Racial Perceptions of Crime and Support for Punitive Policies*. Washington, DC: The Sentencing Project.

Ghandoosh, Nazgol. 2015. *Black Lives Matter: Eliminating Racial Inequity in the Criminal Justice System*. Washington, DC: The Sentencing Project.

Hannon, Lance. 2017. "An Exploratory Multilevel Analysis of Pedestrian Frisks in Philadelphia." *Race and Justice*. Prepublished on September 22.

Harris, David. 2017. "Racial Profiling." In *Reforming Criminal Justice: Policing*, 117. Edited by Erik Luna. Phoenix: Arizona State University.

Huebner, Beth & Bynum, Timothy. 2008. "The Role of Race and Ethnicity in Parole Decisions." *Criminology*, 46, 907.

Klarman, Michael. 2009. "Scottsboro." *Marquette Law Review*, 93, 379.

Nellis, Ashley. 2017. *Still Life: America's Increasing Use of Life and Long-Term Sentences*. Washington, DC: The Sentencing Project.

Oshinsky, David. 1996. *Worse Than Slavery: Parchman Farm and the Ordeal of Jim Crow Justice*. New York: Free Press.

Salman, Josh, Lee, Dag, & Braga, Michael. 2016. "'This Is a Culture War': When It Comes to Punishment, Racial Disparities Are Pervasive." *Sarasota Herald Tribune*. Retrieved from http://projects.heraldtribune.com/one-war-two-races/punishment.

Schmitt, Glenn, Reedt, Louis, & Blackwell, Kevin. 2017. *Demographic Differences in Sentencing: An Update to the 2012 Booker Report*. Washington, DC: U.S. Sentencing Commission.

Spohn, Cassia. 2017. "Race and Sentencing Disparity." In *Reforming Criminal Justice: Punishment, Incarceration, and Release*, 169. Edited by Erik Luna. Phoenix: Arizona State University.

Steinmetz, Kevin & Anderson, Jamaliya. 2015. "A Probation Profana-
tion: Race, Ethnicity, and Probation in a Midwestern Sample." *Race
and Justice*, 6, 325.

U.S. Sentencing Commission. 2011. *Report to the Congress: Mandatory
Minimum Penalties in the Federal Criminal Justice System*. Washington,
DC: U.S. Sentencing Commission.

Q36: ARE THERE OTHER RACIAL OR ETHNIC GROUPS WHO EXPERIENCE DISPROPORTIONATE INCARCERATION?

Answer: African Americans are hardly the only group to experience disproportionate incarceration. Among other disproportionately incarcerated racial and ethnic groups, Hispanics (Latinos) and Native Americans
(American Indians) have received the most attention.

The Facts: Black incarceration rates have dominated both the research
and the public discussion of disparate incarceration in the United States.
However, other racial and ethnic groups have also experienced incarceration rates that are disproportionate to their share of the general population. The incarceration rates of two groups in particular, Hispanics and
Native Americans, have received growing attention in recent years.

Hispanics are imprisoned in federal and state institutions at a rate of
856 inmates per 100,000 adults—about half the black figure but triple the
white (Carson, 2018, 8). By contrast, the Hispanic *jail* incarceration rate
(185 per 100,000) is only a little higher than the white (171) and much
lower than the black (599) (Zeng, 2018, 3). The Hispanic share of the
community supervision population (probation and parole) appears to be
slightly *lower* than the Hispanic share of the general population (Kaeble &
Bonczar, 2016). In the juvenile system, the out-of-home placement rate of
Hispanic youth is about 65 percent higher than is the rate for white youth
(Sentencing Project, 2017a).

According to victim surveys, Hispanic offenders account for about
17 percent of violent crime (Morgan, 2017, 3), which is about the same
as the Hispanic share of the general population and a little less than the
Hispanic share of the prison population (23 percent). In 2016, FBI data
indicate that 18 percent of arrestees in the United States were Hispanic
(Federal Bureau of Investigation, 2017, Table 21), although this data must
be used with caution since ethnicity went unreported for about 21 percent of arrests. Hispanics accounted for 24 percent of arrests for major

violent crime, 21 percent of burglary arrests, 11 percent of fraud arrests, 24 percent of weapons arrests, and 20 percent of drug arrests. The general picture seems to be one of some Hispanic overrepresentation among those arrested for serious crime but to a much less extent than with African Americans. As with African Americans, the Hispanic arrest rates for serious crimes are roughly in line with the Hispanic imprisonment rate. This suggests that criminal justice actors may add relatively little to disparities that arise at the offense and arrest stages.

As of 2016, the federal Bureau of Justice Statistics reports there were nearly 23,000 federal and state prisoners who were categorized as "American Indian or Alaska Native" (Carson, 2018, 25–26). This figure indicates an imprisonment rate for this population of about 857 per 100,000, about the same as the Hispanic rate. However, the jail incarceration rate was substantially higher than that of Hispanics at 359 per 100,000 (Zeng, 2018, 3), giving Native Americans a higher overall incarceration rate than Hispanics. The figure would likely grow even somewhat larger if jails administered by Indian tribes or the federal Bureau of Indian Affairs were included; these facilities hold about 2,500 inmates (Minton & Cowhig, 2017). Native Americans appear to be somewhat overrepresented in the national parole population but somewhat underrepresented in the probation population (Glaze & Bonczar, 2011, 35, 45). In the juvenile system, the out-of-home placement rate of Native American youth is about three times higher than is the rate for white youth (Sentencing Project, 2017b).

Victim surveys indicate that about 0.4 percent of violent crimes are committed by American Indians or Alaska Natives (Morgan, 2017, 3), which is substantially lower than their 0.8 percent share of the general population or their 1.5 percent share of the prison population. However, the Native American arrest figures are considerably higher. The FBI data for 2016 indicate that American Indians and Alaska Natives accounted for 2.0 percent of total arrests, 1.8 percent of arrests for major violent crime, 1.0 percent of burglary arrests, 1.2 percent of fraud arrests, 0.9 percent of weapons arrests, and 1.0 percent of drug arrests (Federal Bureau of Investigation, 2017, Table 21). Thus, there is a substantial overrepresentation of Native Americans in the arrest population, especially with respect to major violent crime, and this overrepresentation seems roughly in line with their overrepresentation in the prison population.

The disproportionate incarceration of Hispanics and Native Americans has not been studied as much as the disproportionate incarceration of African Americans, but likely arises to some extent from a similar set of dynamics. All three groups have suffered a long history of discrimination and negative stereotyping in the United States and continue to experience elevated rates of socioeconomic disadvantage. These factors doubtlessly contribute to the disproportionate arrest rates for all three groups.

As to Hispanics, a growing body of appropriately controlled studies indicates that disparate incarceration cannot be fully explained by reference to offense severity and criminal history. For instance, the U.S. Sentencing Commission has found that Hispanic males in the federal system receive sentences that average 5.3 percent longer than those of similarly situated white males (Schmitt, Reedt, & Blackwell, 2017, 6). Similar results, reflecting a modest but statistically significant tendency toward greater severity for Hispanic defendants, have also been found in various state-level studies (e.g., Ulmer, Painter-Davis, & Tinik, 2014; Bales & Piquero, 2012).

Much less research is available regarding Native Americans. This is likely due in part to their much smaller numbers, but may also reflect the unique complexities of criminal court jurisdiction in cases with Native American defendants. Depending on the state, the location of the crime within the state, the type of crime, and the race of the victim, a Native American might be prosecuted in a state court, a federal court, or one of the hundreds of highly varied tribal courts that exist in the United States (Droske, 2008, 737–38). It is thought that some of the Native American incarceration disparity might result from the fact that in some states, Native American defendants are commonly prosecuted in federal court for engaging in criminal conduct that, if committed by non-Native Americans, would be prosecuted in state court, where penalties tend to be lower. In any event, the highly fractured nature of jurisdiction in Native American cases makes it particularly difficult to develop helpful, appropriate comparisons of sentencing outcomes.

FURTHER READING

Bales, William & Piquero, Alex. 2012. "Racial/Ethnic Differentials in Sentencing to Incarceration." *Justice Quarterly*, 29, 742.

Carson, E. Ann. 2018. *Prisoners in 2016*. Washington, DC: U.S. Department of Justice.

Droske, Timothy. 2008. "Correcting Native American Sentencing Disparity Post-*Booker*." *Marquette Law Review*, 91, 722.

Glaze, Lauren & Bonczar, Thomas. 2011. *Probation and Parole in the United States, 2010*. Washington, DC: U.S. Department of Justice.

Kaeble, Donald & Bonczar, Thomas. 2016. *Probation and Parole in the United States, 2015*. Washington, DC: U.S. Department of Justice.

Minton, Todd & Cowhig, Mary. 2017. *Jails in Indian Country, 2016.* Washington, DC: U.S. Department of Justice.

Morgan, Rachel. 2017. *Race and Hispanic Origin of Victims and Offenders, 2012–15.* Washington, DC: U.S. Department of Justice.

Schmitt, Glenn, Reedt, Louis, & Blackwell, Kevin. 2017. *Demographic Differences in Sentencing: An Update to the 2012* Booker *Report.* Washington, DC: U.S. Sentencing Commission.

Sentencing Project. 2017a. *Fact Sheet: Latino Disparities in Youth Incarceration.* Washington, DC: The Sentencing Project.

Sentencing Project. 2017b. *Fact Sheet: Native Disparities in Youth Incarceration.* Washington, DC: The Sentencing Project.

Ulmer, Jeffrey, Painter-Davis, Noah, & Tinik, Leigh. 2014. "Disproportionate Imprisonment of Black and Hispanic Males: Sentencing Discretion, Processing Outcomes, and Policy Structures." *Justice Quarterly,* 33, 642.

Zeng, Zhen. 2018. *Jail Inmates in 2016.* Washington, DC: U.S. Department of Justice.

Q37: WHAT SHOULD BE DONE TO ADDRESS RACIAL DISPARITIES IN INCARCERATION?

Answer: To the extent that the problem is connected to long-standing, deep-rooted patterns of socioeconomic disadvantage, disparate incarceration defies easy resolution. Additionally, reformers must take care that reduced minority incarceration is not pursued at the cost of increased crime and violence in minority communities. While no good quick fixes seem available, it is possible that some progress might be achieved by raising awareness of implicit racial bias among those who work in the criminal justice system and by requiring policy makers to consider the racial impact of any proposed changes to criminal justice policies.

The Facts: Disparate incarceration means that the costs of mass incarceration—including the stigmatization and diminished life prospects experienced by individuals who have been incarcerated, the financial harm to families, and the psychological and developmental harms to children—are concentrated disproportionately in historically disadvantaged communities, thus perpetuating and compounding legacies of discrimination and marginalization. Disparate incarceration also seems to contribute to the distrust of police and the legal system that exists in some minority communities and that may diminish the effectiveness of law enforcement efforts in those communities. Disparate incarceration thus seems a social problem worthy of policy makers' attention.

The problem, however, defies easy resolution. As detailed in Q35, much of the phenomenon of disparate incarceration can be attributed to disparate offending. The interests of disadvantaged minority communities would hardly be well served by policy changes that had the effect of largely eliminating accountability for violent and other serious crimes in those communities. Reducing minority crime rates may need to be a central part of any strategy that aims to achieve large reductions in minority incarceration. Yet, after decades of research, policy makers still lack a "silver bullet"—proven, easily replicable methods to achieve large, sustained improvements in public safety in high-crime, socioeconomically disadvantaged neighborhoods. There seems only so much that policing can accomplish—especially if we do not wish to see arrest, conviction, and incarceration rates increase. If the goal is to reduce both crime and incarceration on a large scale, there may need to be substantial increases in social investment in disadvantaged communities in pursuit of broad improvements in areas such as education, public health, and employment.

Even to the extent that disparate incarceration results from unfair decisions within the criminal justice system, effective policy solutions still seem elusive. For one thing, as seen in Q35, disparities are not caused by decisions at just one stage of the criminal process, but rather arise in relatively modest ways throughout the system. For another, conscious, deliberate racial discrimination does not seem to be a primary driver of unwarranted disparities. A more significant problem may be implicit racial bias, which, by its very nature as a phenomenon of the unconscious, seems harder to address. Adding to the difficulty is the unfortunate correlation of race with various socioeconomic considerations that are traditionally—and arguably quite appropriately—a routine part of the decision making by police, prosecutors, judges, and corrections officials. For instance, the fact that a defendant has a job is typically regarded as favorable if the defendant is being considered for pretrial release, for admission into a diversion program as an alternative to conventional prosecution, or at sentencing for a community-based sanction in lieu of incarceration. However, since black unemployment rates are substantially higher than white, these seemingly race-neutral practices will tend to exacerbate disparate incarceration. Rooting out the consideration of all factors that have a disparate impact in all criminal justice decision making would be an extremely difficult project, and might well create worse problems than it solves, for example, if most diversion programs then proved unworkable and had to be discontinued.

The history of the federal sentencing guidelines, which were adopted in part to address racial disparities, provides a cautionary tale. Going into effect in 1987, the guidelines greatly reduced judicial sentencing discretion, discouraged the consideration of socioeconomic and related factors by the sentencing judge, and made sentencing decisions overwhelmingly dependent on just offense severity and criminal history (O'Hear, 2017, 99–100). By taking off the table many traditionally recognized mitigating circumstances, the guidelines contributed to a sharp increase in the severity of federal sentences in the 1980s and 1990s, and a related explosion in the size of the federal prison population. Yet, even at those costs, the guidelines proved unsuccessful at wringing racial disparities from the federal sentencing system. Indeed, the gap in average sentences between black and white defendants actually *increased* under the guidelines (109). The most important driver of this disparity was likely the guidelines' particularly harsh treatment of crack cocaine offenses, which were disproportionately associated with black defendants (112). This provides a good example of the potential for facially race-neutral sentencing factors to generate racial disparities. In 2002, on the eve of major changes to the federal sentencing system that reduced the importance of the guidelines, the average sentence in crack cases (mostly involving blacks defendants) was 119 months, while the average sentence in powder cocaine cases (mostly involving white defendants) was only 78 months. There is no reason to think that the guidelines' crack-powder disparity was intended to exacerbate racial disparities, but that was precisely the impact. Racial effects can creep into even the most aggressive efforts to control discretion and eliminate bias in the criminal justice system.

The unintended or incidental character of racial disparities in incarceration helps to explain why constitutional litigation has proven ineffective as a reform strategy. The Fourteenth Amendment to the U.S. Constitution requires "equal protection of the laws," but the Supreme Court has interpreted this provision such that a policy's disparate racial impact does not, in itself, make the policy unconstitutional. In order to have a policy overturned on equal protection grounds, a person must normally show that the policy is racially discriminatory on its face or otherwise reflects a conscious intent to discriminate. Thus, for instance, in *Johnson v. California* (2005), the Supreme Court supported a lawsuit challenging a California policy requiring the racial segregation of some prison inmates. However, in *McKleskey v. Kemp* (1987), the Supreme Court turned aside an equal protection challenge to the death penalty that was based on a statistical demonstration of racial disparities in its administration. In contrast to *Johnson*, where there was a policy that openly discriminated on the basis of race, the disparate impact in McKleskey did not result from any policy that was discriminatory on its face; nor was there otherwise proof of *intentional* discrimination in the adoption or administration of the death penalty.

Arguably, the best response to racially disparate incarceration would be reforms designed in a general way to minimize the unnecessary incarceration of *all* defendants and to diminish the long-term stigma and collateral consequences of *all* convictions. In effect, such reforms would mean that racial disparities in incarceration simply matter less. One imagines, for instance, that there would be far less consternation over a prison population that is two-thirds people of color if the overall size of the population were 500,000, instead of the actual 1.5 million.

On the other hand, some incarceration-reducing reforms threaten to *increase* racial imbalances. Drug treatment courts (DTCs) provide a good illustration. As detailed in Q10, DTCs are found throughout the United States and are generally regarded as a successful innovation that helps to reduce participants' drug use and recidivism rates. However, to the extent that DTCs serve to divert some offenders from prison, those who are white are more likely to benefit than those of color (National Association of Criminal Defense Lawyers, 2009, 42–43). This is because people of color are more likely to have a disqualifying criminal history that keeps them out of a DTC, and because, even if admitted, people of color are more likely to suffer from unemployment, poverty, low educational attainment, and other risk factors that diminish the likelihood of successful treatment. Unfortunately, failing out of a DTC often results in even more incarceration than would have been imposed through conventional case processing. In any event, DTCs throughout the country have struggled to maintain diverse "client" populations. All too often, they are perceived to be a pathway out of incarceration for white offenders only. No matter how well intentioned and successful on their own terms, incarceration-reducing reforms that disproportionately benefit white offenders will do little to reduce racial tensions related to mass incarceration, and may even prove counterproductive.

There are few serious reform proposals that get more directly at the problem of racial disparities in incarceration. Moreover, those reforms that have been adopted in a few jurisdictions in recent years are of uncertain effectiveness. Still, pending further research on their impact, they may merit consideration for replication elsewhere. First, a handful of states have adopted policies requiring the preparation of "racial impact statements" when changes to criminal laws are considered (Ghandoosh, 2015, 20). These are similar, for instance, to environmental impact statements, which require policy makers to assess and consider the consequences of their decisions on the natural environment. Likewise, racial impact statements aim to ensure that policy makers understand the potential for proposed criminal justice policy changes to exacerbate racial disparities.

Second, police departments, courts, and other criminal justice agencies can work to mitigate implicit racial bias. Training programs have been developed that help people to better understand their unconscious biases, and some research indicates that such programs can have a positive impact (Nellis, 2016, 13). It may also help for agencies to work on recruiting and retaining more diverse workforces. Some evidence suggests, for instance, that black police officers may be less prone to racially biased attitudes than whites (Ghandoosh, 2015, 21).

Finally, two states have adopted (although one subsequently repealed) a "racial justice act," which allows defendants who have been sentenced to death to challenge their sentences based on statistical demonstrations of disparities in the administration of the death penalty (Spohn, 2017, 183). In effect, these statutes overrule the Supreme Court's decision in *McKleskey v. Kemp* (noted earlier). It is also possible to imagine more broadly targeted racial justice acts that would force consideration of racial disparities in sentencing outside the death context. For instance, there might be statistically based challenges to life sentences, too, or even more ambitiously to any prison sentence.

FURTHER READING

Ghandoosh, Nazgol. 2015. *Black Lives Matter: Eliminating Racial Inequity in the Criminal Justice System*. Washington, DC: The Sentencing Project.

National Association of Criminal Defense Lawyers. 2009. *America's Problem-Solving Courts: The Criminal Costs of Treatment and the Case for Reform*. Washington, DC: National Association of Criminal Defense Lawyers.

Nellis, Ashley. 2016. *The Color of Justice: Racial and Ethnic Disparity in State Prisons*. Washington, DC: The Sentencing Project.

O'Hear, Michael. 2017. *The Failure of Sentencing Reform*. Santa Barbara, CA: Praeger.

Spohn, Cassia. 2017. "Race and Sentencing Disparity." In *Reforming Criminal Justice: Punishment, Incarceration, and Release*, 169. Edited by Erik Luna. Phoenix: Arizona State University.

8

⬦⬦⬦

Public Opinion, Politics, and Reform

As explained in Chapter 6, contemporary American incarceration rates stand far above international and historical norms. In recent years, motivated primarily by the growing fiscal burdens of mass incarceration, policy makers across the United States from both major parties have embraced reforms that aim to reduce excessive imprisonment. To date, however, few states have made much progress in downsizing their prison populations. A variety of more ambitious reforms could likely achieve larger-scale decarceration with little or no adverse impact on public safety. However, there are concerns that the political prospects for more effective reforms may be limited by entrenched tough-on-crime attitudes among voters.

Q38: DOES PUBLIC OPINION ALWAYS FAVOR TOUGHER PUNISHMENT?

Answer: In public opinion surveys over a period of many years, large majorities have consistently expressed the view that sentencing judges in the United States are too lenient. To a great extent, however, these views likely reflect misinformation regarding what actually happens in typical cases. Other research indicates that, if given more complete information, laypeople tend to exhibit views of sentencing that are similar to those of judges. Additionally, public opinion surveys point to widespread support for offender rehabilitation and more cost-effective criminal justice policies. Overall, the evidence indicates that American voters are not unreservedly punitive, but rather hold more nuanced, and perhaps somewhat contradictory, views regarding crime and punishment.

The Facts: It is not hard to find evidence that the American public holds quite punitive attitudes toward crime. Consider, for instance, results from the General Social Survey. (A leading national opinion survey, the GSS is a project of the independent research organization NORC at the University of Chicago, with principal funding from the National Science Foundation.) Since 1972, survey participants have been regularly asked to opine whether their local courts "deal too harshly or not harshly enough with criminals." Each time, a large majority (ranging from 57 percent to 87 percent, depending on the year) has answered "not harshly enough" (NORC, 2018). Over the years, the GSS has consistently found that majorities nearly as large support the death penalty. Many other surveys asking these and similar questions over the same time period reach similar results (Ramirez, 2013).

Within these overarching tendencies, though, substantial differences among social groups can be observed. In one recent survey, for instance, respondents were asked whether society would be better served by harsher punishment or by greater efforts to rehabilitate those who have been convicted of crimes (Opportunity Agenda, 2014, 20). While a 54 percent majority overall favored harsher punishment, rehabilitation was more commonly embraced by liberals (64 percent), college graduates (58 percent), African Americans (53 percent), and Asian Americans (53 percent). It should also be noted that tough-on-crime attitudes have been slowly declining since the mid-1990s (Enns, 2014).

Many studies have attempted to discern the underlying attitudes that drive support for punitive policies. Unnever and Cullen (2010) have identified three competing theories. First, there is the "crime-distrust" model. From this perspective, people support tough-on-crime policies primarily because they fear crime and because they do not trust that government agencies will successfully mitigate the threat of crime through offender rehabilitation, social welfare programs, or any other alternative to long-term incapacitation and stern deterrence. Second, there is the "moral decline" model. On this view, people embrace punitive policies primarily as a response to a perceived loss of cohesion and moral order in society. Harsh punishment for rule breakers is seen as a way to reaffirm the existence of shared moral values and to strengthen their role as a unifying force in society. Third, there is the "racial animus" model. Proponents of this model argue that racial and ethnic bias continues to play a central role in white support for punitive policies. Crucial to this model is research showing that "a sizable proportion of the American public perceives the crime problem through a racial lens that results in an association of crime with African Americans, especially Black men" (106). Given this racial lens, "punitive attitudes may provide white Americans with a means to control or subordinate black people, or they may simply offer a way to vent anti-black resentments" (106).

After identifying these competing theories, Unnever and Cullen sought to test them through an analysis of how well punitive attitudes correlate with various proxies for each of the three models. Controlling for age, race, sex, political ideology, and a few other demographic variables, the researchers found some support in the survey data for each model. Thus, for instance,

- "the perception of a worsening crime rate consistently predicts a more punitive approach to controlling crime";
- "individuals who believe that society is in a state of moral decline are significantly more likely to support a punitive approach to crime"; and
- "racial resentment . . . significantly predicts greater support for a punitive approach to crime" (114–15).

On the whole, Unnever and Cullen found strongest support for the racial animus model. Several other studies have also found close associations between punitive attitudes and racial resentment (Committee on Causes and Consequences of High Rates of Incarceration, 2014, 122).

If most Americans think that current sentences are not harsh enough, does that validate mass incarceration and perhaps suggest that we should have even *more* mandatory minimums and other tough-on-crime laws? Not necessarily. There are good reasons to take the results of the GSS and other public opinion surveys with the proverbial grain of salt. For one thing, the connection between punitive attitudes and racial bias (conscious or unconscious) is an important consideration.

For another, support for punitive policies may be based on wrong beliefs about the realities of crime and punishment. For instance, Unnever and Cullen found a correlation between punitive attitudes and a belief that crime is getting worse, but most Americans hold mistaken views about crime trends. As discussed in Q31, crime has consistently dropped or remained the same in the United States since the early 1990s. However, in almost every year, the Gallup Poll has found that large majorities of respondents—often two-thirds or more—believe that crime is *increasing* (Opportunity Agenda, 2014, 12).

Sensationalized news coverage of highly atypical crimes likely leaves many Americans with serious misimpressions about crime in other respects, too (Roberts et al., 2002, 78). Surveys indicate that many more Americans base their opinions about crime on what is reported in the news media than on personal experience (Opportunity Agenda, 2014, 18). Yet, the media "disproportionately portrays crime as violent and the people engaging in violent crime as disproportionately non-white and male" (18). Black-on-white crime and male-on-female crime seem especially prone to disproportionately heavy media coverage (Ghandoosh, 2014, 22–23). Such coverage may strengthen racial biases and reinforce the link between punitiveness and racial animus. Additionally, research indicates that exposure to crime news coverage may engender higher levels of fear of crime in some people (22). Similar dynamics may also be associated with the mass consumption of crime-oriented dramatic entertainment and reality TV shows (Roberts et al., 2002, 82–84).

Julian Roberts and his coauthors argue that the media not only influences public perceptions of crime but also public views regarding the proper responses to crime (2002, 84–89). The imperatives of dramatic storytelling (both fiction and nonfiction) tend to push against expansive views of crime in its social context and depictions of broadly targeted reforms that try to address the root causes of crime. Thus, the media reinforces "simple views of the causes of crime" and promotes "decisive, event- and action-oriented responses to crime" (92).

Many researchers believe that if the public had more complete information about crime and punishment, support for punitive views would likely be much less. Perhaps the best evidence for this comes from a number of studies in which lay people have been asked to select a sentence in a particular case after being given some information about the crime and the criminal (Tonry, 2004, 36). After indicating their initial preferences, participants are given addition information about sentencing options and practices, and then asked again for their views. With this additional information, participants tend to moderate their sentences and become more likely to favor community-based alternatives to imprisonment. Indeed, the research indicates that the views of lay people, if well informed, tend to mirror those of lawyers and judges. Further support for this comes from studies of the few jurisdictions in which lay people are actually given the opportunity to impose sentences in some types of cases (Roberts et al., 2002, 94).

Even in the more conventional public opinion surveys, Americans seem far less punitive when the questions are framed differently than just as a choice between "too harshly" versus "not harshly enough." To note a few representative findings from several national polls:

- Eighty-four percent agree that "[s]ome of the money that we are spending on locking up low-risk, non-violent inmates should be shifted to strengthening community corrections programs like probation and parole."
- Fifty-eight percent say that prevention or rehabilitation should be the top priority for dealing with crime, as opposed to only 19 percent who favor longer sentences and more prisons.
- Seventy-nine percent agree that "under the right conditions, many offenders can turn their lives around."
- Sixty-one percent say it is "very important" to put nonviolent offenders in treatment, employment, or education programs.
- Eighty-seven percent agree that "[i]t does not matter whether a non-violent offender is in prison for 18 or 24 [or] 30 months. . . . What really matters is that the system does a better job of making sure that when an offender does get out, he is less likely to commit another crime."
- Seventy-seven percent favor alternatives to prison for nonviolent, nonsexual offenders whose crime did not involve significant property loss (O'Hear & Wheelock, 2015).

Such responses exhibit considerable hope for offender rehabilitation and interest in community-based alternatives to incarceration, especially for nonviolent offenders.

Broadly worded questions about whether "criminals" should be treated more harshly implicitly invite opinions based on the worst sorts of crimes that jump first into mind (influenced, no doubt, by the media tendencies noted earlier). However, when respondents are prompted more specifically to consider less serious crimes, they show a more forgiving side. Similarly, when asked about *juvenile* crimes, large majorities indicate support for rehabilitation and alternatives to imprisonment (Opportunity Agenda, 2014, 38–39).

Or consider public views of the death penalty. Consistent supermajority support for the death penalty in surveys like the GSS is often cited as a leading indicator of American punitiveness. However, when survey respondents are told about life without the possibility of parole as an alternative to capital punishment, support for the death penalty consistently drops by 10 to 20 percentage points, falling a little below the 50 percent mark (Opportunity Agenda, 2014, 36).

Overall, public opinion research indicates that Americans hold nuanced views about crime and punishment—views that reflect conflicting instincts and that are to some extent malleable based on the framing of questions (Pickett & Baker, 2014). As Michael Tonry puts it, Americans have "complex and ambivalent attitudes":

> They believe crimes are the product of bad moral choices, disadvantaged backgrounds, and substance abuse. They want offenders to be punished and to be rehabilitated. They are much more willing to pay more taxes for treatment programs than for prison building. They insist on prison sentences only for the most violent crimes. (Tonry, 2004, 36)

FURTHER READING

Committee on Causes and Consequences of High Rates of Incarceration, National Research Council of the National Academies. 2014. *The Growth of Incarceration in the United States*. Washington, DC: The National Academies Press.

Enns, Peter K. 2014. "The Public's Increasing Punitiveness and Its Influence on Mass Incarceration in the United States." *American Journal of Political Science*, 58, 857.

Ghandoosh, Nazgol. 2014. *Race and Punishment: Racial Perceptions of Crime and Support for Punitive Policies*. Washington, DC: The Sentencing Project.

NORC. 2018. GSS Data Explorer. Interactive website at http://www .norc.org/Research/Capabilities/Pages/gss-data-explorer.aspx.

O'Hear, Michael & Wheelock, Darren. 2015. "Imprisonment Inertia and Public Attitudes toward 'Truth in Sentencing.'" *Brigham Young University Law Review*, 2015, 257.

Opportunity Agenda. 2014. *An Overview of Public Opinion and Discourse on Criminal Justice Issues*. New York: Tides Center.

Pickett, Justin & Baker, Thomas. 2014. "The Pragmatic American: Empirical Reality or Methodological Artifact?" *Criminology*, 52, 195.

Ramirez, Mark. 2013. "Punitive Sentiment." *Criminology*, 51, 329.

Roberts, Julian et al. 2002. *Penal Populism and Public Opinion: Lessons from Five Countries*. New York: Oxford University Press.

Tonry, Michael. 2004. *Thinking about Crime: Sense and Sensibility in American Penal Culture.* New York: Oxford University Press.

Unnever, James & Cullen, Francis. 2010. "The Social Sources of Americans' Punitiveness: A Test of Three Competing Models." *Criminology,* 48, 99.

Q39: ARE THE FISCAL BURDENS OF MASS INCARCERATION CHANGING THE POLITICS OF PUNISHMENT?

Answer: Since 2000, the burgeoning fiscal costs of mass incarceration have received increasing attention from political leaders in both parties. With these costs often characterized as "unsustainable," dozens of states have adopted reforms that are intended to reduce the incarceration of offenders who have been convicted of nonviolent crimes or are otherwise considered low risk. It is not clear, however, whether the American politics of punishment in the early twenty-first century are actually fundamentally different from what they were in the late twentieth century. In general, fiscally motivated reforms have been modest in ambition and have proven more successful in holding down *growth* in imprisonment than in achieving large, durable *reductions* in imprisonment.

The Facts: In the 1990s, both major parties tried to position themselves as tough on crime. The competitive efforts by both Democratic and Republican politicians to gain recognition as "the toughest" pushed legislatures to adopt increasingly harsh and ill-conceived policies, such as California's notorious "three strikes and you are out" law (see Q1). Since 2000, a somewhat different political dynamic has become apparent. Although there has been plenty of tough-on-crime rhetoric—embraced, for instance, to seemingly good effect by Donald Trump as a presidential candidate in 2016—extreme proposals no longer seem to move so quickly and easily through legislatures. If anything, the legislative current has been in the opposite direction, with all or nearly all states adopting reforms intended to divert nonviolent offenders from prison, reduce prison terms, and move inmates back into the community more quickly when it is safe to do so (O'Hear, 2017a, xiv). Even the California three-strikes law was finally softened in 2012.

Cost considerations have figured quite prominently in the pro-reform arguments. It is probably no accident that the new political dynamic first became apparent at about the time of the 2001 recession, which stressed state budgets across the nation, while another reform wave gathered strength in the wake of the Great Recession of 2007–2009.

Given the remarkable growth of corrections spending in the late twentieth century, it is hardly surprising that the fiscal burdens of mass incarceration have become a central part of the political discourse regarding criminal justice policy. In real dollars, the total cost of state, federal, and local corrections in the United States quintupled between 1980 and 2009, reaching more than $80 billion (Committee on Causes and Consequences of High Rates of Incarceration, 2014, 315–16). This rate of growth exceeded almost every other significant component of state spending over that time, including the budgets for education, public assistance, and transportation (314). In most states, corrections spending has become the third-largest category of general fund expenditures behind only education and Medicaid.

In the face of these budgetary challenges, fiscal conservatism has led even many Republicans to voice concern over excessive incarceration and to embrace reform. For instance, Right on Crime, a leading reform organization, declares in its "Statement of Principles":

> Conservatives correctly insist that government services be evaluated on whether they produce the best possible results at the lowest possible cost, but too often this lens of accountability has not focused as much on public safety policies as other areas of government. . . .
>
> Conservatives are known for being tough on crime, but we must also be tough on criminal justice spending. That means demanding more cost-effective approaches that enhance public safety. A clear example is our reliance on prisons, which serve a critical role by incapacitating dangerous offenders and career criminals but are not the solution for every type of offender.

Signatories of the Statement of Principles include former Republican governors and presidential hopefuls Jeb Bush, Mike Huckabee, and Rick Perry; former Republican Speaker of the House Newt Gingrich; former Republican U.S. attorney general Edwin Meese, III; former Republican U.S. education secretary and "drug czar" William Bennett; influential anti-tax crusader Grover Norquist; and leading "family values" activists such as Gary Bauer, Tony Perkins, and Ralph Reed.

With incarceration-reducing reforms now gaining bipartisan support in Congress and state legislatures across the United States, it is clear that the American politics of punishment are no longer what they were in the

1990s. Yet, while the fiscal burdens of mass incarceration have reshaped the political dynamics in some respects, it is less clear whether the changes should be regarded as truly fundamental.

There are many reasons to doubt that the new money-focused reform movement will achieve any large-scale rollback of mass incarceration. First, the modest scope of what has been accomplished thus far should be noted. The total drop in the nation's state and federal prison populations between its peak in 2009 and 2016 amounted to a reduction from 1.6 million inmates to 1.5 million inmates. Moreover, a single state, California, accounted for more than 37 percent of the entire national prison population reduction. That state, notably, was forced into exceptionally aggressive reforms by a federal court order, and not principally by arguments about saving money (O'Hear, 2017a, 191–94). Additionally, it should be appreciated that recent successes in reducing imprisonment follow a long period of declining crime rates in the United States; based on crime trends alone, some shrinkage in prison populations should have occurred even without any policy changes.

A closer examination of the sorts of reforms that have been most commonly adopted since 2000 makes clear why imprisonment reductions have not been more impressive. These reforms have particularly sought to divert nonviolent drug offenders from prison (O'Hear, 2017a, 26–58). However, as seen in Q32, mass incarceration has not truly been driven by the War on Drugs. It is (relatively) politically easy to change policies regarding the incarceration of nonviolent offenders, but such reforms are unlikely to fundamentally alter the corrections picture in the United States.

Additionally, recent reforms have generally been structured so as to give frontline criminal justice actors new *options*, without actually requiring that they be utilized (199). Prosecutors are given new treatment-oriented diversion programs as an alternative to conventional charging; mandatory minimums are lifted, leaving judges with the option of ordering probation instead of imprisonment; parole rules are modified so as to empower parole officials to release more prisoners earlier; and compassionate release laws are adopted so to create new possibilities for elderly and disabled inmates to get out early. Such reforms are politically expedient for legislators because they do not require that any particular offender receive a break. If an offender is spared incarceration or released early and then commits a terrible new crime, legislators can point the finger of blame at whatever agency or official showed lenience. However, these sorts of reforms tend to have only modest impact in practice because the frontline actors understand full well the potential blame dynamics. They tend accordingly to exercise their expanded discretion in risk-averse ways—especially, again, with the offenders who are thought to pose any threat of violence.

A deep public fear of predatory violence, including sexual assaults, played a vital role in the politics of punishment in the late twentieth century, and there is little reason to think that the enhanced fiscal sensitivities of the early twenty-first century have altered, or are capable of altering, the powerful, seemingly instinctual preferences of so many people for harshly punitive treatment of those who commit serious violent crimes. As documented in Q38, public opinion surveys show that respondents sharply distinguish between violent and nonviolent offenders in their policy views. Survey results also point to some ambivalence about the goal of reducing corrections spending (O'Hear & Wheelock, 2015). For instance, in a recent survey of voters in Wisconsin, a nationally important swing state, respondents were asked to assess the importance of various objectives for the criminal justice system. While extremely large majorities of 88 percent or more said that the goals of "improving public safety" and "ensuring that criminals get the punishment they deserve" were very important, only 51 percent said the same of "reducing the amount of money we spend on imprisoning criminals" (O'Hear & Wheelock, 2016). Such results help to explain why policy makers have been so reluctant to reduce punishment for violent offenders in the name of cost cutting. But, until sentences for violent offenders are addressed, there is little likelihood of truly rolling back mass incarceration (Clear & Austin, 2017).

There are other difficulties, too, with building a reform agenda around the objective of cutting corrections costs. In truth, there is little money to be gained from reduced incarceration unless a prison is closed (O'Hear, 2017b, 199–200). With the exception of elderly and seriously ill inmates, the marginal costs of housing and feeding each individual prisoner are normally quite low, but the costs of staffing and maintaining a prison building are high. Yet, despite the fiscal benefits, it can be very difficult politically for policy makers to close an institution. In order to avoid not-in-my-backyard resistance, prisons have typically been built in struggling communities that welcomed them as drivers of economic development. These communities (and their legislative representatives) can hardly be expected to take closures lying down. This helps to explain why legislatures have been more prone to adopt reforms intended to prevent projected *increases* in imprisonment than reforms aiming to *reduce* current incarceration rates. Of course, correctional officers' unions, private prisons, and other corrections-related contractors can also form a potent lobbying force against incarceration-reducing reforms (see Q20). Moreover, even if the politics of cutting corrections budgets can be managed during a time of fiscal crisis, that provides no assurance that policy makers will act with comparable boldness when states are flush with cash. In the wake of a remarkably long period of economic growth in the United States, we might expect some slowing of reform momentum.

It is not clear what would produce a more fundamental change in the politics of punishment. In the interests of holding down growth in corrections budgets, policy makers (like the respondents in public opinion surveys (see Q38)) seem willing to take a chance on rehabilitation and community-based sanctions for nonviolent offenders, but these offenders were never a major focal point of tough-on-crime politics, policies, and practices. Perhaps greater change would come if voters had better information about the actual risks posed by the individuals who have been convicted of violent crimes. On the whole, these individuals actually have lower recidivism rates than drug and property offenders, and when they do recidivate the new crime is usually nonviolent (O'Hear, 2017b, 206).

The available evidence strongly suggests that sentences for violent crime could be much shorter without much negative impact on public safety (Clear & Austin, 2017, 71–73). Indeed, given what is known about the tendency of imprisonment to increase recidivism for some offenders (see Q16) and the possibility that cost savings from reduced imprisonment might be redirected into various chronically underfunded programs that are known to reduce risk (see Q9–10, 16), there is a plausible argument that *less* imprisonment (even of those who have committed violent crimes) might make for *more* public safety. But how open are members of the public to being influenced by research findings that cut against deeply held beliefs—beliefs that are routinely reinforced by discussions and depictions of crime and punishment in the mass media (see Q38)?

Some argue that the politics will not really change unless certain ethical principles of human dignity and equality are more deeply embraced in the United States (Tonry, 2016, 466). It is certainly true that public discourse regarding crime—especially that of a violent or sexual nature— has throughout the mass-incarceration era tended to portray offenders as fundamentally depraved and different from the "law-abiding" public (O'Hear, 2017a, 14–15). In such a rhetorical environment, it is difficult to perceive a shared humanity with offenders and to give their well-being—or even that of their family members—any serious consideration in thinking about sentencing and corrections policies. Yet, without some measure of compassion for these individuals, it is questionable whether fiscal pressures alone will be sufficient to bring down American incarceration rates to international or historical norms.

FURTHER READING

Clear, Todd & Austin, James. 2017. "Mass Incarceration." In *Reforming Criminal Justice: Punishment, Incarceration, and Release*, 55. Edited by Erik Luna. Phoenix: Arizona State University.

Committee on Causes and Consequences of High Rates of Incarceration, National Research Council of the National Academies. 2014. *The Growth of Incarceration in the United States*. Washington, DC: The National Academies Press.

O'Hear, Michael. 2017a. *The Failure of Sentencing Reform*. Santa Barbara, CA: Praeger.

O'Hear, Michael. 2017b. *Wisconsin Sentencing in the Tough-on-Crime Era: How Judges Retained Power and Why Mass Incarceration Happened Anyway*. Madison: University of Wisconsin Press.

O'Hear, Michael & Wheelock, Darren. 2015. "Imprisonment Inertia and Public Attitudes toward 'Truth in Sentencing.' " *Brigham Young University Law Review*, 2015, 257.

O'Hear, Michael & Wheelock, Darren. 2016. "Public Attitudes toward Punishment, Rehabilitation, and Reform: Lessons from the Marquette Law School Poll." *Federal Sentencing Reporter*, 29, 47.

Tonry, Michael. 2016. "Equality and Human Dignity: The Missing Ingredients in American Sentencing." *Crime and Justice*, 45, 459.

Q40: WHAT REFORM MEASURES MIGHT BEST REDUCE EXCESSIVE INCARCERATION?

Answer: The most effective strategy for ending mass incarceration would focus on dramatically reducing the number of offenders spending decade-plus periods of time in prison—a reality that many researchers believe is rarely justified from a public safety perspective. This goal should be pursued through a combination of shorter sentences on the front end and more flexible early release options on the back end. Other potential reform objectives include dramatically reducing the number of very short incarceration sentences, dramatically reducing the number of probationers and parolees incarcerated for violating conditions of community supervision, and increasing the funding for prison- and community-based programming that has been shown to reduce recidivism rates. As an overarching matter, reforms must take into account and seek to address the tendency of frontline criminal justice decision makers to manage offenders in excessively risk-averse ways.

The Facts: There are many reasons to question the wisdom of American mass incarceration. Some of the key concerns include:

- The chronic overcrowding found in many American prisons exacerbates the psychological harms of incarceration and diminishes the reach and effectiveness of rehabilitative programs (see Q14, Q17);
- Imprisonment increases the recidivism risk for some inmates (see Q16);
- Children are adversely affected by the incarceration of a parent, including through an increased risk of juvenile delinquency (see Q21);
- The experience and stigma of imprisonment commonly have serious negative effects on the lives of returning citizens and their families for many months or even years after release (see Q24);
- The experience of imprisonment may be especially difficult and cruel for mentally and physically ill, juvenile, and elderly inmates (see Q19, Q27, Q28, Q30);
- The current U.S. incarceration rate stands several times higher than international and historical norms (see Q31);
- Current incarceration levels could likely be cut substantially without an adverse impact on public safety (see Q33);
- High levels of incarceration among historically disadvantaged racial and ethnic groups perpetuate and amplify their disadvantage, contributing to the problems of distrust in some communities of the police and other legal institutions (see Q37); and
- Mass incarceration imposes large fiscal burdens on state governments and reduces the money available for other good purposes, including programs that might prove more effective over the long run at reducing crime rates (see Q39).

Despite the potential benefits, the political feasibility of reform is far from clear. While Americans are not as unrelentingly punitive as they are sometimes depicted (see Q38), a major rollback of mass incarceration would require changes in the punishment of individuals who have been convicted of violent crimes—a population toward which the public harbors very negative views (see Q39).

Assuming there is a political will to undo mass incarceration, a number of more specific reform objectives might be pursued. Most helpful would likely be a sharp reduction in the number of long-term prison inmates.

Although most incarceration sentences are for three years or less, the comparatively small number of decade-plus sentences play an outsize role in driving mass incarceration. The inmates with the longest sentences "stack up" over the years and, depending on the state, tend to account for about one-third to one-half of prisoners at any given time. This segment of the prison population has been identified as an especially inviting reform target, both because its elimination or near-elimination would constitute a truly large-scale reversal of mass incarceration and because these super-sized sentences tend to deliver relatively little public safety benefit over the long run. Based on the well-established patterns of life-course crime-desistance, long-term incapacitation is unnecessary for most offenders, including many of those who have been convicted of high-level felonies (Committee on Causes and Consequences of High Rates of Incarceration, 2014, 5).

Reducing the number of long-serving inmates can be accomplished through reforms at both the "front" and "back" ends of the system. Front-end reforms aim to reduce the nominal sentence lengths imposed by judges. For instance, there is a strong argument in favor of eliminating all mandatory minimum prison terms (Tonry, 2014, 516). Critics describe mandatory minimums as crude and clumsy devices, basing punishment on a very small number of factors and ignoring others that often bear in important ways on the gravity of an offense and the dangerousness of an offender. While unlimited judicial sentencing discretion is not necessarily the best policy choice, either, presumptive sentencing guidelines have been touted as offering a more nuanced and flexible approach to regulating discretion (see Q1).

In addition to eliminating minimums, reformers have also endorsed reducing maximum sentences. To be sure, maximums are rarely imposed. Still, they function as important benchmarks in practice. The apparent reasonableness of, say, a probationary sentence or of a prison term of two or three years varies dramatically depending on whether the maximum term is five, ten, twenty, or fifty years. And it has been well documented that maximums in the United States tend to be high by international standards (see Q31). In Germany, for instance, life sentences are limited to aggravated intentional homicide, and sentences are otherwise generally limited to fifteen years (Weigend, 2016, 84). To the extent that there are offenders who remain demonstrably high-risk at the end of a fifteen-year term, that risk could be addressed through a period of intense supervision in the community post-release, potentially including the technologically advancing electronic monitoring systems that show growing promise as a risk-reduction measure (see Q9). Civil commitment might also be an option—ideally with more scientifically rigorous standards than are currently employed with sex offenders (see Q29).

Back-end reforms focus on mechanisms for early release such as parole, good time, earned time, and compassionate release (see Q22, Q30). Properly administered, such mechanisms incentivize good behavior and rehabilitative effort behind bars and help to move inmates back into the community as soon as it is safe to do so (see Q23). There is also another reason for early release reform to be included in any mass *decarceration* strategy: if sentences are simply reduced on the front end, the continued long-term imprisonment of those sentenced under the old system means that real progress in reducing incarceration rates will take many years.

The eligibility criteria for early release programs were sharply restricted in almost all states in the 1980s and 1990s, especially for prisoners convicted of violent or sexual offenses. However, these offenders are not categorically more dangerous than others (Durose, Cooper, & Snyder, 2014), and there seems no good public safety reason to subject them to different early release rules. Moreover, since the generally applicable rules almost always require that a certain percentage of prison terms be served before release is possible, the offenders with the most serious crimes (and hence the longest judge-imposed sentences) will still normally spend considerably more time behind bars than those who have committed less serious crimes.

Fairness to victims might constitute a more compelling objection to liberalizing early release (see Q30). In deference to victims, any early release program should be administered with transparency, which should include providing clear notice to victims at the time of sentencing that any prison term imposed is subject to later adjustment and additional notice well in advance of the actual release date, combined with information about how the offender will be supervised after release. It would also be appropriate to place constraints on how "early" an early release can occur. Many good-time programs offer a maximum "discount" in the range of 25–35 percent (O'Hear, 2017, 64), which may be sufficient to preserve a meaningful degree of certainty for victims.

In addition to reforms targeting the longest-serving inmates, advocates of reform say that there are other changes in sentencing policies and practices that could help to draw down incarceration rates without sacrificing public safety. Most short terms of incarceration (say, less than two years) could probably be replaced with intermediate sanctions (see Q9). Reformers argue that short terms behind bars can do a great deal of harm to offenders and their families—even a few days or weeks can mean a loss of employment or housing—with little offsetting benefit. The natural process of maturation is unlikely to progress much in just a few weeks or months, while good rehabilitative programs are apt to take longer than is available to the transient inmate. Indeed, few jails, where sentences of a year or less are typically served, even offer much programming. There should be little surprise, then, that recidivism rates seem to be highest for offenders sentenced to one year (see Q16). Reform advocates assert that if the offense is not sufficiently serious, or the offender sufficiently dangerous, to warrant a lengthier term of incarceration, then a sentence that is less disruptive to the offender's life should normally be selected. As discussed in Q9-Q11, a growing body of research suggests that electronic monitoring, day reporting centers, restorative justice, and problem-solving courts can be effective, risk-reducing community-based alternatives to incarceration for many offenders.

The difficulty with intermediate sanctions is making sure that they really are used as an alternative to incarceration. There has been a temptation for prosecutors and judges to use these sanctions as a tougher alternative to straight probation, leaving the incarceration-bound offender population untouched by reforms. Presumptive guidelines regarding the use of intermediate sanctions may help to mitigate this "net-widening" phenomenon.

Another frequent reform target is the revocation of community supervision (parole and probation). Perhaps as many as one-half of prison admissions each year result from revocations (Clear & Austin, 2017, 61). Most revocations are unaccompanied by a new sentence, which suggests that the revocation was either for a technical rules violation or for some type of very minor criminal activity, such as the consumption of a controlled substance (see Q25). Typically involving only a very short term of incarceration, such revocations have been cited by some prisoner reformers as disruptive and counterproductive for the same reasons as short sentences of incarceration. In recent years, several states have adopted reforms to encourage greater use of non-revocation sanctions for rules violations (see Q25). However, such reforms also present net-widening risks; that is, new sanctions may be used to increase the punishment that is imposed for the least serious violations, rather than softening the punishment for violations that would have otherwise resulted in revocation. In addition to, or in lieu of, new intermediate sanctions for rules violations, states might work on reducing the number and onerousness of supervision conditions and the length of supervision terms.

Yet another strategy for reducing revocations, as well as recidivism-fueled prison admissions more generally, would be to increase the funding for evidence-based rehabilitative programs both in the community and in correctional institutions. Research confirms that certain kinds of programs can reduce the recidivism rates of certain groups of offenders (see Q16). However, while reformers say that these gains are worth pursuing, it is important to realize that programming alone can make only a modest dent in mass incarceration (Clear & Austin, 2017, 70). This is because not all offenders can benefit from programming, and because even the best programs can only be expected to cut recidivism rates by about 20 percent.

Any reform effort that aims to roll back mass incarceration also must come to grips with an important overarching challenge: the powerful incentives that exist for criminal justice decision makers (prosecutors, judges, parole boards, and corrections officials) to act in excessively risk-averse ways. All of these actors know that taking a chance on an offender can be a career killer. If a prosecutor drops a felony charge in a plea deal, or a judge imposes a probationary sentence, or a parole board member supports early release, heavy public criticism may result, *especially* if the offender who caught the break then commits a major crime. Such negative publicity especially threatens the reputations and careers of elected judges and district attorneys.

The pressures to err on the side of higher levels of control over offenders helps to explain why repealing mandatory minimums does not necessarily result in less severe sentences in practice (O'Hear, 2017, 48–49, 116); why states that retained parole in the 1980s and 1990s tended to experience no less imprisonment growth than those that abolished it (9); and why net widening has been such a problem for intermediate sanctions.

Presumptive guidelines for prosecutors, judges, parole boards, and corrections officials—that is, guidelines that must normally be followed unless a good reason is given for deviation—can help to counter these tendencies to risk-aversion by providing political cover to decision makers in this regard. Presumptive guidelines for sentencing judges have a well-established track record of success in a handful of states (Committee on Causes and Consequences of High Rates of Incarceration, 2014, 76–78). It is less clear how well presumptive guidelines can work in other contexts, but the experience with sentencing guidelines may provide a basis for experimentation in other areas.

In the past, sentencing guidelines have been drafted with a variety of different goals in mind. If the objective is to end mass incarceration, then new guidelines must be developed around that goal in an analytically rigorous way. In this regard, drafters may benefit from the improving science of offender risk assessment (see Q23). In general, guidelines should try to limit incarceration, both at the sentencing stage and in early release decisions, to offenders who present high risks that cannot be managed effectively in the community.

Other reforms might also help to address some of the perverse incentives that exist in the criminal justice system. For instance, judges and prosecutors are locally based decision makers for whom prison sentences are essentially cost free; when an offender is sent to prison, state taxpayers assume financial responsibility for the sentence. Criminologists Franklin Zimring and Gordon Hawkins call this the "correctional free lunch" for judges and prosecutors (O'Hear, 2017, 182–83). If the free lunch were discontinued, and local taxpayers were billed by the state for use of the state prison system, then judges and prosecutors would have greater incentives to take the costs of imprisonment into account in their decision making. Otherwise, at election time, local voters might have some pointed questions for elected judges and district attorneys about why their tax bills are increasing. Such political dynamics might partly offset the existing pressures that push in the direction of excessive risk aversion.

FURTHER READING

Clear, Todd & Austin, James. 2017. "Mass Incarceration." In *Reforming Criminal Justice: Punishment, Incarceration, and Release*, 55. Edited by Erik Luna. Phoenix: Arizona State University.

Committee on Causes and Consequences of High Rates of Incarceration, National Research Council of the National Academies. 2014. *The Growth of Incarceration in the United States*. Washington, DC: The National Academies Press.

Durose, Matthew, Cooper, Aaron, & Snyder, Howard. 2014. *Recidivism of Prisoners Released in 30 States in 2005: Patterns from 2005 to 2010*. Washington, DC: U.S. Department of Justice.

O'Hear, Michael. 2017. *The Failure of Sentencing Reform*. Santa Barbara, CA: Praeger.

Tonry, Michael. 2014. "Remodeling American Sentencing: A Ten-Step Blueprint for Moving Past Mass Incarceration." *Criminology & Public Policy*, 13, 503.

Weigend, Thomas. 2016. "No News Is Good News: Criminal Sentencing in Germany since 2000." *Crime and Justice*, 45, 83.

Index

About the Author

Michael O'Hear is a professor at Marquette University Law School, where he teaches criminal law and procedure. His books include *The Failure of Sentencing Reform and Wisconsin Sentencing in the Tough-on-Crime Era: How Judges Retained Power and Why Mass Incarceration Happened Anyway.* He is also the author of more than sixty scholarly articles and book chapters on criminal law and sentencing and an editor of the journal *Federal Sentencing Reporter.*